Acts Through Ephesians

Wuest's Expanded Translation of the Greek New Testament: Volume II

Acts

through

Ephesians

KENNETH S. WUEST, LITT. D.

Teacher of New Testament Greek
The Moody Bible Institute

WM. B. EERDMANS PUBLISHING COMPANY
GRAND RAPIDS   MICHIGAN

WUEST'S EXPANDED TRANSLATION
OF THE GREEK NEW TESTAMENT,
VOLUME II, ACTS THROUGH EPHESIANS

BY KENNETH S. WUEST

© *Wm. B. Eerdmans Publishing Company,* 1958

Set up and printed, March, 1958

LIBRARY OF CONGRESS CATALOG CARD NUMBER: 56-12804

CONTENTS

A PERSONAL WORD TO THE READER   9

PREFACE TO THE BOOK OF ACTS   13

THE EXPANDED TRANSLATION OF ACTS   17

PREFACE TO PAUL'S LETTER TO THE ROMANS   97

THE EXPANDED TRANSLATION OF ROMANS   101

PREFACE TO THE CORINTHIAN LETTERS   135

THE EXPANDED TRANSLATION OF FIRST
CORINTHIANS   137

THE EXPANDED TRANSLATION OF SECOND
CORINTHIANS   173

PREFACE TO PAUL'S LETTER TO THE GALATIANS   197

THE EXPANDED TRANSLATION OF GALATIANS   201

PREFACE TO PAUL'S LETTER TO THE EPHESIANS   213

THE EXPANDED TRANSLATION OF
EPHESIANS   215

DEFINITION OF TERMS   227

INDEX OF CHAPTER AND VERSE DIVISIONS   243

Acts Through Ephesians

A PERSONAL WORD TO THE READER

This is a commentary translation the purpose of which is to clarify the text of the Authorized Version where its condensed phraseology needs the explanation which an expanded translation is able to afford. It is to be used in connection with that version, never in its place.

In order correctly to evaluate and understand the translation work found in this book, the reader is urged to consult the prefatory chapters in *The Gospels: An Expanded Translation* entitled, "The Advantages of an Expanded Translation," "The Supreme Importance of the Doctrine of Verbal Inspiration in the Translation of the Greek New Testament," and "A Personal Word to the Reader."

The reader can use this translation, first, to make a study of one of the Books of the Bible, for instance, Romans, by using the Authorized Version as the standard translation and endeavoring to understand it more clearly by consulting this expanded translation for the light it will shed upon it; second, to read this expanded translation as one would read any other book, following the rules of synthetic Bible reading in order to obtain a comprehensive grasp of a particular Book in its entirety. Those rules are:

1. Read the Book *continuously,* that is, read as much of the Book as possible at each session.

2. Read it *independently,* without consulting study helps.

3. Read it *repeatedly.* After each successive reading, the grand sweep of its contents becomes clearer.

4. Read it *reverently,* in conscious dependence upon the Holy Spirit for His illumination.

THE
EXPANDED TRANSLATION
OF THE
BOOK OF ACTS

PREFACE TO THE BOOK OF ACTS

This expanded rendering of the Greek text is a commentary translation to be used alongside of the Authorized Version as an aid in its understanding. For instance, take the question Paul asked the disciples at Ephesus, "Have ye received the Holy Ghost since ye believed?" (Acts 19:2, A.V.). The English word "since" has both a temporal and a causal meaning. One could understand the question to mean, "Have ye received the Holy Ghost since that time when ye believed?", the teaching being that the Holy Spirit is not given the believer in response to his initial act of faith in the Lord Jesus as Saviour, but some time after that act. Or the question could be, "Have ye received the Holy Ghost as a result of your initial act of faith?", the teaching then being that the Holy Spirit is given to the sinner as a result of believing. The difference between these two questions is the difference between heresy and true doctrine, the difference between confusion in the local assembly and that order and unity which true doctrine provides. The solution to this difficulty is found in the Greek construction. The finite verb is "received," the participle, "believed." It is a causal participle. The rule of Greek syntax here is that the ground of action in the verb is found in the participle. That is, the act of receiving the Holy Spirit has its cause in the act of believing. That settles the matter. This translation and interpretation is just as sure as the mathematical rule which says that two and two make four. This is an illustration of the scientific accuracy with which this expanded translation has been produced.

Take the matter of the filling with the Spirit. The expression is found in Acts 2:4, 4:31, 6:5, 7:55, 9:17. The word "filled" when used with reference to the Holy Spirit means "controlled." The Spirit is not a substance to fill an empty receptacle, the human heart (which is not an empty receptacle but a symbol of the free will, the emotions, and the reason of the believer). The Spirit is a divine Person to control another person, the believer. The references cited are not references to separate and repeated fillings with the Spirit. To so interpret them is to accuse the early Christians of being controlled at other times by the evil nature. The believer never acts alone. He acts either in the power of the

13

evil nature, or in the power of the Holy Spirit. The translation "They were all controlled by the Holy Spirit" (2:4) and "And Stephen being under the control of the Holy Spirit" (7:55) gives the reader a correct understanding of "filled with the Spirit." The expression is descriptive of the normal spiritual condition of the person referred to, that of being controlled by the Holy Spirit.

As another instance take the place where the A.V. offers a contradiction to the reader owing to its inability to bring out clearly the meaning of the Greek text, this inability being due to the minimum number of words it had at its disposal. In Acts 9:7 Luke records the fact that the men with Paul heard the voice of the Lord Jesus. In 22:9 he records Paul's speech in which Paul states that the men did not hear the voice. The Greek grammar involved is as follows: the word "voice" in 9:7 is in the genitive case, which means that the men heard the voice as a mere sound but did not understand the words; the word "voice" in 22:9 is in the accusative case, which means that the men did not hear the voice so as to understand the words, but only as a sound. Thus, the contradiction is resolved in an expanded translation.

Again, since this expanded translation is based upon a more correct Greek text than that used by the translators of the A.V., it is able to offer the reader some renderings necessary to the correct understanding of some passages. Luke reports (A.V.) that as soon as Paul was saved "he preached Christ in the synagogues that he is the Son of God" (9:20). But the fact that the Messiah would be the Son of God is taught in the Old Testament. To this the Jews would have offered no opposition. The correct text here is "Jesus." It was the fact that Paul announced that Jesus of Nazareth is the Son of God which aroused the bitter opposition of the Jews.

The sarcastic, caustic question which the Athenian philosophers asked with reference to Paul is given by the A. V. as follows: "What will this babbler say?" The expanded translation offers: "What would he desire to be saying, granted he was able to say anything, this ignorant plagiarist, picking up scraps of information here and there, unrelated in his own thinking, and passing them off as the result of his own mature thought?"

In the account of our Lord's ascension to heaven, the A.V. reports Luke as saying, "A cloud received Him out of their sight" (Acts 1:9). The Greek word "received" means "to take up under in order to raise up, to bear on high." The expanded translation offers: "A cloud came under Him in order to bear Him up on

high out of their sight." This identifies the cloud, not as an ordinary cloud in the sky, but as the Shekinah Glory sent down to bring the Lord Jesus to heaven through the kingdom of Satan and his demons in the lower atmosphere.

And so one could go on enumerating the advantages of this expanded translation as an aid to the understanding of the A.V. But we will allow the reader to find more of these for himself.

The first historical narrative indeed I produced con-   **1-5**
cerning all things, O Theophilus, which Jesus began and
continued both to be doing and to be teaching until the
day in which He was taken up, having previously given
a commandment to the apostles through the intermediate
agency of the Holy Spirit, those apostles whom He had
selected out for himself, to whom also He presented himself as one who was living after His suffering by many
indubitable proofs through a period of forty days, being
seen by them at successive intervals and speaking of the
things concerning the kingdom of God. And being assembled together with them He charged them not to go away
from Jerusalem, but to be waiting for the promise of the
Father which you heard from me, because John indeed
baptized by means of water, but as for you, by the agency
of the Holy Spirit you will be baptized not many days
from now.

Then indeed having assembled together, they went to   **6-8**
asking Him, saying, Lord, at this time are you restoring
to its former state the kingdom to Israel? He said to
them, It is not yours to know the chronological events
in the passing of time nor the strategic, epochal periods
of time which the Father placed within the sphere of His
own private authority. But you shall receive power of
the kind which God has and exerts after the Holy Spirit
has come upon you. And you shall be those who testify
of what they have seen and experienced, my witnesses,
both in Jerusalem and in all Judaea and in Samaria and to
the end of the earth.

And having said these things, while they were look-   **9-11**
ing, He was taken up, and a cloud came under Him in
order to bear Him up on high out of their sight. And
while they were looking with fixed and protracted attention up to heaven as He was proceeding on His way, behold, also two men in brilliant white apparel had taken
their position alongside of them and were standing there,
who also said, Men, Galilaeans, why have you taken your
stand, looking up to heaven? This Jesus, He who was
taken up from you into heaven, shall come in like manner as you saw Him proceeding into heaven.

12-14   Then they returned to Jerusalem from the mount called
Olivet which is near Jerusalem a sabbath day's journey. And when they entered the city, they went up to
the upper room where they had taken up their residence
for the ensuing time, both Peter and John and James and
Andrew, Philip and Thomas, Bartholomew and Matthew,
James the son of Alphaeus, and Simon the Zealot, and
Judas the brother of James. These all continued to give
their persistent attention with absolute unanimity to prayer which was characterized by its definiteness of purpose,
together with the women and Mary the mother of Jesus
and with His brethren.

15-17   And in these days Peter having arisen in the midst of
the brethren said [and there was a group of persons
gathered together, about one hundred and twenty], Men,
brothers, it was a necessity in the nature of the case for
the scripture to be fulfilled which the Holy Spirit spoke
on a previous occasion through David's mouth concerning Judas, the one who became guide to those who seized
Jesus, for he was numbered among us and received his
portion of this ministry.

18-20   Now, this man acquired a piece of ground, the pur-
chase price having its source in wages obtained by wrong-
doing, and having fallen flat on his face, he cracked open
at the waist with a crashing noise and all his inner organs
gushed out. And it became known to all the residents
of Jerusalem, so that that piece of ground came to be
called in their own language, Akeldamach, that is, a
bloody piece of ground, for it stands written in the Book
of Psalms, Let his place of abode become deserted, and
let there not be he who establishes his permanent residence in it, and his office let another person of a different
character take.

21-26   Therefore, it is a necessity in the nature of the case
that of those men who have accompanied us during all
the time the Lord Jesus went in and went out in our presence, beginning from the time of John's baptism until the
day when He was taken up from us, there be one of these
appointed as one who bears testimony with us that he was
a personal witness of His resurrection. And they nomi-

nated two, Joseph, the one called Barsabas, who was surnamed Justus, and Matthias. And having prayed, they said, Lord, you who have an experiential knowledge of the hearts of all, appoint the one of these two whom you selected out to receive the place of this ministry and apostleship, from which ministry and apostleship Judas fell away to proceed to his own private, unique place. And they handed out lots to be placed in an urn with respect to them, and the lot fell to Matthias, and he was numbered with the eleven apostles.

1-4 And when the day of Pentecost was in process of being fulfilled, they were all together in the same place. And suddenly there came an echoing sound out of heaven as of a wind borne along violently. And it filled the whole house where they were sitting. And there appeared to them tongues that had the appearance of fire, these tongues being distributed among them, and one of these tongues took up a position upon each of them. And all were controlled by the Holy Spirit and began to be uttering words in languages different from their own native language and different from those spoken by the others, even as the Spirit kept giving them ability to speak forth, not in words of everyday speech but in words belonging to dignified and elevated discourse.

5-11 And there were in Jerusalem Jews who were in residence there, devout men who reverenced God, from all nations of those under heaven. Now, when this sound was heard, the multitude came together and was at a loss to understand this, because they were hearing each one of them uttering words in his own dialect. And they were astounded to the point of being beside themselves, and went to wondering, saying, Look. To be sure. Are not all these who are speaking Galilaeans? And as for us, how can it be possible that we are hearing each one in our own private dialect in which we were born, Parthians and Medes, and Elamites, and those who had taken up residence in Mesopotamia, and also in Judaea and Cappadocia, in Pontus and Asia, also in Phrygia and Pamphylia, in Egypt, and in the parts of Libya about Cyrene, also sojourners from Rome, both Jews and Gentile con-

19

verts to Judaism, Cretes and Arabians, we are hearing them uttering in our languages the mighty works of God?

12, 13 And they were all astounded to the point of being beside themselves, and were wholly at a loss what to think, saying one to another, What does this desire to be? But others of a different class, mocking, were saying, They have been filled brimful with sweet wine with the result that they cannot hold any more.

14-18 But Peter having taken his stand with the eleven raised his voice and said to them in words which belonged to dignified and elevated discourse, Men of the Jewish race, and all those who are residents of Jerusalem, let this be known to you, and give ear to my words, for, as for you, these are not intoxicated as you suppose, for it is nine o'clock in the morning. But this is that which has been spoken through the intermediate agency of the prophet Joel and is on record, And it shall be in the last days, says God, that I will abundantly bestow my Spirit upon all flesh. And your sons shall speak forth by divine inspiration, also your daughters. And your young men shall see visions. And your old men shall dream with dreams. Yes, and upon men and women who are the slaves of others and yet belong to me, in those days I will abundantly bestow my Spirit and they shall speak by divine inspiration.

19-21 And I will bring forth miracles of a startling, amazement-awakening character in the heaven above and miracles upon the earth whose purpose it is to attest the workings and words of God, blood and fire and vapor of smoke. The sun shall be turned into darkness and the moon into blood before the day of the Lord comes, that great, conspicuous day. And it shall be that everyone whoever shall call upon the Name of the Lord shall be saved.

22-24 Men, Israelites. Hear these words at once. Jesus, the Nazarene, a man who has been demonstrated to you by God to be that which He claims to be, this demonstration taking the form of miracles that show the power of God, and miracles that are a startling, imposing, amazement-awakening portent, and miracles that have for their pur-

pose the attestation of the divine mission of the one who performs them, which miracles God performed through His intermediate agency in your midst even as you yourselves know positively; this One, having been delivered up by the counsel of God which [in the council held by the Trinity] had decided upon His destiny, even by the foreordination of God which is that act fixing His destiny, by wicked hands you crucified and killed, whom God raised up, having loosed the pangs of death because it was not possible for Him to be mastered by it.

For David says concerning Him, I was beholding the **25-28** Lord always before my face, because He is at my right hand in order that I might not be agitated and disturbed, thrown out of my sober and natural state of mind. On this account my heart was made glad and my tongue rejoiced exceedingly. Yes, moreover also my flesh shall still pitch its tent upon hope, there to rest, because you will not leave my soul surviving in that place in the unseen world reserved for the human dead. Neither will you permit your Holy One to see corruption. You made known to me the courses of thought, feeling, and action of life [that life, the eternal life given a believer in salvation]. You will fill me with joy with your countenance.

Men. Brothers. I may speak to you with utter free- **29-36** dom of speech concerning our progenitor David, that he came to his end in death and was entombed. And his sepulchral memorial is among us even to this day. Therefore, being a foreteller of future events, and knowing that God had sworn with an oath to him that from his offspring He would seat One upon his throne, he having seen this beforehand, spoke concerning the resurrection of the Christ [the Messiah], that neither was He left surviving in that place in the unseen world reserved for the human dead, nor did His flesh see corruption. This Jesus God raised up, whose witnesses we all are, bearing testimony to what we have seen and heard and learned concerning Him. Therefore, by the right hand of God exalted, and having received from the presence of the Father the promise of the Holy Spirit, He bestowed this which you are both seeing and hearing; for David did

not ascend into heaven, but he himself says, The Lord
said to my Lord, Take your seat at my right hand until
I make your enemies the footstool of your feet. Assuredly therefore, let the whole house of Israel be knowing
that God made Him both Lord and Christ, this Jesus
whom you crucified.

37-41   Now, having heard this, they were stung to the heart
with poignant sorrow. And they said to Peter and the
rest of the apostles, What shall we do, men, brothers?
And Peter said to them, Have a change of mind, that
change of mind being accompanied by abhorrence of and
sorrow for your deed, and let each one of you be baptized upon the ground of your confession of belief in the
sum total of all that Jesus Christ is in His glorious Person, this baptismal testimony being in relation to the fact
that your sins have been put away, and you shall receive
the gratuitous gift of the Holy Spirit, for to you is the
promise and to your children and to all who are at a
distance, as many as the Lord our God shall with a divine
summons call to himself. And with many other words he
solemnly affirmed, and kept on exhorting them, saying,
Be saved from this perverse generation. Then those who
received his word with approval were immersed. And
there were added to their number on that day about three
thousand souls.

42-47   And they were giving constant attention to the teaching of the apostles and to that which they held in common with them, and to the breaking of the bread and to
the gatherings where prayers to God were offered. And
a reverential fear came upon every soul. And many miracles that excited amazement and attesting miracles were
performed by the apostles. And all those who believed
were gathered together as a unit and were holding all
things in joint-participation, and were selling their houses
and lands and other possessions and kept on distributing
them to all, according as anyone was having a need. And
daily they continued to remain in the temple, in perfect
unanimity, breaking bread at home, partaking of food
together in gladness and simplicity of heart, praising God
and having the good will of the people. And the Lord
kept on adding to them daily those who were being saved.

Now Peter and John were going up into the temple
at the hour of prayer, three o'clock in the afternoon. And
a certain man whose lameness was due to prenatal causes
was being carried, whom they were accustomed to place
daily at the door of the temple, the gate which is called
Beautiful, for the purpose of asking alms from those who
were entering the temple, who having seen Peter and
John about to go into the temple, went to asking for a
benefaction. And Peter having looked at him with a
piercing gaze together with John said, Look at once on
us. And he began to fix his attention on them, expecting
to receive something from them. Then Peter said, Silver
and gold coins I do not have, but that which I have, this
I give to you. In the Name of Jesus Christ the Nazarene,
start walking and keep on walking. And having firmly
grasped his right hand, he raised him up. And instantly
his feet and ankle bones were made strong. And leaping
up he stood and went to walking about. And he entered
the temple with them, walking about, leaping and
praising God. And all the people saw him walking about
and praising God. And they recognized him as being
the one who customarily sat at the Beautiful Gate of the
temple for alms. And they were filled with amazement
and were in a state of mental imbalance because of that
which had happened to him. And while he was holding
firmly to Peter and John, the entire crowd ran together
to them in the covered colonnade, the one called
Solomon's, completely flabbergasted.

And Peter, having seen this, answered the people;
Men, Israelites, why are you marvelling at this, or why
are you fixing your attention upon us as though by means
of our own power or piety we have made him to be walking? The God of Abraham and Isaac and Jacob, the God
of our fathers glorified His servant, Jesus, whom you
indeed delivered up and denied before the face of Pilate
when it was that one's verdict to release Him. But, as for
you, you denied the Holy One and the Just One, and demanded a man who was a murderer to be granted to you
as a favor, and killed the Author of the life whom God
raised out from among those who are dead, of whom, as
for us, we are those who bear testimony to what we have

seen and heard and learned concerning Him. And upon the ground of our faith in His Name, this man whom you are attentively gazing at with a critical, discerning eye and whom you positively identify as the person you know — His Name made him strong, and the faith which is exercised through Him gave to him this entire soundness in the sight of all of you.

17-21   And now brothers, I know positively that in ignorance you did it, even as also your chief men. But the things which God announced fully beforehand through the mouth of all the prophets that His Christ should suffer, He thus fulfilled. Therefore repent at once, instantly changing your attitude, and perform a right-about-face in order that your sins may be obliterated, in order that there may come epoch-making periods of spiritual revival and refreshment from the presence of the Lord, and in order that He may send off on a mission to you Christ Jesus who has been appointed, this appointment being in the interest of your well-being; whom it is a necessity in the nature of the case for heaven indeed to receive until times when all things will be restored to their pristine glory, things regarding which God spoke through the mouth of His holy prophets who lived in bygone times.

22-26   Moses indeed said, A prophet from among your brethren the Lord your God shall raise up for you who is like me. Him you are to hear with reference to all things whatever He may say to you. And it shall be that every soul which is of such a nature that he will not hear that prophet shall be utterly destroyed from among the people. And indeed, all the prophets since Samuel, and those who followed, one after another, as many as spoke, also announced these days. As for you, you are the sons of the prophets and of the covenant which God covenanted with your fathers, saying to Abraham, And by means of your race all the nations of the earth shall become the recipients of benefits. To you first, God, having raised up His Servant, sent Him on a mission to confer benefits upon you in turning away each one of you from your pernicious deeds.

And while they were speaking to the people, the **1-4**
priests and the captain of the temple police and the Sadducees burst suddenly upon them and stood there in a
hostile attitude, being greatly displeased because they
were teaching the people and announcing in the case of
Jesus the resurrection from among the dead. And they
laid their hands upon them and placed them in custody
where they would be guarded until the next day, for it
was already evening. But many of those who heard the
Word believed. And the number of male individuals
came to be about five thousand.

And it came to pass on the next day that their rulers **5-14**
and elders and men learned in the sacred scriptures were
gathered together in Jerusalem, also Annas the chief
priest and Caiaphas and John and Alexander, and as
many as were relatives of the chief priest. And having
stood them in their midst, they went to inquiring of them,
By what sort of power or by what manner of name did
you do this? Then Peter, being controlled by the Holy
Spirit, said to them, Rulers of the people and elders, as
for us, since we are being examined regarding a good
deed done to an infirm man, by what means this man has
been made whole, let it be known to you all and to all
the people of Israel, that by means of the Name of Jesus
Christ, the Nazarene, whom, as for you, you crucified,
whom God raised out from among those who are dead,
by means of this One this man stands in your presence
sound in body. This is the stone which was utterly despised and treated with contempt by you, the builders,
which has become the cornerstone. And there does not
exist in any other the salvation, for there is not even another name under heaven which has been given among
men by means of which we can be saved, the need for this
salvation being a necessity in the nature of the case. And
viewing with a practiced eye the free and fearless confidence of Peter and John as manifested in their uninhibited and unreserved manner of speaking, and comprehending the fact that they were without formal education and that they were not professional men but lay-
men, they began to wonder and kept on wondering, and
they began to recognize them as those who were with

Jesus. And seeing the man who was standing with them, the one who had been healed, they kept on having not even one thing to say against it.

15-18   But having ordered them to go off outside of the council, they went to conferring with one another, saying, What shall we do to these men? for that indeed a miracle which has for its purpose the attestation of the divine source of a message given by the one who performs the miracle, and one which is known, has been done through their agency, is known to all those who are residing in Jerusalem. And we are unable to deny it. But, in order that it may not be caused to spread the more among the people, let us with sternest threats forbid them to be speaking upon the basis of this name to even one of the people. And having called them, they commanded them not to be speaking at all nor to be teaching upon the basis of the Name of Jesus.

19-22   But Peter and John, answering, said to them, Whether it is right in the sight of God to be yielding obedience to you rather than to God, you be the judges, for, as for us, we are not able not to be speaking the things which we saw and heard. And having sternly threatened them in addition, they released them, finding not even one thing relative to the particular way in which they might punish them because of the people, for all glorified God for that which had taken place, for the man was more than forty years old upon whom this attesting miracle of healing had been wrought.

23-31   And having been released, they went to their own associates and reported as many things to them as the chief priests and the elders had said. And they having heard this, with one accord raised their voice to God and said, O Lord, absolute in power, you who made the heaven and the earth and the sea and all the things in them, who by the mouth of our father David your servant through the Holy Spirit said, Why did the Gentiles take on lofty airs and behave arrogantly, and the people devise futile things? The kings of the earth set themselves in array and the rulers formed a coalition to the same end, that of antagonism against the Lord and against His Anointed One,

for of a truth, there joined together in this city, against your holy servant Jesus, whom you anointed, both Herod and Pontius Pilate with the Gentiles and with the people of Israel, to do as many things as your hand and counsel determined beforehand should come to pass. And as to the present circumstances, Lord, look upon their threatenings and grant at once to your bondslaves the ability to be speaking your word with all fearless confidence and freedom of speech while you stretch out your hand to heal, and grant that attesting miracles and miracles which arouse wonder may be done through the Name of your holy servant Jesus. And having prayed, the place in which they were gathered was shaken. And they were all controlled by the Holy Spirit and went to speaking the word of God with fearless confidence and freedom of speech.

And in the multitude of those who believed there was   32-37
one heart and soul. And not even one was saying that anything of the things he possessed was his private property, but they had all things in common. And with great power the apostles of the Lord were constantly giving their testimony of the resurrection. And great grace was upon all of them, for there was no one among them who was in need, for as many as were possessors of lands or houses, selling them, kept on bringing the equivalent values of the things that were being sold and kept on placing them at the feet of the apostles, and distribution was constantly being made to each one according as he was having a need. And Joseph, who by the apostles was surnamed Barnabas, which latter name by interpretation means Son of Encouragement, a Levite, of the land of Cyprus, possessing a field, having sold it, brought the money and placed it at the feet of the apostles.

But a certain man named Ananias with his wife Sap-   1-6
phira sold a possession and set apart part of it for himself, his wife also knowing of this together with him. And having brought a certain part, he placed it at the feet of the apostles. And Peter said, Ananias, how is it that Satan exercised control over your heart with the result that you lied to the Holy Spirit and set apart for yourself a portion of the value of the land? While it remained, did it not remain your own? And having sold it, was

it not under your authority? Why did you resolve upon this deed in your heart? You did not lie to men but to God. And Ananias, having heard these words, having fallen down, expired. And there came a great fear upon all those who heard. And having arisen, the younger men covered him with a shroud, and having carried him out, buried him.

7-11   Now, there elapsed an interval of about three hours, and his wife, not knowing of that which had taken place, entered. And Peter answered her, Tell me at once whether you both sold the land for so much? And she said, Yes, for so much. And Peter said to her, Why is it that it was agreed by both of you craftily to make trial of and put to the proof the Lord's Spirit [to see whether He would condone or condemn this act]? Behold, the feet of those who buried your husband are at the door, and they shall carry you out. And she fell down immediately at his feet and expired. And the younger men, having entered, found her dead. And having covered her with a shroud, they buried her with her husband. And there came a great fear upon the whole assembly and upon all who heard these things.

12-16   And by the hands of the apostles, attesting miracles and miracles which excite wonder and amazement, many of them, were constantly being performed among the people. And they were in perfect unanimity, all of them, in Solomon's covered colonnade. And of the rest, not even one was daring to be entering into fellowship with them, but the people were esteeming them highly. And those believing on the Lord were the more constantly being added to the number, crowds both of men and women, with the result that also into the streets they were carrying out those who were ill and placing them upon small couches for the sick and upon pallets in order that the shadow of Peter as he was coming might overshadow some of them. Moreover, there kept on congregating also the multitude of those from the environs of Jerusalem, carrying sick ones and those who were being troubled by unclean spirits; such as these were being healed, all of them.

Then having arisen, the chief priest and all those with **17-25**
him, the sect which is of the Sadducees, were filled with
jealousy. And they laid their hands upon the apostles and
put them in the public prison. But an angel of the Lord
during the night opened the doors of the prison, and
having brought them out said, Be going on your way,
and having taken a stand, be speaking in the temple to
the people all the words of this life. And having heard
that, they went about daybreak into the temple and began teaching. Now the chief priest and those with him,
having come, called together the Sanhedrin and all the
council of elders of the sons of Israel, and they sent to
the prison-house to have them brought. But the officers
having come, did not find them in the guard-house. And
having returned, they made an announcement, saying,
The prison-house we found to have been shut, and it was
locked, in a state of perfect security, and the guards
standing at the doors. But having opened them, we found
not one person inside. Now, when they heard these
words, the captain of the temple guard and the chief
priests continued to be entirely at a loss concerning them
as to what might become of this. Then a certain one
having come, brought word to them saying, Look. The
men whom you put in the prison are in the temple, standing there and teaching the people.

Then the captain, having gone with the officers, was **26-28**
bringing them without a show of force or violence, for
they were fearing the people lest they be stoned. And
having brought them, they stood them in the midst of
the council. And the chief priest questioned them, saying,
With a charge we commanded you not to be teaching in
the name of this fellow, and look, you have filled Jerusalem with your teaching, and purpose to bring upon us
the blood of this fellow.

Then, answering, Peter and the apostles said, It is a **29-32**
necessity in the nature of the case to be obeying God
rather than men. The God of our fathers raised up Jesus, whom, as for you, you killed, hanging Him upon a
cross. This One God exalted to His right hand as the
Chief Leader and the Saviour, to give repentance to Israel and the putting away of sins. And as for us, we are

those who are bearing testimony concerning these words, and so is the Holy Spirit whom God gave to those who obey Him.

33-36   Now when they heard this, their hearts were, as it were, sawn in two with vexation and rage. And they were consulting with one another with a view to killing them. Then there arose a certain one in the council, a Pharisee named Gamaliel, a teacher and interpreter of the law, held in honor by all the people. He ordered that the men be put outside for a brief period. And he said to them, Men, Israelites, be taking heed to yourselves with regard to what you are about to be doing to these men, for before these days there arose Theudas, saying that he was somebody, with whom a number of men, about four hundred, took sides, who was killed, and all, as many as obeyed him, were broken up and dispersed and came to nothing.

37-42   After this man there arose Judas of Galilee in the days of the census and drew away people after him. That one also perished, and all, as many as obeyed him, were scattered abroad. And with reference to the present things I am saying to you, stand off from these men and let them alone, because if this counsel or this work be of men, it will be overthrown. But assuming that it is of God, you are not able to destroy them, lest perchance you even be found to be those who are fighting God. And they permitted themselves to be persuaded by him. And having called the apostles, having beaten them, they ordered them not to be speaking in the Name of Jesus, and released them. They then went on their way rejoicing from the presence of the Sanhedrin, rejoicing that they were deemed worthy to be dishonored for the sake of the Name. And all through every day in the temple and at home they did not cease teaching and giving out the good news that the Christ is Jesus.

1-7   And in these days when the number of the disciples was multiplying, there arose a low, undertone murmuring of the Hellenists who were conferring together, secretly complaining against the Hebrews, the complaint being that their widows were being neglected in the daily

provision of food. Then the Twelve, having called to themselves the entire number of the disciples, said, It is not fitting that we should neglect the word of God, to be occupied with the distribution of food. Now, look, brethren, for men from among yourselves who are accredited, seven of them, controlled by the Spirit and filled with broad and full intelligence whom we shall appoint over this business. But as for us, to prayer and the ministry of the Word we shall give constant attention. And the word pleased the entire multitude. And they selected out from their number Stephen, a man full of faith and controlled by the Holy Spirit, and Philip, and Prochorus, and Nicanor, and Timon, and Parmenes, and Nicolas, a proselyte from Antioch, whom they stood before the apostles, and they, having prayed, laid their hands upon them. And the word of God kept on increasing, and the number of the disciples in Jerusalem kept on multiplying greatly. And a large number of the priests were becoming obedient to the Faith.

And Stephen, full of grace and of power, was con-   **8-15** stantly performing great miracles among the people that aroused wonder and amazement, and miracles that had for their purpose the attestation of the message of the one performing the miracle as one that was inspired of God. Then there arose certain ones from the synagogue which is called the synagogue of the Libertines [those who had once been slaves but were set free by Rome], and certain ones from the synagogues of the Cyrenians and of the Alexandrians and from those of Cilicia and of Asia disputing with Stephen, and they continued to be unable to stand up against his wisdom and the Spirit by whom he was speaking. Then they secretly instructed and instigated men who said, We have heard him saying slanderous words against Moses and God. And they stirred up the people and the elders and the men learned in the sacred scriptures as a mass, and moved them to a concerted point of view, and having come upon him suddenly, they seized him and brought him to the council of the Sanhedrin, and presented false witnesses saying, This man does not cease from continually speaking words against this place which is holy and against the law, for

we have heard him saying that Jesus, the Nazarene, this
fellow will destroy this place and will change the customs
which Moses delivered to us to keep, and the recollection
of this is still vivid in our memory. And all those sitting
in the council, having gazed intently upon him, saw his
face as if it were an angel's face.

1-7   Then the chief priest said, These things, are they
factual, as has been stated? And he said, Men, brethren,
and fathers, hear me. The God of the glory appeared to
our father Abraham when he was in Mesopotamia, before he took up his residence in Charran and said to him,
Come out of your country at once and away from your
relatives and come into the country which I will indicate
to you. Then, having come out of the country of the Chal-
daeans, he took up his residence in Charran. And from
that place, after his father died, He transferred him to
this land in which you now are residing. And He did
not give him an inheritance in it, nor even the space which
a human foot covers. Yet He promised to give it to him
as a permanent possession and to his offspring after him,
this promise made at the time when he did not have a
child. And God spoke to this effect, that his offspring
shall be temporary residents in a foreign land belonging
to another, and that they shall enslave his offspring and
oppress them four hundred years. And the nation for
which they will slave, as for myself, I will bring to the
bar of justice and punish, God said. And after these
things, they shall come out and render sacred service and
worship to me in this place.

8-10   And He gave him a covenant, the rite of circumcision
being its seal and sign. And thus he begat Isaac, and circumcised him on the eighth day. And Isaac begat Jacob,
and Jacob begat the twelve progenitors of the twelve
tribes. And these aforementioned founders, burning up
with envy of Joseph, sold him into Egypt. But God was
with him and delivered him out of all his tribulations.
And He gave him favor and wisdom in the sight of Pharaoh, king of Egypt. And he appointed him governor
over Egypt and his whole house.

Then there came a famine over the whole of Egypt   11-16
and Chanaan, and great affliction. And our fathers were
not finding fodder for their cattle. And when Jacob
heard that there were provisions in Egypt he sent off on
a mission our fathers first. And during their second visit
Joseph was made known to his brothers, and the identity of Joseph's nationality became evident to Pharaoh.
And Joseph having sent, summoned to himself Jacob his
father and all his relatives, seventy-five souls. And Jacob came down into Egypt, and he himself ended his
days, also our fathers, and were carried over to Sychem
and placed in the tomb which Abraham bought for a sum
of money from the sons of Emmor in Sychem.

But as the time of the promise which God had sworn   17-21
to Abraham was drawing near, the people increased and
multiplied in Egypt until there arose a king of a different
kind over Egypt who did not know Joseph. This one
dealt craftily against our nation and oppressed our fathers
so that they threw out their babies to the end that they
might not be preserved alive, during which time Moses
was born. And he was comely in the sight of God, and
was nourished in the house of his father three months.
And when he was thrown out the daughter of Pharaoh
took him up and nourished him for her own son.

And Moses was instructed in all the wisdom of the   22-29
Egyptians, and he was powerful in his words and deeds.
And when he was forty years old, it came into his heart
to pay a visit to his brethren, the sons of Israel, for the
purpose of acquainting himself with their needs and with
a view to helping them in their difficulties. And having
seen a certain one being ill treated, he defended him and
avenged the one who was being roughly treated, having
cut down the Egyptian. Now, he was supposing that his
brethren understood that God through his hand was giving them deliverance. But they did not understand. And
on the next day he appeared to them while they were
fighting and tried to reconcile them with a view to peace,
saying, Men, you are brothers. Why are you wronging
one another? But the one who was wronging his neighbor pushed him away, having said, Who constituted you
a ruler and an arbitrator over us? As for you, you are

not desiring to kill me even as you killed the Egyptian
yesterday, are you? Then Moses fled at this word and
became a temporary resident in the land of Madian where
two sons were born to him.

30-41   And after forty years had passed by, there appeared
to him in the uninhabited region of Mount Sinai an angel in a flaming fire of a bush. And Moses, having seen
it, went to wondering at the spectacle. And as he was
approaching it for the purpose of considering it attentively, the Lord's voice came, As for myself, I am the
God of your fathers, the God of Abraham and Isaac
and Jacob. But Moses becoming terrified, was not daring
to attentively consider it. Then the Lord said to him,
Take off your sandals at once from your feet, for the
place upon which you have taken a stand is holy ground.
I have surely seen the affliction of my people which are
in Egypt, and I heard their groaning, and I came down
to rescue them. And now, come. I will send you to
Egypt. This Moses whom they denied, saying, Who constituted you a ruler and an arbitrator? this man God sent
on a mission as both a ruler and a deliverer in cooperation with the angel who appeared to him in the bush. This
one led them out, having performed miracles which arouse
wonder and amazement and miracles whose purpose is
that of attesting the divine source of the message and mission of the one who performed them, performing them
in Egypt and at the Red Sea and in the uninhabited region
for forty years. This is the aforementioned Moses, the
one who said to the sons of Israel, A Prophet to you God
will raise up from your brethren who is like me. This is
he who was in the called-out assembly [called out of
Egypt] in the uninhabited region with the angel who was
speaking to him in Mount Sinai and with our fathers, who
received the living, divine utterances to give to you, to
whom our fathers were not desirous of becoming obedient, but thrust him away from themselves and turned
back in their hearts to Egypt, having said to Aaron, Make
us at once gods who will go before us. For this Moses
who led us out of the land of Egypt, we do not have any
positive knowledge as to what has happened to him. And
they made a calf in those days and offered a sacrifice to

the idol, and they kept on rejoicing in the works of their hands.

Then God turned His back upon them and delivered **42, 43** them up to be rendering religious service to the sun, moon, and stars of heaven, even as it stands written in the book of the prophets, You did not offer as sacrifices beasts slaughtered for sacrifice and sacrifices to me for forty years in the uninhabited region, house of Israel, did you? Yes, you raised up the tent of Moloch and the star of your god Remphan, the images which you made for the purpose of worshipping them. And I will cause you to be removed beyond Babylonia.

The tent of the testimony was for our fathers in the **44-47** uninhabited region even as He appointed when He was speaking to Moses that he should make it according to the pattern which he had seen, which tent also our fathers in their turn having received, brought in with Joshua when they entered the territory possessed by the Gentiles, whom God expelled from before our fathers until the days of David who found favor before God and asked as a personal favor that he be permitted to find a habitation for the house of the God of Jacob. But Solomon built Him a house.

Nevertheless, the Most High does not reside in things **48-53** made by hands, even as the prophet says, The heaven is my throne. The earth is the footstool for my feet. What sort of a house will you build me, says the Lord, or what is the place of my rest? Did not my hand make all these things? Stiffnecked, stubborn, headstrong, obstinate, and uncircumcised in heart and ears, as for you, incessantly do you strive against the Holy Spirit. As your fathers did, so also do you. Which of the prophets did not your fathers persecute? And they killed those who announced beforehand concerning the advent of the Just One, of whom, as for you, you now became the betrayers and the murderers, you who are of such a character as to have received the law as it was ordained by angels, and did not guard it so as not to violate it and to observe it.

And having heard these things they were cut to the **54-VIII 1** heart, and they began to gnash their teeth at him. And

Stephen being under the control of the Holy Spirit, having fixed his gaze into heaven, saw God's glory and Jesus standing at the right hand of God, and said, Behold, I see the heavens which have been opened, and the Son of Man standing on the right hand of God. And having cried out with a great voice, they covered their ears and rushed upon him in concert, and having thrown him outside of the city, they went to stoning him. And the witnesses put aside their outer garments beside the feet of a young man called Saul. And they kept on stoning Stephen as he was calling upon the Lord and saying, Lord Jesus, receive my spirit. And having knelt down, he cried with a great voice, Lord, do not place this sin against them. And having said this, he fell asleep. And Saul was together with the others approving of his death, taking pleasure with them in his death and applauding it.

1, 2   Then on that day there arose a persecution, a great one, against the assembly at Jerusalem. And all were scattered throughout the regions of Judaea and Samaria except the apostles. And men of piety and reverence toward God carried Stephen to his burial and made great lamentation over him, this lamentation accompanied by the beating of the breast.

3-8   But Saul kept on ravaging and devastating the Church, entering house after house, dragging both men and women by their feet along the street, consigning them to prison. Then those who were scattered abroad went about proclaiming the good news of the Word. And Philip, having gone down to the city of Samaria, proclaimed to them the Christ. And the people with one accord kept on giving heed to the things spoken by Philip, hearing them and seeing the attesting miracles which he was constantly doing, for in the case of many who had unclean spirits, the spirits came out shouting with a great voice. And many who were paralyzed and lame were healed. And there arose much joy in that city.

9-11   But there was a certain man whose name was Simon, who previous to this in the aforementioned city was practicing his magical arts in the form of charms and incan-

tations and astounding the people of Samaria to the point of being beside themselves in a mental imbalance, saying that he was some great personage, to whom they were continually giving heed, all of them from the least to the greatest, saying, This man is the [impersonated] power of God, that power which is called great [since in him it is seen in an outstanding way]. And they kept on giving heed to him because for a considerable length of time he had rendered them beside themselves with amazement by means of his magical arts.

Now, when they believed Philip as he was proclaim-   **12, 13**
ing the good news concerning the kingdom of God and the Name of Jesus Christ, they were being baptized, both men and women. Moreover Simon himself also believed, and having been baptized, continuing as an adherent of Philip, viewing with an interested and critical eye both the attesting miracles and also the great miracles which excited wonder as they were being performed, was being rendered beside himself with amazement.

Now, the apostles who were in Jerusalem, having   **14-17**
heard that Samaria had received the word of God, sent on a mission to them Peter and John, who, after they had come down, prayed for them in order that they might receive the Holy Spirit, for not yet had He fallen upon any one of them, but they had been baptized only into the Name of the Lord Jesus. Then they laid their hands upon them and they received the Holy Spirit, one after another, as each one submitted to the laying on of the apostles' hands.

And Simon having seen that through the laying on   **18-25**
of the hands of the apostles the Spirit was being given, offered them money, saying, Give to me also at once this authority in order that on whomsoever I lay my hands, he may be receiving the Holy Spirit. But Peter said to him, May your money accompany you in your destruction, because the gift of God you thought to acquire with money. You do not have a part nor a lot in this matter concerning which I am speaking, for your heart is not straightforward and sincere in the sight of God. Therefore repent at once of this your wickedness and beseech

the Lord if perhaps the purpose of your heart may be forgiven you, for I plainly see that you are in the gall of bitterness and in the bond of iniquity. Then Simon answering said, As for you, you beseech the Lord on my behalf in order that none of the things of which you have spoken may come upon me. Then after they had borne their testimony and had spoken the word of the Lord they proceeded on their return journey to Jerusalem and kept on proclaiming the good news in many villages of the Samaritans.

26, 27 And an angel of the Lord spoke to Philip, saying, Arise at once and be going on your way in a southerly direction along the road which goes down from Jerusalem to Gaza. This road is in an uninhabited region. And having arisen, he proceeded on his journey.

27-33 And behold. A man, an Ethiopian, a eunuch, a royal official of great authority serving under Candace, queen of the Ethiopians, who was in charge of all her treasure, who had gone to Jerusalem for the purpose of worshipping, was now returning and sitting in his chariot and reading the prophet Isaiah. And the Spirit said to Philip, Go towards this chariot at once and join yourself to it. And having run towards it, Philip heard him reading Isaiah the prophet. And he said, Do you really understand the things which you are reading? And he said, How am I able to unless someone guides me? And he urged Philip to come up and sit with him. Now, the contents of the scripture which he was reading were this: In the same manner as a sheep, to slaughter He was led. And in the same manner as a lamb before the one who is shearing it is without a sound, in the same manner He does not open His mouth. In His humiliation the equitable administration of justice due Him was denied Him. His nativity who shall set forth, for His life is taken from the earth?

34-40 And the eunuch answering Philip said, I beg of you, concerning whom is the prophet saying this, concerning himself or concerning some other person of a different character? And Philip opened his mouth and beginning from this scripture announced the good news to him con-

cerning Jesus. And as they were proceeding along the road they came to a certain water, and the eunuch says, Look, water. What is there that hinders me from being baptized? And he gave orders for the chariot to stand still. And the two descended into the water, both Philip and the eunuch. And he baptized him. And when they came up out from the water, the Lord's Spirit caught away Philip, and the eunuch saw him no longer, and he proceeded along his road rejoicing. And Philip was discovered at Azotus. And passing through, he proclaimed the good news to all the cities until he came to Caesarea.

And Saul, still breathing in a personally produced at-   **1, 2** mosphere of threatening and slaughter against the disciples of the Lord, having gone to the chief priest, asked from him as a personal favor letters to Damascus, to the synagogues, in order that if he found certain ones who belonged to the Way [that characteristic course of conduct exemplified by believers in the Christ of Christianity], both men and women, he might bring them bound to Jerusalem.

And as he was proceeding on his journey he was   **3-9** drawing near to Damascus. And suddenly there flashed around him a light out of heaven. And having fallen upon the ground he heard a voice saying, Saul, Saul, why are you persecuting me? And he said, Who are you, Sir? And as for myself, I am Jehoshua, whom, as for yourself, you are persecuting. But arise at once and go into the city and it shall be told you that which is a necessity in the nature of the case for you to be doing. And the men who were journeying with him stood speechless, hearing indeed the voice as a sound only and not understanding the words, moreover not seeing anyone. And Saul arose from the ground, but having opened his eyes he was seeing nothing. And leading him by the hand, they brought him into Damascus. And he was three days without sight. And he did not eat nor did he drink.

And there was a certain disciple in Damascus named   **10-14** Ananias. And the Lord said to him in a vision, Ananias. And he said, Behold, I am here, Lord. And the Lord said to him, Having arisen, proceed to the street called

the Straight Street, and inquire in the home of Judas for one whose name is Saul, a citizen of Tarsus; for behold, he is praying, and he saw a man whose name is Ananias who came and laid his hands upon him in order that he may recover his sight. And Ananias answered, Lord, I heard from many concerning this man, how many evil things he did to your saints in Jerusalem. And here he has delegated authority from the chief priests to bind all those who are calling on your Name.

15-19   But the Lord said to him, Be going on your way, because this man is a selected-out instrument of mine for the purpose of bearing my Name both before Gentiles and kings and the sons of Israel, for, as for myself, I will show him how many things it is necessary in the nature of the case for him to suffer on behalf of my Name. Then Ananias went off and entered the city. And having placed his hands upon him he said, Saul, brother, the Lord has sent me on a mission, Jehoshua, He who appeared to you on the road as you were coming, in order that you may recover your sight and be controlled by the Holy Spirit. And immediately there fell off from his eyes something having the appearance of incrustations. He recovered his sight, and having arisen, he was baptized, and having taken nourishment, he was strengthened.

19-21   Then he was with the disciples in Damascus for certain days. And immediately in the synagogues he proclaimed Jesus, his message being that this very person is the Son of God. And all those hearing continued to be amazed to the point of being beside themselves with wonder, and kept on saying, Is not this man he who made havoc among those who in Jerusalem are calling upon this Name, and who came here for this purpose, in order that having bound them he might bring them to the chief priests?

22-25   And Saul kept on being endued with power to a greater degree, and he bewildered Jews, those residing in Damascus, proving that this very person is the Christ. And when a considerable number of days had elapsed, the Jews consulted together with a view to putting him

out of the way. But their plot became known to Saul. And they kept on watching the gates both day and night in order that they might make away with him. Then the disciples, having taken him at night, sent him down through [a window in] the wall, having lowered him in a large basket.

And having come to Jerusalem, he kept on trying to **26-31** keep company with the disciples. And all were fearing him, not believing that he was a disciple. But Barnabas, coming to his help, brought him to the apostles and related in detail to them how on the road he saw the Lord and that He spoke to him, and how in Damascus he spoke out boldly in the Name of Jesus. And he was with them, going in and going out in Jerusalem, speaking boldly in the Name of the Lord, and he kept on both speaking and disputing with the Jews who had adopted Greek culture. But they kept on attempting to make away with him. And the brethren, having come to know of this, brought him down to Caesarea and sent him forth to Tarsus on a mission. So then the Church throughout Judaea and Galilee and Samaria was in possession of unbroken tranquillity, being constantly built up and proceeding on its way in the fear of the Lord, and by means of the instrumentality of the exhortation and encouragement of the Holy Spirit was multiplied as to its membership.

Now, it came to pass that as Peter was passing **32-35** through all parts, he came down also to the saints who were residing in Lydda. And there he found a certain man named Aeneas who for eight years had been lying prostrate on his bed, he being completely paralyzed. And Peter said to him, Jesus Christ is healing you right now. Arise at once and immediately spread your bed out evenly for comfort, doing this for yourself. And immediately he arose. And all those who were residing in Lydda and Saron saw him, who were such as turned to the Lord.

Now, in Joppa there was a certain woman disciple **36, 37** named Tabitha, which name being interpreted is Dorcas, the name Dorcas meaning gazelle, the creature with the beautiful eyes. This woman was abounding in good

works and in the giving of alms to the needy, in which
activities she was constantly engaged. And it came to
pass that in those days she became ill and died. And
having bathed her, they placed her in a room in the upper part of the house.

38-43   Now, Lydda being near Joppa, the disciples having
heard that Peter was there, sent two men on a mission to
him with the following urgent request, Do not delay to
come through to the place where we are. And Peter, having arisen, went with them, whom when he came, they
brought up into the upper room. And all the widows
stood by him weeping audibly and exhibiting the under-
garments and the long flowing outer robes, as many as
Dorcas was accustomed to make while she was with
them. And Peter, having put them all outside and having
kneeled down, prayed. And having turned to the corpse
he said, Tabitha, arise at once. And she opened her eyes,
and having seen Peter, she sat up. And having given her
his hand, he raised her up to a standing position. And
having called the saints and the widows, he presented her
alive. And this became known throughout the whole of
Joppa, and many believed on the Lord. And it came to
pass that he was the guest in Joppa for a considerable
length of time of a certain Simon, one who made his living by tanning hides.

1-6   Now, there was a certain man in Caesarea named
Cornelius, a centurion from the military cohort which
was called the Italian cohort, a pious man and one who
feared God with all his household, who gave many alms
to the Jewish people and who made supplication to God
always. He saw in a vision clearly and distinctly, about
three o'clock in the afternoon, an angel of God who came
to him and said to him, Cornelius. And having fixed
his gaze upon him and having become afraid, he said,
What is it, Sir? And he said, Your prayers and your
alms ascended as a memorial before God. And now send
men at once to Joppa and fetch a certain Simon who is
surnamed Peter. This man is being entertained as a
house-guest by a certain individual, Simon, a tanner,
whose house is on the seashore.

And when the angel who spoke to him had gone, having called two of his household slaves and a pious soldier who were numbered among those who were in continual attendance upon him, and having narrated to them the entire matter, he sent them off on a mission to Joppa. Now on the next day as those were on their journey and nearing the city, Peter went up to the house-top [the oriental veranda which was used for meditation and prayer] to engage in prayer, the time, about noon. And he became very hungry and was desiring to eat. And while they were preparing the meal, he entered into a new experience, that of an individual whose attention has been drawn to and concentrated upon one thing to the degree that he might as well be outside of his body so far as his physical senses registering anything is concerned. And he views with a critical eye heaven having been opened and a certain container descending, this object being like a sheet, a great one, being let down to the earth by means of four ropes attached to the four corners, in which there were all kinds of four-footed animals and reptiles of the earth and birds of the heaven. And there came a voice to him, Having arisen, Peter, kill at once and eat. But Peter said, By no means, Lord, because not yet have I eaten anything which is unhallowed or unclean. And a voice spoke a second time to him, The things which God cleansed, as for you, stop declaring unhallowed. And this occurred three times. And immediately the container was taken up into heaven.

Now, while Peter was completely at a loss as to what the vision which he saw might be, behold, the men who were sent off on a mission by Cornelius, having made diligent inquiry regarding the home of Simon, stood at the gate, and having called, inquired whether Simon, the one surnamed Peter, was staying there as a guest. And while Peter was earnestly pondering in his mind the matter concerning the vision, the Spirit said, Behold, two men are looking for you. But, having arisen, go down at once and be going on your way with them without any hesitation as to whether it is lawful or not, because, as for myself, I have sent them on a mission. Then Peter, having gone down to the men, said, Behold, as for my-

self, I am he for whom you are looking. What is the reason for your being here? And they said, Cornelius, a centurion, a man who is upright and who fears God and who is being highly recommended by the entire nation of the Jews, was divinely commanded by a holy angel to send for you to come to his home and to hear words from you.

23-27 Then he invited them in and extended to them the hospitality of the home. On the next day, having arisen, he went with them, and certain of the brethren of Joppa accompanied him. On the following day they entered Caesarea. Now, Cornelius was looking for them with eager expectation and hope, having called together his relatives and intimate friends. And when it came to pass that Peter entered, Cornelius having met him, having fallen at his feet, prostrated himself in an expression of profound respect. But Peter raised him up saying, Stand up. As for myself, I also am myself a man. And as he was conversing with him he entered and found many gathered together.

28, 29 And he said to them, As for you, you understand that it is a violation of established order for a man, a Jew, to enter into close relations with or come to a foreigner. And yet to me God showed that I am not to be calling any man unhallowed or unclean. Wherefore I also came without debating the issue, having previously been sent for. I am inquiring therefore, for what reason did you send for me?

30-33 And Cornelius said, Four days ago I was observing the afternoon prayer hour at three o'clock in my home, and behold, a man stood before me in brilliant apparel and said, Cornelius, your prayer was heard and your benefactions to others in need are held in remembrance as a memorial before God. Send therefore at once to Joppa and call here Simon who is surnamed Peter. This man is a house-guest in the seaside home of Simon, a tanner. I sent to you, and as for you, you have done well in coming. Now then, as for us, we all are present before God to hear all things which have been commanded you by the Lord.

And Peter, having opened his mouth, said, Of a truth **34-38**
I am in the process of comprehending the fact that God
does not show partiality to anyone because of his looks
or circumstances, but in every nation he who fears Him
and does uprightly is acceptable with Him. The word
which He sent to the sons of Israel, proclaiming as good
news peace through Jesus Christ, this One is Lord of all,
as for you, you know, which word went throughout the
whole of Judaea, beginning from Galilee after the time of
the baptism which John preached; Jesus, the one from
Nazareth, how God anointed Him with the Holy Spirit
and with power, who went about doing good and healing
all who were being oppressed by the devil, because God
was with Him.

And as for us, we are those who are bearing testi- **39-43**
mony to the things we saw, all those things He did both
in the land of the Jews and in Jerusalem, whom they also
killed and suspended on a cross. This One God raised up
on the third day and appointed that He should become
clearly identified, not to all the people, but to witnesses
who had been designated beforehand by God, to us, who
were such as ate and drank with Him after He arose from
the dead. And He charged us to make a proclamation to
the [Jewish] people and to bear testimony that this is
the One who was appointed by God to be the Judge of
the living and the dead. To this One all the prophets
bear testimony, that through His Name everyone who
places his trust in Him receives remission of the penalty
of sins.

While Peter was speaking these words, the Holy **44-48**
Spirit fell upon all those who were hearing the Word.
And the believers who belonged to the circumcision, as
many as came with Peter, were amazed to the point of
being beside themselves with consternation, because also
upon the Gentiles the gift of the Holy Spirit had been
bestowed with the result that now He was in their possession, for they were hearing them speaking by means
of languages [other than their own and not naturally
acquired], and extolling God. Then answered Peter, No
one can forbid the water in order that these may be baptized, who are such as received the Holy Spirit even as

also we, can he? Then he ordered that they be baptized
in the Name of Jesus Christ. Then they asked him to
be their guest for certain days.

1-10   Now, the apostles and the brethren who resided
throughout Judaea heard that the Gentiles also received
the word of God. And when Peter went up to Jerusalem
those of the circumcision disputed with him saying, You
went into men who were uncircumcised and ate with
them. And Peter having begun, went to expounding the
matter in its sequence of events, saying, As for myself,
I was in the city of Joppa praying, and I being in a state
in which my attention was withdrawn from everything
else and fixed on things divine, saw a vision, a certain
container like a great sheet descending, being let down
out of heaven by four great strips of cloth. And it came
even to me, and having fastened my gaze upon it, I considered it attentively. And I saw the four-footed animals
of the earth and the wild beasts and the birds of heaven.
And I heard also a voice saying to me, Having arisen,
Peter, kill at once and eat. And I said, By no means,
Lord, because that which is unhallowed or unclean, never
yet did it enter my mouth. But there answered a second
time a voice out of heaven, The things which God cleansed,
as for you, stop calling them unhallowed. And this
was done three times. And all was drawn up again into
heaven.

11-18   And behold. Immediately, three men had come to the
house in which we were, sent on a mission from Caesarea
to me. And the Spirit told me to go with them without
even one bit of hesitation as to its propriety. Moreover,
there came with me also these six brethren, and we entered into the house of the man. Then he reported to us
how he saw the angel in his house stand and say, Send at
once a mission to Joppa and bring back Simon, the one
surnamed Peter, who will speak words to you by which,
as for yourself, you shall be saved and everyone of your
household. Now, when I began to be speaking, the Holy
Spirit fell upon them even as upon us at the beginning.
Then there was brought to my remembrance the word
of the Lord how He was saying, John indeed baptized
by means of water, but as for yourselves, you will be

baptized by means of the Holy Spirit. Therefore, in view of the fact that God gave the equal gift to them as also to us who believed on the Lord Jesus Christ, as for myself, who was I that I would be able to hinder God? And having heard these things, they were silent and glorified God saying, Then also God gave repentance to the Gentiles resulting in life.

19-21 Therefore, those who were scattered abroad, scattered as seed by the distress and affliction which arose on account of Stephen, passed through the country as far as Phoenicia and Cyprus and Antioch, speaking the Word to nobody except only to Jews. Now, there were certain ones of these, men of Cyprus and Cyrene, being such as those who having come to Antioch, began speaking also to the Jews who had acquired Greek culture, announcing as glad tidings the Lord Jesus. And the Lord was with them, and a large number who believed, turned to the Lord.

22-26 Then the word concerning them reached the ears of the assembly at Jerusalem. And they sent off on a mission Barnabas to go as far as Antioch, who, having come and having seen the grace of God, rejoiced and went to exhorting all that with purpose of heart they should live in close fellowship with the Lord; for he was a good man and controlled by the Holy Spirit and full of faith. And there was added to the Lord many people. Then he went off to Tarsus for the purpose of hunting up Saul, and having found him, he brought him to Antioch. And it came to pass that even for a whole year they were gathered together with them in the assembly and taught many people. And the disciples were first given the name, Christian, at Antioch.

27-30 And in these days there came down from Jerusalem, prophets to Antioch. And having arisen, one of them, by name, Agabus, made known through the agency of the Holy Spirit that there was about to be a famine over the whole of the Roman empire, which occurred at the time of Claudias. And the disciples, according as any one of them was prospered, determined, each one of them, to send things which would minister to the needs of those

brethren who were residing in Judaea, which thing also
they did, having sent them to the elders by the hand of
Barnabas and Saul.

1-4   Now, at that strategic, significant period [in the
growth of the Church and the success of the gospel mes-
sage], Herod the king laid his hands upon certain of
those who belonged to the Church for the purpose of mal-
treating them. And he put James, the brother of John,
out of the way, beheading him with a sword. And having seen that it was a pleasing thing to the Jews, he proceeded to seize Peter also. Now, it was the days of bread
baked without yeast. And having apprehended him, he
put him in prison, having delivered him into the custody
of sixteen soldiers who were to guard him constantly,
purposing as the result of mature consideration after the
passover to set him before the people for the purpose of
being tried in their courts.

5-9   Therefore, on the one hand, Peter was continually
guarded in the prison, but on the other hand, prayer was
continually and earnestly being directed by the Church to
God concerning him. Now, when Herod was about to
bring him out, on that night Peter was slumbering between two soldiers, securely bound by two chains, and
guards were at the door who were maintaining a constant
watch. And behold, the Lord's angel came suddenly and
stood by him, and a light shone in his cell. And having
gently tapped Peter's side, he raised him up, saying, Arise
quickly. And his chains fell off his hands. Then the angel said to him, Put on your belt and bind on your sandals. And he did this. And he said to him, Throw your
outer garment around yourself and keep on following
with me. And having gone out, he kept on following,
and he did not know that it was true, namely, that which
was taking place through the agency of the angel, but
he was of the opinion that he was seeing a vision.

10   Now, after they had gone through the guards posted
at the first and second stations, they came up against the
iron gate which leads into the city, which opened to them
automatically, and having gone out they went on along
one street, and immediately the angel departed from him.

And Peter, having come to himself, said, Now I know **11-17**
truly that the Lord dispatched His angel on a mission
and delivered me out of Herod's hand and from every
expectation of the people of the Jews. And having taken
in his situation clearly, he went to the home of Mary the
mother of John, the one surnamed Mark, where there
were many who had come together and were praying.
And after Peter had knocked on the door of the passageway, there came a female slave to answer the knock,
her name, Rhoda. And having recognized the voice of
Peter, in her joy she failed to open up the passageway,
but having run in she announced that Peter was standing before the entrance. But they said to her, You are
raving mad. But she strongly and consistently asserted
that thus it was. But they kept on saying, It is his angel
[his guardian angel, assuming his form and voice, a Jewish belief]. But Peter remained and kept on knocking.
And having opened the door, they saw him and were beside themselves with astonishment. And having beckoned
to them with his hand to keep quiet, he related in detail
to them how the Lord had brought him out of the
prison, and said, Report these things to James and the
brethren. And having gone out, he proceeded to a different place.

Now, day having come, there was no small commo- **18,19**
tion among the soldiers as to what then had become of
Peter. And after Herod had made a careful search for
him and did not find him, having questioned the guards,
he ordered that they be led away to execution, and having gone down from Judaea to Caesarea, he spent some
time there.

Now, Herod was having a violent quarrel with the **20-25**
Tyreans and Sidonians that had lasted for some time.
And they with one accord came to him, and having won
the favor of Blastus, the king's chief valet, they kept on
requesting peace, because their country received its supplies of food from the country of the king. And on an
appointed day Herod, having arrayed himself in royal
apparel, having seated himself upon the judgment seat,
was making an address to them. And the people kept on
shouting, The voice of a god and not of a man. And

immediately an angel of the Lord afflicted him with a disease because he did not give God the glory. And having reached that stage in the disease where worms were eating him, he expired. But the word of God kept on growing and multiplying. And Barnabas and Saul returned from Jerusalem, and having completed their ministry, took with them John whose surname was Mark.

1-3 Now, there were in Antioch in the assembly which was there, prophets and teachers, as Barnabas and Simeon, the one called Niger, and Lucius and Cyrenian, Manaean who had been reared with Herod the tetrarch, and Saul. Now, as they were ministering to the Lord in sacred things and were fasting, the Holy Spirit said, Now, therefore, set apart for me at once Barnabas and Saul for the work to which I have called them to myself. Then, having fasted and prayed and having laid their hands upon them, they sent them away.

4-12 So then they themselves, having been sent out by the Holy Spirit, went down to Seleucia. And from there they sailed away to Cyprus, and having come to Salamis, they went to making the word of God known in the synagogues of the Jews. And they were also having John as their attendant and assistant. And having gone through the whole island until they came to Paphos, they found a certain man, one who practiced the magical arts, a false prophet, a Jew, his name, Bar-jesus, who was with the proconsul, Sergius Paulus, a man of understanding. This man having called Barnabas and Saul to himself, desired to hear the word of God. But Elymas the soothsayer [for thus is his name by interpretation, the wise one] kept on standing up against them, seeking to turn away the proconsul from the Faith. But Saul, who also is called Paul, controlled by the Holy Spirit, having fixed his gaze upon him, said, O full of every craftiness and every unscrupulousness, son of the devil, enemy of every righteousness, will you not cease perverting the right ways of the Lord? And now, behold, the Lord's hand is upon you, and you will be blind, not seeing the sun for a time. And immediately there fell upon him a dimness of the eyes and darkness. And walking about, he went to seeking someone to lead him by the hand. Then the proconsul,

having seen that which had taken place, believed, being astonished to the point of a loss of self-control at the teaching of the Lord.

Now, having put out to sea from Paphos, Paul and his associates came to Perga of Pamphylia, but John having withdrawn from them, returned to Jerusalem. Then, they themselves having gone on through the country from Perga, came to Antioch, the Pisidian Antioch, and having gone into the synagogue on the day of the sabbath, seated themselves. And after the reading of the law and the prophets, the rulers of the synagogue sent to them saying, Men, brethren, if, as is the case, you have any word of exhortation to the people, you are invited to speak.

13-15

Then Paul, having arisen and having beckoned with his hand, said, Men, Israelites, and those who fear God [the latter, Gentile proselytes], give me your attention. The God of this people Israel selected out [from the rest of humanity] our fathers and exalted the people during their temporary residence in the land of Egypt, and with a high arm He brought them out of it, and for about forty years He tenderly cared for them in the uninhabited region, and having destroyed seven nations in the land of Canaan, He divided their land, distributing it by lot among them as an inheritance for about four hundred and fifty years. And after these things He gave them judges until Samuel the prophet.

16-20

And after this they requested a king, and God gave them Saul, the son of Kish, a man of the tribe of Benjamin, for forty years. And having deposed him, He raised up David for them as king, to whom He bore testimony and said, I found David, the son of Jesse, a man after my heart who will do all things which are my desires. Of this man, God from his family according to promise brought to Israel a Saviour, Jesus, John having previously heralded to all the people, Israel, before His entry upon His ministry, a baptism associated with repentance. And when John was finishing the course of his office [as herald], he kept on saying, What do you conjecture that I am? As for myself, I am not He. But behold.

21-25

There comes One after me, the sandals of whose feet I am not worthy to unloose.

26-41   Men, brethren, sons of the family of Abraham and those among you who fear God, to us the word of this salvation was sent forth, for those who are residing in Jerusalem and their rulers, having been ignorant of this One and of the voices of the prophets which every sabbath are read, in condemning Him fulfilled this word, and though not having found even one cause of death in Him, they asked Pilate as a personal favor that He be put out of the way. And when they fulfilled all the things which stand written concerning Him, having taken Him down from the cross, they laid Him in a tomb. But God raised Him out from among the dead. He was seen for many days by those who had come up with Him from Galilee to Jerusalem, who now are as to their nature those who are testifying to what they have seen of Him to the people. And, as for us, we are bringing good news to you of the promise which was made to our fathers, that God has completely fulfilled this to our children, having raised up Jesus [as the Messiah], as also in the second psalm it stands written, As for you, you are my Son. As for myself, today I have begotten you. Now that He raised Him up from among those who are dead, no longer destined to return to corruption, thus has He spoken, and the record is a permanent one, I will give to all of you the holy things of David, the trustworthy things, because also in another psalm He says, You will not appoint your Holy One to see corruption, for indeed, David during his own generation having ministered in the sphere of the counsel of God, fell asleep [died], was buried with his fathers, and saw corruption. But He whom God raised up did not see corruption. Let it be known therefore to you, men, brethren, that through this One to you is being announced the putting away of sins, and from all things from which you were not able by the law of Moses to be justified, by this One everyone who believes is justified. Therefore, be bewaring lest there come upon you that which has been spoken by the prophets and is on permanent record, Behold, you despisers, and you who wonder and perish, because as for myself, I am accomplishing

a work in your days, a work which you will by no means
believe if anyone keep on narrating it in full to you.

Now, as they were going out they kept on begging   **42-52**
that on the next sabbath these words might be preached
to them. Then after the congregation had dissolved,
many of the Jews and the proselytes who were worshipping followed with Paul and Barnabas who, speaking to
them, were urging them to be continuing in the grace of
God. And on the next sabbath almost the entire city
was gathered together to hear the word of God. Then the
Jews, having seen the crowds, became filled with jealousy
and went to speaking against the things which were being spoken by Paul, saying slanderous and evil things.
And having become bold, Paul and Barnabas said, To you
it was required in the nature of the case for the word of
God to be spoken first. Since now you are thrusting it
away from yourselves and are judging yourselves not
worthy of life eternal, behold, we are turning ourselves to
the Gentiles, for thus has the Lord commanded us; I
have appointed you as a light of Gentiles in order that
you may be for salvation to the end of the earth. Now,
the Gentiles hearing this were rejoicing and glorifying
the word of the Lord. And as many as had been appointed to life eternal believed. And the word of the Lord was
being carried in different directions and to different places
throughout the entire country. But the Jews urged on
the devout women, those of high position and the leading men of the city, and raised up persecution against
Paul and Barnabas, and threw them out of their boundaries. But having shaken off the dust of their feet against
them, they came to Iconium. And the disciples were
continually filled with joy and controlled by the Holy
Spirit.

And it came to pass in Iconium that they entered the   **1-7**
synagogue of the Jews together and spoke in such a manner that a large company of both Jews and Gentiles believed. But the Jews who were unwilling to be persuaded
and thus withheld belief, stirred up the minds of the Gentiles and rendered them antagonistic toward their brethren. So then for a long time they stayed there, speaking
boldly in reliance upon the Lord who bore testimony

upon the basis of His word to His grace by granting attesting miracles and miracles exciting wonder to be done constantly through their hands. But the population of the city was split up into factions, and some on the one hand were with the Jews and others on the other hand were with the apostles. Now, when there arose a hostile intention on the part of both Gentiles and Jews with their rulers to treat them in a shameful manner and to stone them, having become aware of it, they fled for refuge to the cities of Lycaonia, Lystra, and Derbe, and to the surrounding region, and there they were engaged in proclaiming the good news.

8-10   And a certain man who was without strength in his feet, his lameness having its source in a prenatal condition, who never yet had walked, was sitting there at Lystra. This man was listening to Paul speak, who, having fixed his gaze attentively upon him and having seen that he was having faith to be healed, said in a great voice, Stand upright upon your feet. And he leaped up with a single bound and went to walking about.

11-13   And the crowds having seen what Paul did, raised their voice in the language of Lycaonia saying, The gods, having assumed the likeness of men, came down to us. And they began calling Barnabas, Zeus, and Paul, Hermes, since he himself was the leader in the discourse. And the priest of Zeus, whose temple was before the city, having brought oxen and garlands to the gates, was desiring to offer sacrifice with the crowds.

14-18   But the apostles, Barnabas and Paul, having heard of this, having torn in two pieces their outer garments, leaped into the midst of the crowd, shouting out and saying, Men, why are you doing these things? And as for us, we are men who possess the same kind of feelings that you have, proclaiming the good news that you should turn from these things that are futile, ineffectual in accomplishing the purpose for which they were intended, to God who is alive, who made the heaven and the earth and the sea and all the things which are in them, who in the generations gone by permitted all the nations to be proceeding along their ways of life. And yet He did not

leave himself without a witness in that He did good, giving to you rain from heaven and fruitful seasons, filling your hearts with food and good cheer. And saying these things they with difficulty restrained the crowds from offering sacrifice to them.

Then there arrived Jews from Antioch and Iconium, **19-22** and having persuaded the crowds and having stoned Paul, they dragged him by his feet outside of the city, thinking that he had died. However, after the disciples had gathered around him, he arose suddenly and went into the city. And on the next day he went forth with Barnabas to Derbe. And proclaiming the good news in that city and having made many disciples through their teaching, they returned to Lystra and Iconium and Antioch, establishing and strengthening the souls of the disciples, exhorting them to be persevering in and holding true to the Faith, and exhorting them that it is a necessity in the nature of the case to enter the kingdom of God through many tribulations.

And having appointed for them elders in every assem- **23-28** bly, having prayed in connection with fasting, they commended them to the Lord on whom they had believed. And having gone throughout Pisidia, they came to Pamphylia, and having spoken the Word in Perga, they went down to Attalia, and from there they sailed away to Antioch, from which place they had been committed to the grace of God for the work which they fulfilled. And reaching their destination and gathering the assembly together, they went to reporting as many things as God had done in helping them, and that He opened to the Gentiles a door of faith. And they stayed with the disciples not a little time.

And certain men having come down from Judaea **1-4** began teaching the brethren, and these were their words, Unless you are circumcised after the custom of Moses, you are not able to be saved. And there having come no little discord and questioning to Paul and Barnabas as they faced them, they [the brethren] appointed Paul and Barnabas and certain others of them to go up to the apostles and elders at Jerusalem concerning this question in dis-

pute. They therefore having been furnished with the requisites for the journey by the assembly, proceeded on their way through Phoenicia and Samaria, narrating in full the turning of the Gentiles [from idolatry to God], and they were constantly giving great joy to all the brethren. And having come to Jerusalem, they were formally and cordially received by the assembly and the apostles and the elders, and they reported as many things as God had done in helping them.

5   But there suddenly rose up [among the assembled believers] certain ones from the religious sect of the Pharisees who believed, saying that it was a necessity in the nature of the case for them to be circumcised and to be commanding them to keep the law of Moses.

6-12   Both the apostles and the elders had come together for the purpose of looking into this matter. And after there had been much debate, Peter, having arisen, said to them, Men, brethren. As for you, you know that a good while ago God made a choice among us to the effect that through my mouth the Gentiles should hear the story of the good news and believe. And God who knows the hearts, bore attesting testimony to them by having given them the Holy Spirit even as also to us. And He made no distinction at all between both us and also you, in answer to their faith having cleansed their hearts. Now, therefore, why are you putting God on trial [to see whether He has committed an error or not] by putting a yoke upon the neck of the disciples which neither our fathers nor we were able to endure? But through the grace of the Lord Jesus we believe that we are saved in the like manner as also those. Then the entire group lapsed into silence and went to listening to Barnabas and Paul recounting in detail as many attesting miracles and miracles that excite wonder and amazement which God performed among the Gentiles through their intermediate agency.

13-18   And after they became silent, James answered, saying, Men, brethren, may I have your attention. Simeon related in detail how that God for the first time exercised His overseeing care in taking out from the Gentiles a

people for His Name. And to this agree the words of the prophets, even as it has been written and as a result is on record, After these things I will return and I will build again the hut of David which has fallen down and now lies in ruins. And I will build again the things belonging to it which are lying about in utter ruin. And I will build it anew, in order that those left remaining of mankind may seek out the Lord, also all the Gentiles upon whom my Name has been pronounced, says the Lord who makes these things known from the beginning of the world.

Wherefore, as for myself, my judgment is that we are not to be troubling those from among the Gentiles who are turning to God, but that we write them to be holding themselves off from the pollutions of the idols and from fornication and from eating the flesh of an animal which was killed without the shedding of its blood, and from this blood; for Moses from the time of generations long past has those in every city who proclaim him, being read in the synagogues every sabbath.   **19-21**

Then it seemed good to the apostles and the elders together with the entire assembly to send men who had been selected out of their own number to Antioch with Paul and Barnabas, namely, Judas, the one called Barsabas, and Silas, men who exercised leadership among the brethren, writing through them as follows: The apostles and the elders, brethren, send greetings to those brethren who are of the Gentiles in Antioch and Syria and Cilicia. In view of the fact that we heard that certain ones of our number perplexed and disturbed you with words, throwing your souls into confusion, to whom we did not give any express injunctions, it seemed good to us, having arrived at a unanimous agreement, to send men who have been selected out from our number to you with our beloved Barnabas and Paul, men [Barnabas and Paul] who have jeopardized their lives on behalf of the Name of our Lord Jesus Christ. We have sent therefore Judas and Silas, and they themselves will report the same things verbally, for it seemed good to the Holy Spirit and to us to lay no greater burden upon you than these things which are necessary, that you abstain from eating the flesh of animals left over from the pagan sacrifices, and   **22-29**

blood and the flesh of animals killed without the shedding of their blood, and from fornication, from which if you carefully keep yourselves, it shall be well with you. Farewell.

30-35   So they, having been sent off, went down to Antioch, and having gathered together the whole assembly, delivered the letter. And having read it, they burst into exultant joy because of the encouragement it brought them. And both Judas and Silas, also being prophets themselves, through much discourse exhorted the brethren and encouraged them besides. And having been there for some time, they were sent off with peace from the brethren to those who had sent them on the mission. But Paul and Barnabas continued their stay in Antioch with many others, teaching and giving out as good news the word of the Lord.

36-41   And after certain days Paul said to Barnabas, Now, therefore, retracing our steps, let us look in on our brethren for the purpose of seeing what they are in need of and supplying that need, city by city in which we publicly proclaimed the word of the Lord, observing how they are getting along. Now, Barnabas, after thinking the matter over, kept on insisting that they take along with them also John, the one called Mark. But Paul kept on considering it the part of wisdom with reference to this one who withdrew from them from Pamphylia and did not go with them to the work, not to be taking him. And there arose a sharp contention so that they separated from one another, and Barnabas having taken Mark with him, set sail for Cyprus. And Paul, having chosen Silas for himself, went forth, having been commended to the grace of the Lord by the brethren. And he went through Syria and Cilicia establishing the assemblies.

1-5   And he came also to Derbe and Lystra. And behold, a certain disciple was there named Timothy, a son of a Jewish woman who was a believer. However, his father was a Greek, he [Timothy] constantly being well recommended by the brethren in Lystra and Iconium. This one Paul desired to go forth with him. And having taken him, he circumcised him because of the Jews who were

in those regions, for they all knew that his father was a Greek. And as they were proceeding through the cities they kept on delivering to them the decrees for them to be keeping which had been issued by the apostles and elders in Jerusalem. So then the assemblies were being strengthened with respect to the Faith and increased in number daily.

Then they passed through Phrygia and the Galatian region, having been forbidden by the Holy Spirit to speak the Word in Asia. And having come down to the borders of Mysia, by a trial-and-error method they kept on attempting to discover whether it was right to go to Bithynia. But the Spirit of Jesus did not permit them to do so. And having skirted Mysia they came down to Troas.

6-8

And a vision appeared to Paul during the night. A certain man, a Macedonian, was standing and begging him and saying, Come over into Macedonia at once and give us aid. And when he had seen the vision, immediately we endeavored to go forth into Macedonia, concluding that God had called us to tell them the good news.

9, 10

Then setting sail from Troas we ran a straight course before the wind to Samothracia, and on the morrow, to Neapolis. And from there we went to Philippi which was the first Macedonian city of the district, a [Roman] colony [its citizens, Roman citizens]. Now, we were in this city, staying certain days. And on the day of the sabbath we went outside the gate along the river bank where we supposed there was a place of prayer. And having seated ourselves, we went to speaking to the women who had come together. And a certain woman, by name Lydia, a seller of purple fabrics, from the city of Thyatira, who worshipped God, was listening, whose heart the Lord had opened up wide so that she kept her mind concentrated upon the things which were spoken by Paul. Now, when she was baptized and her household, she begged us, saying, Since you have judged me to be a believer on the Lord, having come into my home, be my guest for a while. And she, by her entreaties, persuaded us to accept her hospitality.

11-15

16-18   And it came to pass that as we were proceeding to
the place of prayer, a certain female slave possessing a
spirit [a demon], a pythian spirit [associated with the
demonology of the pagan Greek religions], encountered
us, who was of such a nature that she provided her masters with a profitable business by acting as a seer and delivering prophecies and oracles. This woman, having followed after Paul and us, cried out saying, These men
are slaves of God, the Most High God, such as are making known to you the way of salvation. And this she
kept on doing many days. But Paul, thoroughly annoyed
and indignant, was worn out, and having turned around
to the spirit, said, I charge you in the Name of Jesus
Christ to come out of her at once. And he came out that
same hour.

19-24   Now, her masters, having seen that the hope of their
gain had vanished, having seized Paul and Silas, dragged
them by their heels into the market place to the civil rulers, and having brought them to the magistrates said,
These men are causing a great deal of trouble in our city,
being Jews, and are promulgating customs which it is not
lawful for us to be receiving nor to be doing, since we
are Romans. And the crowd rose up together against
them, and the magistrates, having torn off their clothing,
were issuing orders to be beating them with rods. And
having inflicted many stripes upon them they threw them
into prison, charging the jailer to be guarding them
safely, who, having received such an order, threw them
into the inner prison and made their feet secure in an
instrument of torture having five holes, four for the
wrists and ankles and one for the neck.

25-34   Now, about midnight Paul and Silas while they were
praying were also singing praises to God, mingling peti-
tion with songs of praise, and the prisoners were listening to them, enjoying their singing. And suddenly there
was an earthquake, a great one, so that the foundations
of the prison were caused to totter. And all the doors
were instantly opened, and the bonds of all were loosened.
And the jailer, having been roused out of sleep and having seen the doors of the prison opened, having drawn

out his sword, was about to be killing himself, supposing
that the prisoners had escaped. But Paul shouted in a
loud voice, saying, Do not begin to do yourself one bit
of harm, for we are all here. Then, having asked for a
light, he sprang in, and having become terrified, fell down
before Paul and Silas, and having brought them outside,
said, Sirs, what is it necessary in the nature of the case
for me to keep on doing in order that I may be saved?
And they said, Put your trust at once and once for all
in the Lord Jesus, and as for yourself, you shall be saved,
also your household. And they spoke to him the word of
God together with all those in his home. And having
taken them in that same hour under his care, he bathed
their stripes, washing away the coagulated blood. And he
himself was immediately immersed and all those who belonged to him. And having brought them up into his
home, he put them at his own table and set food before
them. And he rejoiced, having believed in God with his
whole household.

And day having come, the magistrates sent the lictors   **35, 36**
on a mission saying, Release those men at once. Then
the jailer reported these words to Paul, The magistrates
have sent men with a commission to release you. Therefore, now having gone out, be proceeding on your way
in peace.

But Paul said to them, Having beaten us publicly, we   **37-40**
who are uncondemned, men who are Romans, they threw
us into prison. And, as for us, in secret are they now
thrusting us out? No indeed, but having come themselves,
let them bring us out. Then the lictors reported to the
magistrates these words. And they became afraid, having
heard that they were Romans. And having come, they
begged them, and having brought them out, they went to
asking them to go away from the city. And having come
out of the prison, they went to the home of Lydia, and
having seen the brethren, they encouraged them and went
off.

Now, after traveling through Amphipolis and Apol-   **1-3**
lonia, they came to Thessalonica, where there was a synagogue of the Jews. And Paul according to his custom

61

went in to them, and for three sabbaths reasoned with them upon the basis and from the source of the scriptures, making these plain to the understanding and setting them forth as proof of the fact that it was a necessity in the nature of the case for the Christ [Messiah] to suffer and to be raised out from among the dead, and that this Man is the Christ [the Messiah], this Jesus whom, as for myself, I am proclaiming to you.

4-9   And certain of them were persuaded and were allotted [by God] to Paul and Silas [as disciples], a great multitude of the devout Greeks, and not a few women who were of the very first rank. But the Jews, motivated by jealousy, having taken to themselves certain pernicious men belonging to the loungers in the market place, and gathering a crowd, put the city in an uproar, and having attacked the house of Jason, they were seeking to bring them [Paul and Silas] before the people. But not having found them, they went to dragging Jason by the feet and certain brethren to the city officials, shouting, These who turned the Roman empire upside down, have arrived here also, whom Jason received as his guests. And these, all of them, are doing things contrary to Caesar's decrees, saying that there is another king of a different nature, Jesus. And they stirred up the people and the city officials hearing these things. And having put Jason and the rest under bond, they released them.

10-14   And the brethren immediately sent off both Paul and Silas by night to Berea, who, having arrived there, went into the synagogue of the Jews. Now, these were more noble-minded than those in Thessalonica, who were such that they received the Word with all readiness of mind, daily scrutinizing the scriptures whether these things were so. Many of them indeed therefore believed, and of the Greek women, the ones who were of rank, and of men not a few. But when the Jews of Thessalonica came to know that in Berea also the word of God was proclaimed by Paul, they went there also, stirring up and agitating the crowds. And then immediately the brethren sent Paul off to be proceeding as far as the sea. And both Silas and Timothy remained there.

Now, those who conducted Paul brought him up to **15**
Athens. And having received a command for Silas and
Timothy to the effect that they should come to him as
quickly as possible, they went off.

Now, while Paul was waiting for them in Athens, his **16-21**
spirit was constantly provoked and irritated in him, viewing with a critical eye the city which was full of idols.
Then indeed he went to reasoning in the synagogue of the
Jews and with the devout persons in the town square
which was used as the public forum every day with those
whom he happened to meet. And certain also of the Epi-
curean and Stoic philosophers kept on encountering him
for the purpose of disputing with him. And some went
to saying, What would he desire to be saying, granted he
was able to say anything, this ignorant plagiarist, picking
up scraps of information here and there, unrelated in his
own thinking and passing them off as the result of his
own mature thought? But others began saying, He seems
to be a proclaimer of foreign divinities; because he was
announcing as good news Jesus and His resurrection. And
having taken him, they brought him to the Court of Areopagus [the seat of the ancient and venerable Athenian
court which decided the most solemn questions connected
with religion], saying, May we come to know what this
teaching is, new as to its character, which you are pro-
pounding, for you are bringing certain startling and be-
wildering things to our ears? Therefore it is our reasoned desire that we come to know what the intent of
these things is. Now, all Athenians and the foreigners
residing there devoted their leisure time in not even one
other thing of a different character than to be telling or
listening to something that was newer in its nature.

Then Paul, having stood up in the midst of the Court **22-31**
of Areopagus, said, Men, Athenians, my critical, understanding eye tells me that in all things you are more di-
vinity-fearing [than the rest of the Greeks]. For when
passing through [your city], looking attentively at the
objects of your worship, I found an altar upon which
was written, TO AN UNKNOWN GOD. That therefore which you are unknowingly worshipping, this, as
for myself, I am announcing to you. The God who made

the universe and all the things in it, this God being the natural Lord of heaven and earth, does not take up His residence in sanctuaries made by hands, neither is He served by the hands of mankind as though needing any certain thing in addition to what He already has, and this in view of the fact that He himself is constantly giving to all life and breath and all things. And He made out of one source material every nation of mankind to inhabit the entire surface of the earth, having marked out the limitations of strategic, epochal periods of time which have been appointed and the fixed boundaries of their occupancy, in order that they should be seeking this aforementioned God, if so then they will grope after Him and find Him, though He is not far from each one of us, for in Him we derive our life and have motion, as also certain of your poets have said, For of Him are we also offspring. Therefore, since we are the offspring of God, we are not under moral obligation to be thinking that this aforementioned Being possessing divine attributes is like gold or silver or stone, a carved work of art and of man's invention. Now, therefore, the times of ignorance God having allowed to pass unnoticed, with reference to the present set of circumstances He declares to men that everyone everywhere should be repenting, because He appointed a day in which He is about to be judging the inhabitants of the earth with an equitable administration of justice by means of a Man whom He appointed, furnishing a guarantee to all in that He raised Him out from among those who are dead.

32-34 And having heard of a resurrection out from among the dead, some began to mock, but others said, We will hear you concerning this yet again. Under these circumstances Paul went out from their midst. But certain men having clung to him, believed, among whom was Dionysius, one of the judges of the Court of Areopagus, and a woman named Damaris, and others with them.

1-3 After these things, having gone out of and away from Athens, he came to Corinth. And having found a certain Jew named Aquila, a man from Pontus recently having come from Italy, and Priscilla his wife, because Claudias had given orders that all the Jews were to be expelled

from Rome, he went to them. And because he was of
the same occupation, he lived at their home. And they
were working at their occupation, for they were by
trade makers of small, portable tents used by shepherds
and travellers.

And he continued reasoning in the synagogue every   **4-11**
sabbath, and kept on trying to persuade both Jews and
Greeks. Then, when both Silas and Timothy had come
down from Macedonia, Paul was wholly occupied with
and absorbed in the Word, solemnly affirming to the
Jews that the Christ [the Messiah] is Jesus. But when
they began to offer an organized and concerted opposition, and began to revile him, he, having shaken off his
garments as an expression of extreme contempt for them
and an expression of his refusal to have any further intercourse with them, said to them, Your blood be upon
your head. As for myself, I am clean [from your blood,
having discharged my duty with a clear conscience].
From this moment as particularized by what has just
taken place, to the Gentiles I will go. And having removed from there he went into the house of a certain
man whose name was Titus Justus, who revered God,
whose home was next to the synagogue. And Crispus,
the chief ruler of the synagogue, believed on the Lord
with his entire household. And many of the Corinthians
hearing, were believing and were being baptized. And
the Lord said to Paul during the night through a vision,
Stop being afraid, but continue to be speaking and do not
begin to be silent, because, as for myself, I am with you,
and not even one person will assault you to do you harm,
for I have a large group of people in this city. And he
took his seat there as a teacher for a year and six months,
teaching the word of God.

Now, when Gallio was proconsul of Achaia, the Jews   **12-17**
made a concerted assault upon Paul and brought him to
the place where legal cases were tried, saying, This fellow, by the means of persuasion, is stirring up the men
to worship God in a manner contrary to the law. And
when Paul was about to be opening his mouth, Gallio
said to the Jews, If it were a matter of wrong-doing
against someone or pernicious villainy, O Jews, reason

would dictate that I should have borne patiently with you. But since it is a parcel of questions concerning a word and names and your own law, you yourselves be seeing to it. As for myself, a judge of these things I do not after mature consideration desire to be. And he drove them away from his judgment seat. Then they all, having seized Sosthenes, the chief ruler of the synagogue, began beating him before the judgment seat. And of these things, not even one was a concern to Gallio.

18-23 And Paul, having remained there yet a considerable length of time, having bidden the brethren farewell, started to sail to Syria, and with him Priscilla and Aquila, having cut his hair short after the manner of the shearing of a sheep, for he had been under a vow which he had taken upon himself. And he came down to Ephesus and left them there, and he himself, having gone into the synagogue, reasoned with the Jews. But when they went to asking him to remain a longer time, he did not consent to do so, but having bidden them farewell and having said, I will return again to you if God so desires it, he sailed from Ephesus. And having landed at Caesarea, having gone up [to Jerusalem] and having paid his respects to the assembly, he went down to Antioch. And having spent some time there, he went off, going through the region of Galatia and Phrygia in that order, stabilizing all the disciples.

24-28 And a certain Jew named Apollos, a native of the city of Alexandria, a learned and eloquent man, came down to Ephesus, being a powerful man in the scriptures. This man had been instructed in the way of the Lord, and being fervent in his spirit was speaking and teaching accurately the things concerning Jesus, knowing only John's baptism. And this man began to be speaking out boldly in the synagogue. Now, Priscilla and Aquila, having heard him, took him to themselves and expounded the way of God more accurately to him. And when he desired to go through into Achaia, the brethren wrote, encouraging the disciples to receive him, and he, having come, threw himself into the work with those who had believed through grace, giving them much help, for he argued the case down to a finish and conclusively refuted

the Jews publicly, proving through the medium of the scriptures that the Christ [the Messiah] is Jesus.

Now, it came to pass that while Apollos was at Cor-   1-7
inth, Paul having gone through the upper districts came to Ephesus. And having found certain disciples he said to them, The Holy Spirit, did you receive Him as a result of your initial act of faith? And they said to him, In fact, we did not hear that there was a Holy Spirit. And he said, Upon what basis then were you baptized? And they said, Upon the basis of John's baptism. Then Paul said, John baptized with a baptism that had to do with repentance, saying to the people that they should believe on the One who comes after him, that is, on Jesus. And having heard this they were baptized into the Name of the Lord Jesus. And after Paul had placed his hands upon them the Holy Spirit came upon them, and they began speaking in languages [other than their own and unacquired], and began to prophesy. And all the men were about twelve.

And having entered the synagogue, he kept on speak-   8-13
ing boldly for three months, reasoning and persuading concerning the kingdom of God. But when some became stubborn and obstinate and were non-persuasible, speaking evil of the Way before the crowd, having withdrawn from them, he separated his disciples from them, daily reasoning in the school of Tyrannus. And this went on for two years, so that all those residing in Asia heard the word of the Lord, both Jews and Greeks. And God kept on performing miracles by the hand of Paul, miracles demonstrating the power of God, not the ordinary kind known to the apostles and completely different from the deeds of the Jewish exorcists, but uncommon, extraordinary ones, so that even to the sick were being brought from his body handkerchiefs and work aprons, and the diseases left them. And the spirits, the pernicious ones, proceeded out of them. Then certain also of the Jews who went from place to place employing a formula of conjuration to expel demons, attempted also to be naming over those who had pernicious spirits the Name of the Lord Jesus, saying, I adjure you by the Jesus whom Paul is proclaiming.

14-17   Now, there were seven sons of a certain Sceva, a Jew, a chief priest, doing this. And the pernicious spirit answering said to them, This Jesus I recognize and with this Paul I am acquainted. But as for you, who are you? And the man in whom the pernicious spirit was, having leaped upon them, having gained the mastery over them, overpowered them so that they fled out of that house with their clothing in shreds and having been wounded. And this became known both to all Jews and Gentiles, those residing in Ephesus. And fear fell upon all of them. And the Name of the Lord Jesus was being extolled and highly esteemed.

18-20   And many of those who were true believers kept on coming, openly confessing, and by fully declaring them, making a clean sweep of their practices. And a considerable number of those who practiced the magical arts, having brought their books together, kept on throwing book after book into the fire before all. And they added up their total cost and found it to be fifty thousand pieces of silver. So mightily did the word of the Lord keep on growing and gaining strength.

21, 22   When these things were fulfilled, Paul purposed in his spirit [his own mind], having gone through Macedonia and Achaia, to proceed on his way to Jerusalem, having said, After I have been there, it is a necessity in the nature of the case for me also to see Rome. Then, having sent on a mission into Macedonia two who were his aids, Timothy and Erastus, he himself stayed for a time in Asia.

23-27   And there arose at that strategic, epochal time no small tumult concerning the Way, for a certain individual, Demetrius by name, a silversmith, making miniature silver temples of Diana containing an image of the goddess, was furnishing no little business for the artisans, and having called them together also with the workmen of the associated trades, he said, Men, you know that from this occupation we have our wealth. And you are clearly seeing and hearing that not only in Ephesus but almost throughout all of Asia this fellow, Paul, having persuad-

ed them, turned away a great number of people, saying
that they are not gods, those being made by hands. Moreover, not only is our department of trade in danger of
coming into disrepute, but also the temple of the great
goddess Artemis is in danger of being considered as nothing and is destined also to be deprived of her magnifi-
cence, whom all of Asia and the Roman empire worships.

Moreover, also having heard these things, having be-   **28-37**
come filled with a boiling rage, they kept on continuously
crying out, saying, Great is Artemis of the Ephesians.
And the city was filled with the confusion, and they
rushed with one accord into the theatre, having seized
Gaius and Aristarchus of Macedonia, Paul's travel com-
panions. And when Paul was desiring to go into this
great mass of people assembled in this public place, the
disciples kept on forbidding him to do so. Moreover, also
certain of the chief officers of Asia, wealthy men who
supervised the Greek games and festivals, being his
friends, having sent to him, kept on begging him not to
take the risk of entering the theater. So then some kept
on crying one thing and some another, for the assembly
had been called together in an irregular way, and was as
a result in a state of confusion, and the majority did not
know on what account they had come together. Then
they brought Alexander out of the crowd, the Jews thrusting him forward. And Alexander, having beckoned with
his hand, was desiring to present his verbal defense to
the people. But having come to recognize that he was a
Jew, one voice arose from all for about two hours, crying, Great is Artemis of the Ephesians. Then the city
recorder [the officer who drafted decrees, had charge of
the city treasury, and had control of the town meeting],
having quieted the people, said, Men, Ephesians, who is
there then of men who does not know that the city of the
Ephesians is warden of the temple of the great Artemis
and of her heaven-fallen image? Therefore, these things
being such that they are indisputable, it is needful for
you to restrain yourselves and to be doing nothing rashly,
for you brought these men here who are neither despoil-
ers of temples nor those who have by contemptuous
speech come short of the reverence due our goddess.

38-41   So then, if, as is the case, Demetrius and the crafts-
men with him have a matter against anyone, court-meet-
ings are now going on and there are proconsuls. Let them
accuse one another. But if you are inquiring concerning
anything of a nature further than accusations, it shall be
decided in a legally constituted assembly. For indeed we
are in danger of being called in question concerning this
day's riot, there being not even one bit of cause for it, and
with reference to it. We shall not be able to give an
account concerning this disorderly riot. And having said
these things, he dismissed the assembly.

1-5   And after the uproar ceased, Paul, having sent after
the disciples to come to him, having exhorted them, having taken his leave of them, went off for the purpose of
proceeding to Macedonia. And having passed through
those parts and having exhorted them in much discourse,
he went to Greece. And having spent three months
there, a plot having been laid against him by the Jews
as he was about to set sail for Syria, he became of the
opinion that he should return through Macedonia. And
there accompanied him Sopater, the son of Pyrrhus of
Berea, and of the Thessalonians Aristarchus and Secun-
dus; and Gaius of Derbe, and Timothy; and the Asians,
Tychicus and Trophemus. And these having gone on
ahead were waiting for us at Troas.

6-12   Now, as for us, we sailed away from Philippi after
the days of bread baked without yeast, and came to them
at Troas in five days, where we stayed seven days. And
on the first day of the week, when we were gathered
together to break bread, Paul was discoursing to them,
about to go forth next day. And he prolonged his discourse until midnight. Now there were many oil lamps
in the upper room where they were gathered together.
And there was sitting on the window sill a certain young
man named Eutychus, being gradually overcome by a
deep sleep. While Paul was continuing his discourse
longer, having finally been completely overcome by sleep,
he [Eutychus] fell down from the third story and was
picked up dead. And Paul, having gone down, fell upon
him and having embraced him, said, All of you stop
your wailing, for his life is in him. And having gone

up and having broken the bread [of the Lord's Supper],
and having eaten, and having communed with them for
a long while until daybreak, thus he went off. And they
brought the lad alive. And they were not a little
comforted.

Now, as for us, having gone on ahead to the boat,   **13-16**
we set sail for Assos, there intending to pick up Paul,
for he had ordered it so, intending himself to travel on
foot. And when he was meeting us at Assos, having
taken him on board, we came to Mitylene. And from
there we set sail and on the next day arrived at a point
opposite Chios. And on the following day we put in
at Samos. And on the succeeding day we came to
Miletus, for Paul had resolved to sail past Ephesus in
order that he might not waste time in Asia, for he was
hurrying on if it were possible for him to be at Jerusalem on the day of Pentecost.

And from Miletus, having sent to Ephesus, he called   **17-21**
the elders of the assembly to himself. Then, when they
came to him, he said to them, As for you, you know that
from the first day when I set foot in Asia, how I was
with you in close association for the entire time, serving
the Lord as His slave with every humility and with tears
and trials which befell me by reason of the plots of the
Jews; how I did not shrink from declaring to you anything that was profitable, and to teach you publicly and
from house to house, testifying both to Jews and Greeks
repentance toward God and faith in our Lord Jesus.

And now, behold, as for myself, having been com-   **22-24**
pletely bound in my spirit, I am proceeding to Jerusalem,
not knowing the things that shall befall me in it, except
that the Holy Spirit in city after city is bearing testimony to me, saying that bonds and afflictions are awaiting me. But I esteem my life of absolutely no account
as precious to myself in order that I [like a Greek
athlete] may finish my race, even the ministering work
which I received from the presence of the Lord Jesus
to bear testimony to the good news of the grace of God.

And now, behold, as for myself, I know positively   **25-31**
that as for you all, you shall no longer see my face, all

of you among whom I went about proclaiming the kingdom. On this account I call you to bear witness on to-day's day to the fact that I am pure from the blood of all, for I did not shrink from declaring to you the entire counsel of God. Be constantly maintaining a careful watch over yourselves with a view to guarding yourselves, also do the same with respect to all the flock in which the Holy Spirit appointed you as spiritual overseers, shepherding the Church of God which He bought for himself through the agency of the blood, the blood which is His own unique blood, possessed by himself alone. As for myself, I know positively that after my departure [from you now] there shall enter in among you rapacious wolves, not sparing the flock. And from among yourselves there shall arise men mouthing things which have been distorted and corrupted for the purpose of drawing away the disciples after themselves. Therefore, be exercising the most punctilious care, remembering that for three years, night and day, I did not cease admonishing each one with tears.

32-38   And now, as to the present things, I commend you to the Lord and to the word of His grace which has power to build you up, and to give you the inheritance among all those who have been set apart for God. Not even one person's silver or gold or apparel did I covet. You yourselves know from experience that these hands ministered to my necessities and to the necessities of those with me. In all things I gave you an example, that in this manner, working to the point of exhaustion, it is a necessity in the nature of the case to lend a helping hand yourselves to those who are weak, helping them to help themselves in their difficulties, and to be remembering the words of the Lord Jesus, that He himself said, There is more spiritual prosperity in constantly giving than in constantly receiving. And having said these things, having kneeled upon his knees, together with them all, he prayed. And there was much audible weeping by all. They were crying like a child cries. And having fallen upon his neck, they kept on kissing him, one after another, being in anguish because of the word

which he had spoken, that no longer would they affection-
ately be gazing upon his face. And they were bringing
him to the boat.

And it came to pass when we set sail, having torn   **1-6**
ourselves away from them, having run a straight course,
we came to Cos, and the next day to Rhodes, and from
there to Patara. And having found a boat crossing over
to Phoenicia, having gone on board, we set sail. And
having sighted Cyprus and having left it on the left
hand, we sailed to Syria, and disembarked at Tyre, for
there the boat was unloading its cargo. And after a
search, having found the disciples, we remained there
seven days, who were such that they kept on saying to
Paul through the intermediate agency of the Spirit that
he should not be setting foot in Jerusalem. And it came
to pass that when we had fulfilled the days, having gone
off, we were going on our way, all of them with wives
and children accompanying us until we were out of the
city. And having kneeled upon our knees on the beach,
having prayed, and having said good-bye to one another,
we went on board the boat. And those returned home
again.

Now, as for us, when we had finished the voyage   **7-12**
from Tyre, we arrived at Ptolemais, and having greeted
the brethren, we remained one day with them. And on
the next day, having gone off, we came to Caesarea, and
having entered the home of Philip the evangelist [the
bringer of good news], he being one of the seven
[deacons], we remained with him as his guests. This
man had four daughters, virgins, exercising the gift of
prophecy. Now, while we were remaining there many
days, a certain man came down from Judaea, a prophet
named Agabus. And having come to us and having taken
the belt belonging to Paul, having bound his own feet and
hands, he said, Thus says the Holy Spirit, The man
who owns this belt, the Jews shall bind in the same manner and deliver him into the hands of the Gentiles. And
when we heard these things, as for us, both we and
those of that place, kept on begging him not to be setting
foot in Jerusalem.

13-17   Then Paul answered, What are you doing, weeping audibly and breaking my heart? For, as for myself, I am holding myself in readiness on behalf of the Name of the Lord Jesus, not only to be bound but also to die in Jerusalem. And he not being persuaded, we lapsed into silence, having said, The will of the Lord, let it be done. And after these days, having packed our luggage, we went on our way up to Jerusalem. And there went also with us certain ones of the disciples from Caesarea, conducting us to a certain Mnason whose guests we were to be, a disciple of long standing. And when we came to Jerusalem, the brethren received us gladly.

18-21   Now, on the next day, Paul went in with us to James. And all the elders were present. And having greeted them he took them through the story of the things God did among the Gentiles through his ministry, rehearsing them one by one. And having heard these things, they glorified God and said to him, You see clearly, brother, how many thousands there are among the Jews of those who have believed. And all are zealous for the law. Now, they have been carefully instructed with reference to yourself that you are teaching all the Jews who live among the Gentiles to apostatize from Moses, saying that they are not to be circumcising their children, neither to order their manner of life after their customs.

22-26   What is it, therefore? They will certainly hear that you have come and are here. This, therefore, do at once, that which we tell you. There are with us four men who have a vow on them. Having taken these to yourself as associates, ceremonially purify yourself in association with them and pay their expenses incurred in taking this vow in order that they may shave their head. And all will know that the things in which they were instructed concerning you are nothing, but that you yourself also are ordering your behavior according to rule, keeping the law. Now, as concerning the Gentiles who have believed, as for us, we wrote, having come to the conclusion that they are to be keeping themselves both from animal flesh which had been sacrificed to idols, and from blood and from flesh of animals which had been killed in such a way that the blood had not been drained out,

and from fornication. Then Paul, having taken the
men to himself the next day, having purified himself
ceremonially together with them, went on into the temple,
declaring the fulfillment of the days of the purification,
until the sacrifice was offered for each one of them.

Now, when the seven days were about to draw to a **27-36**
close, the Jews from Asia having seen him in the temple,
kept on throwing the entire crowd into confusion, and
they laid their hands on him, crying out, Men, Israelites,
be bringing aid. This is the man who is teaching all men
everywhere against the people and the law and this place
and, moreover, also brought Greeks into the temple and
has profaned this holy place. For they had before seen
Trophimus, the Ephesian, in the city with him, whom
they supposed Paul brought into the temple. And the
entire city was thrown into a commotion, and there
occurred a running-together of the people, and having
seized Paul, they were dragging him by the heels outside of the temple. And immediately the doors were
closed. And as they were seeking to kill him, a report
went up to the chiliarch who commanded the cohort
that all Jerusalem was in confusion, who immediately
having taken soldiers and centurions ran down to them.
And having seen the chiliarch and the soldiers, they
ceased beating Paul. Then, the chiliarch having come
near, seized him and ordered that he be bound with two
chains. And he went to inquiring who he might be and
what he had done. And some in the crowd were shouting one thing and others something else. And when he
was not able to come to know the particular thing that
could be relied upon as the truth because of the confusion, he commanded that he [Paul] be brought into
the barracks. And when he came upon the stairs things
came to such a pass that he was being carried by the
soldiers because of the violence of the people, for the
great mass of people was following, crying out, Be doing
away with him.

And as Paul was about to be brought into the bar- **37-XXII 2**
racks he says to the chiliarch, Will you permit me to say
something to you? And he said, Do you know Greek?
As for you, are you not then the Egyptian, that one who

before these days stirred up to sedition and led out into the uninhabited region four thousand men of the Assassins? But Paul said, As for myself, I am indeed a man, a Jew, of Tarsus, a city of Cilicia, a citizen of no undistinguished city. And I beg of you, permit me to speak to my people. And after he had given him permission, Paul, having taken his stand on the stairs, beckoned with his hand to the people. And a sustained silence having come, he addressed them in the Hebrew dialect, saying, Men, brethren, and fathers, hear my defense which I am making to you just now. And having heard that in the Hebrew dialect he was addressing them, they provided him all the more with silence.

2-5   And he said, As for myself, I am a man who is a Jew, having been born in Tarsus of Cilicia, having been brought up with reference to my education in this city, at the feet of Gamaliel having been instructed in accordance with the strictness of the law received from the fathers, being zealous for God even as all you are this day. I who persecuted this Way to the extent of death, binding and delivering to prison both men and women, as also the chief priest bears me witness, also the eldership of the Sanhedrin, from whom having also received letters to the brethren, was journeying to Damascus for the purpose of bringing those who were there in chains to Jerusalem in order that they might be punished.

6-13   And it came to pass that as I was proceeding on my journey and nearing Damascus, about noon, suddenly out from heaven there flashed around me like lightning a great light, and I fell to the ground and heard a voice saying to me, Saul, Saul, why are you persecuting me? And as for myself, I answered, Who are you, Sir? And it said to me, As for myself, I am Jehoshua, the One from Nazareth, whom you are persecuting. And those with me saw indeed the light but did not hear the voice of the One speaking to me so as to understand the words, but heard it merely as a sound. And I said, What shall I do, Lord? And the Lord said to me, Having arisen, be going on your way into Damascus, and there it shall be told you concerning all things which have been appointed for you to do. And when the ability of look-

ing upon surrounding objects was taken away from me because of that light and I was not seeing, being led by the hand by those with me, I came into Damascus. And a certain Ananias, a pious man who reverenced God according to the law, being well recommended by all the Jews who resided there, having come to me and standing over me said to me, Saul, brother, look up at once and recover your sight. And as for myself, I looked up to him that very hour and recovered my sight.

And he said, The God of our fathers chose and **14-16** appointed you to come to know experientially His will and to see with discernment the One who is righteous and to hear the voice of His mouth, because you shall be one who bears testimony for Him to all men concerning the things you have seen and heard. And now, why are you delaying? Having arisen, be baptized and wash away your sins, having previously called upon His Name.

And it came to pass that after I returned to Jeru- **17-21** salem and while I was praying in the temple, I entered into a new experience, that of having my mind drawn off from surrounding objects and wholly fixed on things divine, and I saw Him while He was saying to me, Hurry, and at once get out of Jerusalem, quickly, because they will not accept your testimony concerning me. And as for myself, I said, Lord, they themselves know that I was continually imprisoning and beating in every synagogue those who put their trust in you. And when the blood of Stephen your witness was shed, the witness who bore testimony to you by his death, I myself also was standing by and exulting, and was guarding the clothes of those who were putting him out of the way. And He said to me, Be going on your way, because, as for myself, to Gentiles afar off I will send you forth on a mission.

And they kept on listening to him up to this word, **22-24** and they raised their voice, saying, Be taking away from the earth such a person, for it was not fitting that he should live. And when they were crying out and throwing off their garments and throwing dust into the

air, the chiliarch commanded that he should be brought
into the barracks of the soldiers, having said that he
should be given a judicial examination under the duress
of the torture inflicted by scourging, in order that he
might come to fully know the cause on account of which
they were continually shouting so against him.

25-30   And when they had stretched him out for the lashes,
Paul said to the centurion standing by, A man who is a
Roman and uncondemned, is it legal for you to be
scourging? And the centurion having heard this, having
gone to the chiliarch, brought this report saying, What
are you about to be doing, for this man is a Roman?
And having come, the chiliarch said to him, Be telling
me, as for you, a Roman are you? And he said, Yes.
And the chiliarch answered, As for myself, with a great
sum of money I procured this citizenship. But Paul said,
And as for myself, I am a Roman by heredity. Then
immediately they stood off from him, those who were
about to be examining him. And the chiliarch became
afraid, having come to know that he was a Roman and
because he had put him in chains. Now, on the next day,
desiring after mature consideration to come to know what
the particular thing was of which he was being accused
by the Jews, he unshackled him and commanded the chief
priests and the entire Sanhedrin to assemble. And having brought Paul down, he stood him before them.

1-5   And Paul, having riveted his gaze upon the Sanhedrin,
said, Men, brethren, as for myself, I have conducted
myself as a citizen [of God's commonwealth of Israel]
in all good conscience toward God up to this day. And
the chief priest, Ananias, ordered those standing by to
be striking him upon his mouth. Then Paul said to him,
To be striking you, God is about to be doing, you wall
that has been plastered over and white-washed with lime
[hypocrite that you are who conceals your malice under
an outward assumption of piety]. And as for you, being
what you are, are you sitting as a judge to be pronounc-
ing judgment upon me according to the law, and contrary
to the law are you commanding me to be beaten? And
those standing by said, The chief priest of God, are you
heaping abuse on him? And Paul said, I did not know,

brethren, that he was a chief priest, for it has been written and is at present on record, Concerning the ruler of your people, you shall not speak evil.

Now, Paul having come to see that the one part were **6-11** Sadducees and the other part Pharisees, cried out in the Sanhedrin, Men, brethren, as for myself, a Pharisee I am, a son of Pharisees. Concerning a hope even of a resurrection of dead people I am being judged. As he was saying this a dissension arose between the Pharisees and the Sadducees, and the crowd was split in two, for Sadducees say that there is not a resurrection, neither angel nor spirit, but Pharisees profess the both. And there arose a great clamor, and certain of the men learned in the sacred scriptures who were attached to the Pharisees, having arisen, went to fighting it out, saying, We do not find one bit of evil in this man. And what if a spirit spoke to him, or an angel? And a great dissension arising, the chiliarch having become afraid lest Paul should be torn in pieces by them, commanded the soldiers, having gone down, to take him by force from their midst, and to be bringing him into their barracks. And on the next night the Lord having taken His stand by Paul said, Be having a cheerful courage, for as you testified with reference to the things concerning me in Jerusalem, thus as for you, it is a necessity in the nature of the case also to testify in Rome.

And when day dawned the Jews having entered into **12-15** a conspiracy, invoked God's curse upon themselves if they should violate their vow, saying that they would neither eat nor drink until that time in which they would kill Paul. And there were more than forty who entered this conspiracy. They, having come to the chief priests and the elders, said, We invoked God's curse upon ourselves should we violate our vow, declaring ourselves anathema should we do so, vowing to eat not even one thing until such time as we killed this Paul. Now, therefore, as for all of you, together with the Sanhedrin, suggest at once to the chiliarch that he bring him down to you as though you were about to be judging the things concerning him more accurately. And as for us, before he comes near, we are those who are in readiness to put him out of the way.

16-22   Now, the son of Paul's sister having heard of their ambush, having come and having entered the barracks, reported this to Paul. Then Paul, having called one of the centurions to him, said, Be taking this young man away to the chiliarch, for he has something to report to him. Then, having taken him, he brought him to the chiliarch and said, The prisoner Paul having called me to himself asked that I bring this young man to you who has something to say to you. Then the chiliarch, having taken him by his hand and having withdrawn, went to inquiring of him privately, What is it that you have to report to me? And he said, The Jews agreed among themselves to ask you to bring Paul down to the Sanhedrin tomorrow as though about to be inquiring more accurately concerning him. As for you, therefore, do not permit yourself to be persuaded by them, for there lie in ambush for him more than forty of their men, those who are such that they invoked God's curse upon themselves should they break their vow not to eat nor drink until such time as they have destroyed him. And now they are in readiness, looking for the promise from you. So then the chiliarch dismissed the young man, having charged him to tell not even one person these things which he had made plain to him.

23, 24   And having called to himself a certain two of the centurions, he said, Make ready at once two hundred heavily armed foot soldiers in order that they may proceed to Caesarea, and seventy soldiers of the cavalry unit, and two hundred lightly armed soldiers, about nine o'clock at night, and furnish them beasts of burden in order that having mounted Paul upon one they might bring him safely through to Felix the governor.

25-30   And he wrote a letter having this form: Claudias Lysias, to his Excellency, the governor Felix, greeting. This man, having been seized by the Jews and about to be put out of the way by them, having rushed in in the nick of time with my heavily armed legionnaires, I rescued, having learned that he was a Roman. And desiring to come to know fully the cause on account of which they were bringing a charge against him, I brought him down to the Sanhedrin, their council, whom I found to be accused

concerning questions of their law, but having not even one thing worthy of death or bonds laid to his charge. And when it was pointed out to me that there would be a plot against the man, immediately I sent him to you, having given orders also to his accusers to be telling before you what they have against him.

So then the soldiers, according to the order given them, having taken up Paul, brought him through a night of travel [forty miles] to Antipatris. And on the next day, having left the horsemen to be going with him, they returned to their barracks, and they, having gone on to Caesarea and having delivered the letter to the governor, presented also Paul to him. And having read the letter, he also asked as to what kind of a province [senatorial or imperial] he came from. And having ascertained that he was from Cilicia he said, I will hear fully and adjudicate your cause whenever also your accusers have come; having previously ordered that he be put under guard in the palace of Herod.

31-35

Now, after five days the chief priest with certain elders and a certain prosecuting attorney, Tertullus, came down, who were such that they preferred charges before the governor against Paul. And after he [Paul] was called, Tertullus began to be accusing him, saying, In view of the fact that we are obtaining much peace through you, and evils are constantly being corrected and things set right for our nation through your forethought in all ways and in all places, we accept these, most illustrious Felix, with all gratefulness. But in order that I may not further cut in on your time and detain you [from your beneficent reforms] I beg of you to hear us in your sweet reasonableness, and we will be concise.

1-4

For we found this man to be a pest and a plague and an instigator of insurrections among all the Jews throughout the Roman empire, and a front-rank champion of the heretical sect of the Nazarenes; who also attempted to profane the temple, whom also we seized, whom you will be able, having yourself conducted an investigation concerning all these things, to come to know fully the

5-9

81

things of which, as for us, we are accusing him. And the Jews also joined in the charge, affirming that these things were so.

10-16   And Paul answered, the governor having nodded to him to be speaking, Knowing that for many years you have been a judge of this nation, I confidently present my defense with respect to the things concerning myself, you being able to understand that there are not more than twelve days since I went up to Jerusalem to worship. And neither in the temple did they find me disputing with any certain individual nor stirring up a crowd, nor even in the synagogues nor in the city; neither are they able to substantiate before you the charges concerning which they now are accusing me. But I confess this to you, that in accordance with the Way, which system of belief they call heresy, thus am I serving the God of my fathers, believing all things which stand written according to the law and those things in the prophets, having hope toward God, which hope they themselves also look for, that there shall be a resurrection of both the just and the unjust. And in this also I myself am constantly disciplining myself to be having a conscience which does not cause offense to God and to men at all times.

17-23   Now, after an interval of some years I came, having brought alms to my nation and [sacrificial] offerings, in the presenting of which offerings they found me ceremonially purified in the temple, not with a crowd nor with an uproar. But certain Jews from Asia, who ought to have been present before you and to be bringing accusation if they were having anything against me — Or, let these themselves tell what wrongdoing they found when I stood before the Sanhedrin, except concerning this one voice which, while standing among them, I cried aloud, Concerning a resurrection of dead people I am being judged today by you. Then Felix put them off by deferring the hearing and the deciding of the case, knowing more accurately the things concerning the Way, having said, When Lysias, the chiliarch comes down I will determine the things which pertain to you. He gave orders to the centurion that he should be kept under guard and that

he should relax the severe conditions of imprisonment and make things easier for him, and that he should not forbid any of his own people to be ministering to him.

Now, after certain days, Felix, having come [back] **24-27** with Drusilla his own wife who was a Jewess, sent for Paul and heard him concerning his faith in Christ Jesus. And while he was discoursing concerning righteousness and self-control and the judgment which was about to come, Felix, having become terrified, answered, Be proceeding on your way for the present, and having found an opportune time, I will summon you; at the same time also hoping that money will be given to him by Paul. On this account also he kept on sending for him more frequently and conversing with him. But after two years had gone by, Felix was succeeded by Porcius Festus, and desiring to ingratiate himself with the Jews, he left Paul behind in shackles.

Then, Festus having come into his province, after **1-6** three days, went up to Jerusalem from Caesarea. And the chief priests and the principal men among the Jews laid legal and formal information against Paul before him. And they kept on begging him, asking a personal favor for themselves against him to the effect that he would send for him to be brought to Jerusalem, all the while preparing an ambush to put him out of the way along the road. Now then, Festus answered that Paul was kept in charge in Caesarea and that he himself would proceed there shortly. Let those therefore among you, he says, who are vested with power, having gone with me, assuming that there is anything amiss in this man, bring accusation against him. And having spent not more than eight or ten days among them, having gone down to Caesarea, on the next day having taken his place on the judge's bench, he commanded Paul to be brought.

And after he had come down, the Jews who had come **7, 8** down from Jerusalem took up positions in a circle around him, bringing against him many and weighty accusations which they did not have the ability to prove by argument, while Paul was saying in his defense, Neither against the temple nor against Caesar did I sin in anything.

9-12   But Festus, desiring to ingratiate himself with the Jews, answering Paul, said, Are you willing, having gone up to Jerusalem, there to be judged concerning these things in my presence? Then Paul said, I have taken my stand before the judgment seat of Caesar, and here I stand where it is a necessity in the nature of the case for me to be judged. To Jews I have not done even one wrong thing, as also, as for yourself, you understand very well. Now, therefore, assuming for the moment that I am a wrongdoer or have committed anything worthy of death, I do not refuse to die. But since there does not exist even one thing of those things of which these accuse me, no one has the power to give me up as a favor to them. I lodge my appeal with Caesar. Then Festus, after he conferred with his council, answered, You lodged your appeal with Caesar. To Caesar you shall proceed.

13-21   Now, certain days having elapsed, Agrippa the king and Bernice arrived at Caesarea and paid their respects to Festus. And when they had spent many days there, Festus laid the things concerning Paul before the king, saying, There is a certain man who has been left behind by Felix in shackles, concerning whom when I was in Jerusalem the chief priests and the elders of the Jews informed me, requesting as a personal favor to themselves a condemnatory sentence against him, to whom I answered, It is not a custom with Romans to be giving up to another any man whom he may punish or put to death before the one who is accused have his accusers face to face and have opportunity to present a defense with reference to the accusation. Therefore, having assembled here without one bit of delay the next day, having sat down on the judge's bench, I commanded that the man be brought concerning whom after his accusers stood up, they brought not one accusation with reference to such pernicious things as I surmised, but they were having certain questions against him concerning their own religion and concerning a certain Jesus who was dead, whom Paul has kept on asserting is alive. And as for myself, being perplexed with reference to an inquiry concerning these things, I went to asking him if he would desire to be proceeding to Jerusalem and there be judged concerning

these things. But since Paul had made his appeal to be reserved for the decision of The August One, I commanded that he be kept until I should send him up to Caesar.

Then Agrippa said to Festus, I myself also was wishing to hear the man. Tomorrow, he said, you shall hear him. Therefore, on the next day Agrippa having come, and Bernice, accompanied by much pomp, and having entered the court room, both with chiliarchs and the outstanding men of the city, and Festus having given the order, Paul was brought in. And Festus says, King Agrippa and all those men who are present with us, you see this man concerning whom the entire multitude of the Jews petitioned me both in Jerusalem and here, shouting that in accordance with the necessity in the nature of the case he ought no longer to be living. But as for myself, having learned that he had done nothing worthy of death, and that he himself had appealed to The August One, I determined to be sending him, concerning whom I do not have anything definite to write to my Lord. Because of this I brought him before you all, and especially before you, King Agrippa, in order that after the examination has taken place, I may have something to write; for it seems to me contrary to reason, sending a prisoner, and not indicating the charges against him.   22-27

Then Agrippa said to Paul, Permission is granted you to be speaking on behalf of yourself. Then Paul, having stretched out his hand, went to presenting his verbal defense. Concerning all things of which I am being accused by the Jews, King Agrippa, I have considered myself fortunate that I am about to be presenting my verbal defense today before you, since you are especially expert with reference both to all the customs and also questions regarding the Jews. On this account I beg of you to hear me patiently.   1-3

Now, therefore, the manner of life which was mine from youth, that which was from the beginning among my nation in Jerusalem, all Jews know, having previous knowledge of me from the very first, if they would be willing to be bearing testimony, that according to the sect   4-7

in our religious discipline which was most precise and rigorous in interpreting the Mosaic law and observing even its most minute precepts, I lived as a Pharisee. And now upon the basis of the hope of the promise made by our God to our fathers I stand here being judged, which promise our twelve tribes earnestly night and day rendering sacred service to God are hoping to arrive at, concerning which hope I am being accused by the Jews, O King.

8-11   Why is it being judged by you all an unbelievable thing that God raises dead individuals, as He has done? As for myself, verily, I was of the opinion that it was a necessity in the nature of the case for me to do many things against the Name of Jesus, the one from Nazareth, which also I did in Jerusalem, and many of the saints, as for myself, I shut up in prisons, having received the authority from the chief priests. And when they were being put to death I registered my vote against them. And often in every synagogue while punishing them I kept on attempting to compel them by contemptuous speech intentionally to come short of the reverence due to God, and possessing an insane fury against them beyond measure, I went to persecuting them even to foreign cities.

12-18   Being engaged in these things, while I was proceeding to Damascus with authority and a commission from the chief priests, at midday I saw along the road, O King, a light from heaven above the brilliance of the sun shining about me and those who were travelling with me. And after all of us had fallen down upon the ground, I heard a voice saying to me in the Hebrew dialect, Saul, Saul, why are you persecuting me? It is hard for you to be kicking against the goads. And as for myself, I said, Who are you, Sir? And the Lord said, As for myself, I am Jehoshua, whom, as for yourself, you are persecuting. But arise at once and stand upon your feet. For this purpose I appeared to you, to appoint you as one who ministers and as one who bears testimony both to the things you saw and to the things in which I will appear to you, delivering you from the people and the Gentiles, to whom, as for myself, I will send you on a mission to

open their eyes that they may turn from darkness to light
and from the authority of Satan to God, that they may
receive forgiveness of sins and an inheritance among
those who have been sanctified by faith which is in me.

Wherefore, O King Agrippa, I did not become dis-   **19, 20**
obedient to the heavenly vision, but both to those in
Damascus first and in Jerusalem and in all the region of
Judaea and to the Gentiles I kept on bringing word that
they should be repenting and turning to God, doing works
that weigh as much as the repentance they profess.

On account of these things the Jews, having made me   **21-23**
a prisoner, were attempting to kill me. Therefore, having
the help that is from God until this day, I stand testifying
both to small and great, saying nothing except the things
which the prophets and Moses said are destined to take
place, whether the Christ is to be a suffering Messiah,
whether He being the first to arise from the dead is destined to be proclaiming light to the people and to the
Gentiles.

And as he was saying these things in his defense,   **24-29**
Festus says with a loud voice, You are going insane, Paul.
Your vast learning is turning you around to insanity.
But Paul says, I am not going insane, most illustrious
Festus. But words of truth and soundness of mind am
I uttering; for the King knows about these things before
whom I also am speaking freely, for I am persuaded that
none of these things is hidden from him, for this thing
has not taken place in a secret place. Are you believing,
King Agrippa, the prophets? I know positively that you
are believing. But Agrippa says to Paul, With but [such]
little persuasion you are attempting to make me a Christian. But Paul said, I am praying to God that whether
by little or by much persuasion not only you but also all
who are hearing me today would become such as even I
am, except these chains.

And the king arose and the governor and Bernice and   **30-32**
those seated with them, and having withdrawn, they were
speaking to one another, saying, Not even one thing
worthy of death or bonds is this man doing. Then Agrip-

pa said to Festus, This man could have been released if he had not appealed to Caesar.

1-6   Now, when it was determined that we should sail away to Italy, they gave both Paul and certain other prisoners of a different type into the custody of a centurion named Julius, belonging to the Augustan military cohort. And having gone on board a ship of Adramyttium which was about to be sailing to places along the coast of Asia, we put to sea, there being with us Aristarchus, a Macedonian of Thessalonica. And on the next day we landed at Sidon. And Julius treated Paul kindly, giving him permission to go to his friends to receive care and attention. And having put out to sea from there we sailed under the sheltered protection of Cyprus because the winds were against us. And having sailed across both the sea which is off the coast of Cilicia and that which is off the coast of Pamphylia, we came down to Myra in Lycia. And having found there a ship of Alexandria sailing to Italy, he put us on board.

7, 8   And when we sailed slowly for a considerable number of days and with difficulty down along Cnidus, since the wind did not permit our straight course onwards, we sailed under the protective shelter of Crete off Cape Salmone, and with difficulty coasting along it we came to a certain place called Snug Harbors, which is near the city of Lasea.

9-13   Now, a considerable time having elapsed and the voyage already being dangerous and also because the fast already was past, Paul went to exhorting them, saying to them, Men, I perceive as the result of past experience and observation that the voyage is destined to be with injury and much loss, not only of the cargo and the ship but also of our lives. But the centurion allowed himself to be persuaded by the steersman and the skipper rather than by the things which were being spoken by Paul. And the harbor being unfit as a place in which to spend the winter, the majority gave it as their counsel to put out to sea from there, if somehow they might be able to reach Phenice and there to spend the winter, this being a harbor of Crete looking to the

northeast and southeast. And a south wind having blown gently, thinking that they had obtained their purpose, having hoisted their anchor, they sailed along Crete close in shore.

Now, after no long time there beat down from it **14-20** [mountainous Crete] a wind of typhoon proportions which is called Euraquilo. And the ship having been caught by it and not able to face the wind, having given up to it, we were carried along. And running under the protective shelter of a certain island called Clauda, we were with difficulty able to get possession of the little boat, which, after they had hoisted it up [into the large boat] they went to using things that would aid us, putting chains around the hull of the ship to hold it together. And fearing lest we veer from our course and be driven against the shoals and rocks of the Syrtis, having taken in some of the sails, we were in this manner being borne along. And we being greatly beaten about by the storm, on the next day they began to be throwing the cargo overboard. And on the third day they threw out with their own hands the furnishings of the ship. Now, when neither sun nor stars were shining for many days, and no small storm was pressing down upon us, all hope that we would be saved, which hope was still clinging to us, was at last being stripped away from us.

And when those on board had been long without **21-26** food, then Paul having taken his stand in their midst said, Surely, O men, in view of the very necessity imposed by the circumstances, you should have taken my advice and not have set sail from Crete and to have incurred this harm and loss. And now I advise and exhort you to be of good courage, keeping up your spirits, for there shall be a loss of not even one life among you, but a loss of the ship, for there took a stand at my side this night a messenger of the God whose I am and to whom I render sacred service, saying, Stop fearing, Paul. It is necessary in the nature of the case for you to stand before Caesar. And behold, God has graciously safeguarded for you all those who are sailing with you. On which account be having courage, men, for I trust God that it shall be in the manner as it has been told

me. However, it is a necessity in the nature of the case for us to be driven into a certain island.

27-32   Now, when the fourteenth night came, as we were being driven to and fro in the sea of Adria, about midnight, the sailors began to suspect that some land was drawing near to them, and having let down the lead for the purpose of finding out the depth of the water, they discovered it to be about one hundred and twenty feet. And after a little distance, having again taken a sounding, they found ninety feet. And fearing lest we should be driven somewhere against rocky places, having thrown four anchors out of the back of the ship, they kept on praying for day to come. Now, as the sailors were seeking to abandon ship and had lowered the small boat under pretense of being about to be laying anchors out of the front of the ship, Paul said to the centurion and the soldiers, Unless these remain in the ship, as for you all, you will not be able to be saved. Then the soldiers cut off the ropes of the small boat and permitted it to fall off.

33-38   Now, until that time at which it should become day, Paul kept on exhorting all to take food, saying, This is the fourteenth day in which you are looking ahead with expectation, continuing to be without food, having taken nothing. On which account I beg of you all, please, to take food, for this is for your preservation, for not one hair of your head shall perish. And having said these things and having taken bread, he gave thanks to God in the presence of all, and having broken it, he began to be eating. Then all having taken courage, they themselves took food. There were two hundred and seventy-six souls on the ship. And having eaten food to their entire satisfaction, they began to lighten the ship by throwing its cargo of grain into the sea.

39-41   Now, when day came, they attempted to recognize the land but were unsuccessful, but they began to observe a certain bay having a beach, and they were deliberating with one another whether they would be able to drive the boat into it. And having cast off the anchors they left them in the sea, at the same time loosing the bands

of the rudders, and having spread the foresail to the wind they began to hold the ship's course steadily to the beach. And having come unexpectedly upon a reef against which the waves dashed on both sides, they ran the vessel aground. And the front of the ship struck, remained immovable, but the back of the ship began to break up by reason of the waves.

Now, the counsel of the soldiers was to kill the **42-44** prisoners lest anyone having swum out should escape. But the centurion desiring to bring Paul safely through kept them from their purpose and ordered those who were able to swim, having thrown themselves overboard, to get first to the land, and the rest, some on the one hand upon planks and some on the other hand on pieces of the ship. And in that way it came to pass that all came safely through to the land.

And having been brought safely through, then we **1-6** recognized at once that the island was called Melita. And the inhabitants who were such that they did not speak Greek nor did they possess Greek culture, showed us not the humane and kind treatment with which one meets ordinarily, but an uncommon, extraordinary, humane, and kindly treatment which was the expression of their natural affection for their fellow-man, for, having set fire to a heap of sticks, they took all of us to themselves because of the rain which, having come down upon us, was now a steady downpour and because of the cold. Now Paul, having gathered together a capacity load of dry sticks and having put them upon the fire, a viper having come out by reason of the heat fastened itself upon his hand. And when the inhabitants saw the poisonous creature dangling from his hand, they kept on saying to one another, No doubt this man is a murderer, whom, having been brought safely through out of the reach of the sea, the goddess of Justice did not permit to continue living. Now, therefore, having shaken off the creature into the fire, he suffered not even one bit of harm. Now they kept on expecting that he was about to swell up or to be falling down dead suddenly. But while they were expecting this for a long time and were seeing not even one thing of a harmful

nature happening to him, having changed their minds, they went to saying that he was a god.

7-10   Now, in that place there were the estates of the chief man of the island who was named Publius, who received us hospitably and treated us in a kindly manner as his guests for three days. And it came to pass that the father of Publius was lying prostrate in the grip of an intermittent fever and dysentery, into whose presence Paul having come and having prayed, having laid his hands upon him, he healed him. Now, this having taken place, also the rest of those in the island who were in possession of infirmities came in a steady procession and were being healed, who also honored us with many honors, and when we sailed put on board the things of which we had need.

11-16   Now, after three months we put out to sea in a boat which had passed the winter in the island, a ship of Alexandria, upon the prow of which there were painted the figures of Castor and Pollux [tutelary deities of sailors]. And having landed at Syracuse, we remained there three days, from where having sailed by a circuitous course we came to Rhegium. And after one day a south wind having commenced blowing, we came on the second day to Puteoli, where having found brethren, we were urged to remain with them as their guests seven days. And in this manner we came to Rome. And from there the brethren, having heard of the things concerning us, came to meet us up to the Market of Appius and the Three Hotels, whom when Paul saw he thanked God and took courage. And when we entered Rome, Paul was given permission to live by himself with the soldier who guarded him.

17-19   And it came to pass after three days that Paul called together those first in prominence and authority among the Jews. And they having met together, he went to saying to them, As for myself, men, brethren, although not having done even one thing against the people or the customs of the fathers, yet I was delivered as a prisoner from Jerusalem into the hands of the Romans, who were such that after having examined me, desired

to release me because there was not even one bit of blameworthiness in me deserving of death. But when the Jews were speaking against me, I was compelled to appeal to Caesar, not at all that I was having anything of which to accuse my nation.

Because of this reason therefore I exhorted you to **20-22** see me and to speak with me, for on account of the hope of Israel I am bound around by this chain. And they said to him, As for us, neither did we receive a letter from Judaea concerning you, nor has any one of the brethren, having come, reported or spoken of any perniciousness concerning you. But we think it only right and proper that we hear from you personally the things which you are thinking, for indeed concerning this heresy, we know that everywhere it is being opposed.

And having mutually agreed with him as to the day, **23-27** there came many to the place where he was staying, to whom he continued to give a detailed exposition, solemnly bearing testimony to the kingdom of God, persuading them concerning Jesus both from the Mosaic law and from the prophets, from early morning until evening. And some on the one hand were persuaded by the things, but others on the other hand persisted in their unbelief. And being at odds with one another, they rid themselves of Paul by going off after Paul had spoken a word, just one: Most fittingly and truly did the Holy Spirit speak through the intermediate agency of Isaiah the prophet to your fathers saying, Proceed at once to this people and say, By means of your sense of hearing you will hear and will positively not understand. And while seeing, you will see and will positively not perceive. For the heart of this people was made dull and callous, and with their ears they heard with difficulty, and their eyes they shut, lest at any time they might see with their eyes and hear with their ears and understand with their heart and return and I should heal them.

Let it become known to you therefore that to the **28** Gentiles there has been sent this, the salvation of God, and they themselves will also hear it.

30, 31   And he lived two whole years in his own hired
dwelling. And he kept on receiving all those who came
to him, proclaiming the kingdom of God and teaching
the things concerning the Lord Jesus Christ with all
freedom of speech and fearless confidence, without
hindrance.

THE EXPANDED TRANSLATION OF PAUL'S
LETTER TO THE ROMANS

PREFACE TO PAUL'S LETTER TO THE ROMANS

Only the Greek text of Romans should be the basis of authoritative Christian doctrine as formulated for the Church at large and never a translation in any language, no matter how correct it may be. However, for the Bible student who is not conversant with the Greek text, a reliable translation must suffice as a basis of his personal study of these doctrines. This expanded rendering of the Greek text is designed to serve as a commentary translation to be used alongside of the A. V. A Greek scholar will be able to observe how closely this translator has kept to the original text in an effort to provide the English reader with a dependable translation of this important Book. As examples of its accuracy and clarity and of the help the reader may expect to receive by its use we offer a number of illustrations.

Paul in presenting his doctrine of the total depravity of man says, "even as they did not like to retain God in their knowledge" (1:28). The word "like" is the translation of *dokimazō*, "to put to the test for the purpose of approving, and should the person tested meet the specifications laid down, to put one's approval upon him." Paul had just said (1:18-20) that the human race understood through the law of cause and effect (which law demands an adequate cause for each effect), that the created universe revealed the fact of a Creator to whom worship and obedience were due. By the use of this word he tells us that the world of sinners, knowing of this God, put Him to the test for the purpose of approving Him as the God to be worshipped should He meet their specifications, and after finding that He did not meet them, they rejected Him, turning to the worship of created things. This is a far cry from the word "like." The expanded translation brings out what the A. V., because of its limited number of words, left in the Greek text. What a flood of light is thrown upon this passage by the use of a few more words, all pure translation.

The word "propitiation" (3:25) in its verb form means "to prevent or reduce the anger of, to win the favor of, appease, conciliate." And that is the meaning of the Greek word of which it is the translation. The pagan would bring an offering to his god

in an effort to prevent or reduce his anger and win his favor. But this is not in accord with Christian doctrine. Our God does not need to have His anger placated like that of a peevish Greek god, nor does He need to have His favor purchased by an offering. His love gushes from His heart like water from an artesian well. Here is a case where a pagan word used in the Greek religions had to have its meaning changed to conform to Christian doctrine. The expanded translation offers "an expiatory satisfaction." Our Lord's death was substitutionary on behalf of sinners, and it satisfied the just requirements of God's holy law which we broke.

Again the word "remission" (3:25) is an incorrect rendering of the Greek here. The word *aphesis* refers to the act of "putting away" sins, thus should be translated "remission." The word *paresis* (used here) means "a passing by" of sins for the present, thus should be translated "pretermission." The expanded translation so renders it. God passed by sins until the Cross with the view of paying their penalty Himself, thus maintaining His justice and righteousness. For doctrinal purposes this correction is important. Again, the word "atonement" (5:11, A.V.) will lead the English reader astray in his interpretation. This word in 1611 meant "at-one ment," the making of two estranged parties at one. Today the word refers to the substitutionary death of our Lord by which He paid or atoned for our sins. The Greek word in 5:11 means "reconciliation" and is therefore in harmony with its context. The expanded translation takes care of this obsolete word.

Another Greek word which acquired a New Testament content of meaning is *dikaios*, "righteous," speaking of a righteousness which has a holy God for its standard. Sometimes these words retain their purely pagan meaning, the context indicating that fact. The righteous man of 5:7 is not a saved man, justified in the New Testament sense, but one who is fair in his dealings, law abiding.

This expanded translation offers the student help in Romans 6 by interpreting the word "sin" rather than by translating it. A rule of Greek grammar indicates that the word "sin" in its noun form in this chapter refers, not to acts of sin, but to the sinful nature indwelling the Christian. The Greek definite article before "sin" in 6:1 points back to "sin" in 5:21 where it is said to reign as a king. Acts of sin do not reign as a king. They are the result of something else reigning. Thus it is the sinful nature

which reigns as king. This gives us the key to the better understanding of the entire chapter. The expanded translation offers
"sinful nature." Again, the Greek word in 6:3 (*baptizō*) is trans-
literated in the A.V. rather than translated. Its English spelling
is not its translation. The word refers to the act of placing something in something else. The expanded translation offers "placed,"
referring to the act of the Holy Spirit placing the believer into
vital union with Jesus Christ.

The word "allow" (7:15, A.V.) is used here in its obsolete
sense. The Greek word means "to understand." Paul, a Christian, did not understand his experience. The very thing he did
not want to do, namely, sin, he did do, and the very thing he
wanted to do, namely, good, he did not do. The expanded translation offers "understand," thus clarifying the passage.

In 12:2 the A.V. translates correctly, but leaves much rich
truth behind in the Greek text. The expanded translation offers:
"Stop assuming an outward expression that does not come from
within you and is not representative of what you are in your
inner being but is patterned after this age; but change your outward expression to one that comes from within and is representative of your inner being." The saint is exhorted to stop masquerading in the habiliments of this age, and instead change his
outward expression to one that comes from his renewed inner
being. What wealth of truth is at the command of the student
here which is denied him in the standard translations.

Another example of the meticulous accuracy of statement in the
Greek text, the ambiguity which sometimes characterizes the
standard translations, and the clarity of statement of the expanded
translation is found in Romans 6:12 which in the A.V. reads,
"Let not sin therefore reign in your mortal body, that ye should
obey it in the lusts thereof." Now, does the pronoun "it" refer
back to the word "sin," the evil nature, or to the word "body"?
Pure logic leads us to conclude that it refers to sin, since the sinful
nature could be looked upon as a king reigning (the Greek word
here meaning "to reign as king"), whereas the human body would
not lend itself so well to such a concept. But the accurate and
scientific interpretation of the word of God is not based upon logic
but upon the rules of Greek grammar and syntax. An examination of the Greek text here discloses the fact that the word "sin"
is feminine in gender, the word "body" neuter, and the pronoun
"it" neuter. The rule of Greek syntax requires that a pronoun

agree with its antecedent in gender. All of which means that the word "it" refers back to the word "body," not the word "sin." This is final. There can be no appeal from this ruling. It closes the argument. In the expanded translation the ambiguous language of the A.V. is cleared up by the rendering, "Stop therefore allowing the sinful nature to reign as king in your mortal body with a view to obeying it [the body] in its passionate cravings."

But the reader may ask, "What practical advantage is gained from this meticulously accurate translation aside from the fact that it is actually what Paul wrote?" The answer is that the sinful nature is invisible although most real so far as its existence is concerned. But one cannot successfully fight an unseen enemy in an effort to keep sin out of the life. But the human body is a tangible, visible thing. One can watch what one's eyes look at, one's ears listen to, one's hands do, and where one's feet take one. The sinful act originates in the sinful nature, but by a careful watching of our members can be stopped before it finds expression in action. And that is an important part of the technique for enjoying constant victory over sin which Paul presents. This translator has meticulously followed the rules of Greek grammar and syntax in the production of this expanded rendering of the original text, holding himself very closely to the Greek words and their full content of meaning, even to the place where the English diction at times becomes somewhat cumbersome. But the acid test of the value of any translation is the accuracy and clarity with which it conveys to the reader the meaning of the original. The reader is invited to dip into this reservoir of truth for himself and drink from the fountain of the word of God.

Paul, a bondslave by nature belonging to Christ Jesus, **1-7**
an ambassador by divine summons, permanently separated to God's good news which He promised aforetime
through the intermediate agency of His prophets in holy
writings concerning His Son, who came from the ancestral line of David so far as His humanity is concerned,
who was demonstrated in the sphere of power as Son of
God so far as His divine essence was concerned by the
resurrection of the dead, Jesus Christ our Lord; through
whom we received grace and apostleship in order that
there may be obedience to the Faith among all the Gentiles in behalf of His name, among whom you also are
divinely summoned ones belonging to Jesus Christ, to
all who are in Rome, God's loved ones, divinely summoned
saints. Grace to you and peace from God our Father and
our Lord Jesus Christ.

First, I am constantly thanking my God through Jesus **8-12**
Christ concerning all of you because your faith is constantly being spread abroad in the whole world; for my
witness is God, to whom I render sacred service in my
spirit in the good news concerning His Son, how unceasingly I am making mention of you always at my prayers,
making supplication if somehow now at last I may be
prospered in the will of God to come to you, for I long
to see you in order that I may impart some spiritual gift
to you resulting in your being stabilized, that is, moreover,
that I may be strengthened by you through the mutual
faith which is both yours and mine.

Moreover, I do not desire you to be ignorant, breth- **13-15**
ren, that often I proposed to myself to come to you, but
I was prevented up to this time, in order that I might
procure some fruit also among you even as also among
the rest of the Gentiles. Both to Greeks and to those
who do not possess Greek culture, both to wise and unwise, I am debtor in such a manner that to the extent
of my ability I am eager to proclaim the good news also
to you who are in Rome.

For I am not ashamed of the good news. For God's **16-23**
power it is, resulting in salvation to everyone who believes, to Jew first and also to Gentile, for God's righteous-

ness in it is revealed on the principle of faith to faith, even as it stands written, And the one who is just, on the principle of faith shall live. For there is revealed God's wrath from heaven upon every lack of reverence and upon every unrighteousness of men who in unrighteousness are holding down the truth. Because that which is knowable concerning God is plainly evident in them, for God made it clear to them; for the things concerning Him which are invisible since the creation of the universe are clearly seen, being understood by means of the things that are made, namely, His eternal power and divine Being, resulting in their being without a defense. Because, knowing God, not as God did they glorify Him, nor were they grateful, but they became futile in their reasonings, and their stupid heart was darkened. Asserting themselves to be wise, they became fools and exchanged the glory of the incorruptible God for a likeness of an image of corruptible man and of birds and of quadrupeds and of snakes.

24-27   On which account God delivered them over in the passionate cravings of their hearts to bestial profligacy which had for its purpose the dishonoring of their bodies among themselves; who were of such a character that they exchanged the truth of God for a lie and worshipped and rendered religious service to the creation rather than to the Creator who is to be eulogized forever. Amen. Because of this God gave them over to dishonorable passions, for even their females exchanged their natural use for that which is against nature. And likewise also the males, having put aside the natural use of the females, burned themselves out in their lustful appetite toward one another, males with males carrying to its ultimate conclusion that which is shameful, receiving in themselves that retribution which was a necessity in the nature of the case because of their deviation from the norm.

28-32   And even as after putting God to the test for the purpose of approving Him should He meet their specifications, and finding that He did not, they disapproved of holding Him in their full and precise knowledge, God gave them up to a mind that would not meet the test for

that which a mind was meant, to practice those things which were not becoming or fitting; being filled with every unrighteousness, pernicious evil, avarice, malice, full of envy, murder, wrangling, guile, malicious craftiness; secret slanderers, backbiters; hateful to God, insolent, haughty; swaggerers, inventors of evil things; disobedient to parents, stupid, faithless, without natural affection, merciless; such are those who, knowing the judgment of God that these who practice such things are worthy of death, not only habitually do the same things but also take pleasure in those who practice them.

1-10

Therefore, you are without a defense, O man, everyone who judges, for in that in which you are judging another, yourself you are condemning, for you who judge practice the same things. But we know that the judgment of God is according to truth against those who practice such things. And do you reason thus, O man, who judges those who practice such things, and are doing the same things, that as for you, you will escape the judgment of God? Or, the wealth of His kindness and forbearance and longsuffering are you treating with contempt, being ignorant that the goodness of God is leading you to repentance? But according to your obstinate and unrepentant heart you are storing up for yourself wrath in the day of wrath and revelation of the righteous judgment of God who recompenses each according to his works, to those on the one hand who by steadfastness of a good work seek glory and honor and incorruptibility, life eternal; but to those on the other hand who out of a factious spirit are both also non-persuasible with respect to the truth and persuasible with respect to unrighteousness, wrath and anger. Tribulation and anguish upon every soul of man who works out to a finish the evil, both upon the soul of a Jew first and also upon the soul of a Gentile, but glory and honor and peace to everyone who works out to a finish that which is good, both to a Jew first and also to a Gentile.

11-13

For there is not partiality in the presence of God. For as many as without law sinned, without law shall also perish. And as many as in the sphere of law sinned, through law shall be condemned. For not those who are

instructed in the law are righteous in the presence of God but those who are doers of the law shall be justified.

14-16   For whenever Gentiles, who do not have law, do habitually by nature the things of the law, these not having law, are a law to themselves, they being such that they show the work of the law written in their hearts, their conscience bearing joint-witness and their reasonings in the meanwhile accusing or also excusing one another in the day when God judges the hidden things of men according to my gospel through Jesus Christ.

17-24   Now, assuming, as for you, that you bear the name of Jew, and have a blind and mechanical reliance on the law, and boast in God, and have an experiential knowledge of His will, and after having put to the test for the purpose of approving the things that differ, and having found that they meet your specifications, you put your approval upon them, being instructed in a formal way in the law, you have persuaded yourself and have come to a settled conviction that you are a guide of the blind, a light of those in darkness, a corrector of those who are without reflection or intelligence, a teacher of the immature, having the rough sketch of the experiential knowledge of the truth in the law. Therefore, you who are constantly teaching another, are you not teaching yourself? You who are constantly preaching a person should not be stealing, are you stealing? You who are constantly saying that a person should not be committing adultery, are you committing adultery? You who are turning away constantly from idolatry as from a stench, are you robbing temples? You who are making your boast in the law, through your transgression of the law are you dishonoring God? For the Name of God because of you is reviled among the Gentiles, even as it stands written.

25-29   For, indeed, circumcision is profitable if you are making a practice of law, but if, on the other hand, you are a transgressor of law, your circumcision has become uncircumcision. Therefore, if the uncircumcision habitually guards the righteous requirements of the law, will not his uncircumcision be computed to his account for circumcision? And the uncircumcision which by nature

is fulfilling the law will judge you who with the advantage
of the letter and of circumcision are a transgressor of
law. For, not he who is so in an outward fashion is a
Jew, nor even that which is in an outward fashion in
flesh is circumcision. But he who is so in the sphere of
the inner man is a Jew, and circumcision is of the heart,
in the sphere of the spirit, not in the sphere of the letter,
concerning whom the praise is not from men but from
God.

What pre-eminence or advantage is there therefore   **1, 2**
which the Jew possesses? Or, what profit is there in circumcision? Much every way, for, first of all, because
they were entrusted with the divine utterances of God.

Well then — if, as is the case, certain ones did not   **3, 4**
exercise faith? Their unbelief will not render the faithfulness of God ineffectual, will it? Let no one ever think
such a thing. Let God be found veracious and every
man a liar, even as it stands written, To the end that
you may be acknowledged righteous in your words, and
may come out victor when brought to trial.

But in view of the fact that our unrighteousness estab-   **5-8**
lishes by proof God's righteousness, what shall we say?
God is not unrighteous who inflicts wrath, is He? I am
using a mode of speech drawn from human affairs. Away
with the thought. Otherwise, how will it be possible for
God to judge the world? Moreover, assuming that the
truth of God by means of my lie became the more conspicuous, resulting in His glory, why then yet am I also
being judged as a sinner? And not, as we were slander-
ously reported and even as certain are saying that we
are saying, Let us do the evil things in order that there
might come the good things; whose judgment is just.

What then? Are we better? Not in any way, for we   **9-18**
previously brought a charge against both Jews and Gentiles that all are under sin; as it stands written, There
is not a righteous person, not even one. There is not
the one who understands; there is not the one who seeks
out God. All turned aside; all to a man became useless.
There is not the one who habitually does goodness; there
is not as much as one. Their throat is a grave that stands

open. With their tongues they continually were deceiving. Asps' poison is under their lips; whose mouth is full of imprecations and bitterness; their feet are swift to pour out blood. Destruction and misery are in their paths. The road of peace they did not know. There is not a fear of God before their eyes.

19, 20   But we know absolutely that whatever things the law says, it says to those within the sphere of the law, in order that every mouth may be closed up and the whole world may become liable to pay penalty to God. Wherefore, out of works of law there shall not be justified any flesh in His sight, for through law is a full knowledge of sin.

21-26   But now, apart from law, God's righteousness has been openly shown as in view, having witness borne to it by the law and the prophets; indeed, God's righteousness through faith in Jesus Christ to all who believe, for there is not a distinction, for all sinned and are falling short of the glory of God; being justified gratuitously by His grace through the redemption which is in Christ Jesus, whom God placed before the eyes of all as an expiatory satisfaction through faith in His blood for a proof of His righteousness in view of the pretermission of the sins previously committed, this pretermission being in the sphere of the forbearance of God, also for a proof of His righteousness at the present season, with a view to His being just and the justifier of the one whose faith is in Jesus.

27, 28   Where then is the glorying? It was once for all excluded. Through what kind of a law? Of the aforementioned works? Not at all, but through the law of faith, for our reasoned conclusion is that a man is justified by faith apart from works of law.

29-31   Or, of Jews only is He God? Is He not also of Gentiles? Yes, also of Gentiles, assuming that there is one God who will justify the circumcision out of a source of faith and the uncircumcision through the intermediary instrumentality of faith. Then are we making law of none effect through this aforementioned faith? Let not such a thing be considered. Certainly, we are establishing law.

What then shall we say that Abraham our forefather
found with reference to the flesh? For, assuming that
Abraham was justified out of a source of works, he has
ground for boasting, but not when facing God. For what
does the scripture say? Now Abraham believed God,
and it was put to his account, resulting in righteousness.
Now, for the one who works with a definite result in
view [his wages], the remuneration is not put down on
his account as an undeserved, gratuitous gift, but as a
legally contracted debt. But in the case of the one who
does not work with a definite result in view [salvation]
but who places his trust upon the One who justifies the
person who is destitute of reverential awe towards God,
there is put to his account his faith, resulting in righteousness, even as David also speaks of the spiritual prosperity
of the man to whose account God puts righteousness
apart from works: Spiritually prosperous are those whose
lawlessnesses were put away and whose sins were covered. Spiritually prosperous is the man to whose account
the Lord does not in any case put sin.

Therefore, does this spiritual prosperity come upon
the circumcised one or the uncircumcised one, for we say,
There was put to Abraham's account his faith, resulting
in righteousness? How then was it put to his account, at
the time when he was circumcised or at the time when
he was uncircumcised? Not in circumcision but in uncircumcision. And he received the attesting sign of circumcision as a seal of the righteous character of the faith
which he had in his uncircumcision, resulting in his being
the father of all who believe while in the state of uncircumcision, in order that there may be put to their account
the righteousness; and the father of circumcision to these
who are not of the circumcision only but to those who
walk in the footsteps of the faith of our father Abraham
when he was in uncircumcision.

For not through law was the promise made to Abraham or to his offspring that he should be the heir of the
world, but through a righteousness which pertains to
faith. For, assuming that those who are of the law are
heirs, the aforementioned faith has been voided with the
result that it is permanently invalidated, and the afore-

mentioned promise has been rendered inoperative with the result that it is in a state of permanent inoperation. For the law results in divine wrath. Now, where there is not law, neither is there transgression.

16-22   On account of this it is by faith, in order that it might be by grace, to the end that the promise might be something realized by all the offspring, not by that which is of the law only, but also by that which is of the faith of Abraham who is father of all of us ; even as it stands written, A father of many nations I have established you permanently, before Him whom he believed, before God who makes alive those who are dead and calls the things that are not in existence as being in existence ; who, being beyond hope, upon the basis of hope believed, in order that he might become father of many nations, according to that which has been spoken with finality, In this manner will your offspring be. And not being weak with respect to his faith, he attentively considered his own body permanently dead, he being about one hundred years old, also the deadness of Sarah's womb. Moreover, in view of the promise of God, he did not vacillate in the sphere of unbelief between two mutually exclusive expectations but was strengthened with respect to his faith, having given glory to God, and was fully persuaded that what He had promised with finality He was able also to do ; wherefore also it was put down in his account, resulting in righteousness.

23-25   Now, it was not written for his sake alone, namely, that it was put to his account, but also for our sakes, to whose account it is to be put, to ours who place our faith upon the One who raised Jesus our Lord out from among the dead, who was delivered up because of our transgressions and was raised because of our justification.

1-5   Having therefore been justified by faith, peace we are having with God through our Lord Jesus Christ, through whom also our entree we have as a permanent possession into this unmerited favor in which we have been placed permanently, and rejoice upon the basis of hope of the glory of God. And not only this, but we also are exulting in our tribulations, knowing that this

tribulation produces endurance, and this endurance, approvedness, and this approvedness, hope. And this hope does not disappoint, because the love of God has been poured out in our hearts and still floods them through the agency of the Holy Spirit who was given to us.

For when we were yet without strength, in a strategic season Christ instead of and in behalf of those who do not have reverence for God and are devoid of piety died; for, very rarely in behalf of one of those individuals who is legally exact and precise in his observance of the customs and rules of the society in which he lives will anyone die, yet perhaps in behalf of the one who is generous in heart, always doing good to others, a person would even dare to die. But God is constantly proving His own love to us, because while we were yet sinners, Christ in behalf of us died. **6-8**

Much more therefore, having been justified now by His blood, we shall be saved through Him from the wrath. For though, while being enemies, we were reconciled to God through the death of His Son, much more, having been reconciled, we shall be saved by the life He possesses. And not only so, but we also rejoice in God through our Lord Jesus Christ, through whom now we received the reconciliation. **9-11**

Wherefore, as through the intermediate agency of one man the aforementioned sin entered the world, and through this sin, death; and thus into and throughout all mankind death entered, because all sinned. For until law, sin was in the world, but sin is not put to one's account, there being no law. But death reigned as king from Adam to Moses, even over those who did not sin in the likeness of the transgression of Adam, who is a type of the One who is to come. **12-14**

But not as the transgression, thus also is the gratuitous favor. For since by the transgression of the one the many died, much more the grace of God and the gratuitous gift by grace which is of the one Man, Jesus Christ, to the many will abound. And not as through one who sinned, was the gift, for the judgment, on the one hand, was out of one transgression as a **15-17**

source, resulting in condemnation. But the gratuitous gift, on the other hand, was out of many transgressions as a source, resulting in justification. For in view of the fact that by means of the transgression of the one death reigned as king through that one, much more those who receive the abundance of grace and of the gift of righteousness, in life will reign as kings through the One, Jesus Christ.

18-21 So then, therefore, as through one act of transgression, to all men there resulted condemnation, thus also through one act of righteousness, to all men there resulted a righteous standing that had to do with life. For just as through the disobedience of the one man the many were constituted sinners, thus also through the obedience of the One, the many will be constituted righteous. Moreover, law entered in alongside in order that the transgression might be augmented. But where the sin was augmented, the grace superabounded with more added to that, in order that just as the aforementioned sin reigned as king in the sphere of death, thus also the aforementioned grace might reign as king through righteousness, resulting in eternal life through Jesus Christ our Lord.

1-4 What then shall we say? Shall we habitually sustain an attitude of dependence upon, yieldedness to, and cordiality with the sinful nature in order that grace may abound? May such a thing never occur. How is it possible for us, such persons as we are, who have been separated once for all from the sinful nature, any longer to live in its grip? Do you not know that all we who were placed in Christ Jesus, in His death were placed? We therefore were entombed with Him through this being placed in His death, in order that in the same manner as there was raised up Christ out from among those who are dead through the glory of the Father, thus also we by means of a new life imparted may order our behavior.

5-10 For in view of the fact that we are those who have become permanently united with Him with respect to the likeness of His death, certainly also we shall be those who

as a logical result have become permanently united with Him with respect to the likeness of His resurrection, knowing this experientially, that our old [unregenerate] self was crucified once for all with Him in order that the physical body [heretofore] dominated by the sinful nature might be rendered inoperative [in that respect], with the result that no longer are we rendering a slave's habitual obedience to the sinful nature, for the one who died once for all stands in the position of a permanent relationship of freedom from the sinful nature. Now, in view of the fact that we died once for all with Christ, we believe that we shall also live by means of Him, knowing that Christ, having been raised up from among those who are dead, no longer dies. Death over Him no longer exercises lordship. For the death He died, He died with respect to our sinful nature once for all. But the life He lives, He lives with respect to God.

Thus, also, as for you, you be constantly counting **11-14** upon the fact that, on the one hand, you are those who have been separated from the sinful nature, and, on the other, that you are living ones with respect to God in Christ Jesus. Stop therefore allowing the sinful nature to reign as king in your mortal body with a view to obeying it [the body] in its passionate cravings. Moreover, stop putting your members at the disposal of the sinful nature as weapons of unrighteousness, but by a once-for-all act and at once, put yourselves at the disposal of God as those who are actively alive out from among the dead, and put your members as weapons of righteousness at the disposal of God, for [then] the sinful nature will not exercise lordship over you, for you are not under law but under grace.

What then? Shall we sin occasionally, because we are **15-20** not under law but under grace? Away with the thought. Do you not know that to whom you put yourselves at the disposal of as slaves resulting in obedience, slaves you are to whom you render habitual obedience, whether slaves of the sinful nature resulting in death, or obedient slaves [of Christ] resulting in righteousness? But God be thanked, that [whereas] you were slaves of the evil nature, you obeyed out from the heart as a source a type

of teaching into which you were handed over. And having been set free once for all from the sinful nature, you were constituted slaves to righteousness. I am using an illustration drawn from human affairs because of the frailties of your humanity. For just as you placed your members as slaves at the disposal of uncleanness and lawlessness resulting in lawlessness, thus now place your members as slaves at the disposal of righteousness resulting in holiness. For, when you were slaves of the sinful nature, you were those who were free with respect to righteousness.

21-23   Therefore, what fruit were you having then, upon the basis of which things now you are ashamed? For the consummation of these things is death. But now, having been set free from the sinful nature and having been made bondslaves of God, you are having your fruit resulting in holiness, and the consummation, life eternal. For the subsistence pay which the sinful nature doles out is death. But the free gift of God is life eternal in Christ Jesus our Lord.

1-6   Or, are you ignorant, brethren, for I am speaking to those who have an experiential knowledge of law, that the law exercises lordship over the individual as long as he lives? For the woman subject to a husband is permanently bound by law to her husband during his lifetime. But if her husband dies she is released from the law of her husband. So then, while her husband is living, an adulteress she will be called if she is married to another man. But if her husband is dead, she is free from the law, so that she is not an adulteress, though being married to another man. So that, my brethren, as for you, you also were put to death with reference to the law through the intermediate agency of the body of Christ, resulting in your being married to another, to the One who was raised up from among the dead, in order that we might bear fruit to God. For when we were in the sphere of the sinful nature, the impulses of the sins which were through the law were operative in our members, resulting in the production of fruit with respect to death. But now we were discharged from the law, having died to that in which we were constantly being held down,

insomuch that we are rendering habitually a slave's obedience in a sphere new in quality, that of the Spirit, and not in a sphere outworn as to usefulness, in a sphere of that which was put in writing.

What therefore shall we say? The law, is it sin? **7-15** Away with the thought. Certainly I did not come into an experiential knowledge of sin except through the instrumentality of law, for I had not known evil desire except that the law kept on saying, You shall not desire evil. But the sinful nature, using the commandment as a fulcrum, brought about in me every kind of evil craving. For without law, the sinful nature was dead. But I was alive without law aforetime. But the commandment having come, the sinful nature regained its strength and vigor, and I died. And the commandment which was to life, this I found to be to death; for the sinful nature, using the commandment as a fulcrum, beguiled me and through it killed me. So that the law is holy, and the commandment holy, and righteous, and good. Therefore, that which is good, to me did it become death? Away with the thought. But the sinful nature, in order that it might become evident that it is sin, through that which is good [the commandment] brought about death in me, in order that the sinful nature [its impulses and workings] through the intermediate agency of the commandment may become exceedingly sinful. For we know that the law is spiritual. But as for myself, I am fleshly [being dominated by the sinful nature], permanently sold under the sinful nature. For that which I do, I do not understand. For that which I desire, this I do not practice. But that which I hate, this I am doing.

In view of the fact then that what I do not desire, **16-20** this I do, I am in agreement with the law that it is good. And since the case stands thus, no longer is it I who do it, but the sinful nature which indwells me; for I know positively that there does not dwell in me, that is, in my flesh, good; for the being desirous is constantly with me; but the doing of the good, not; for that which I desire, good, I do not; but that which I do not desire, evil, this I practice. But in view of the fact that that

which I do not desire, this I do, no longer is it I who do it, but the sinful nature which indwells me does it.

21-23   I find therefore the law, that to me, always desirous of doing the good, to me, the evil is always present. For I rejoice in the law of God according to the inward man. But I see a different kind of a law in my members, waging war against the law of my mind, making me a prisoner of war to the law of the sinful nature which is in my members.

24, 25   Wretched man, I. Who shall deliver me out of the body of this death? Thanks be to God, through Jesus Christ our Lord. Therefore, I myself with my mind serve the law of God but with my flesh the law of sin.

1-4   Therefore, now, there is not even one bit of condemnation to those who are in Christ Jesus, for the law of the Spirit, that of the life in Christ Jesus, freed you once for all from the law of the sinful nature and of death. For that which is an impossibility for the law, because it was weak through the sinful nature, God having sent His Son in likeness of flesh of sin, and concerning sin, condemned sin in the sinful nature, in order that the righteous requirement of the law may be brought to completion in us who, not as dominated by the sinful nature are ordering our behavior but as dominated by the Spirit.

5-8   For those who are habitually dominated by the sinful nature put their minds on the things of the sinful nature, but those who are habitually dominated by the Spirit put their minds on the things of the Spirit. For to have the mind dominated by the sinful nature is death, but to have the mind dominated by the Spirit is life and peace; because the mind dominated by the sinful nature is hostile to God, for it does not marshall itself under the command of the law of God, neither is it able to. Moreover, those who are in the sphere of the sinful nature are not able to please God.

9-13   But, as for you, you are not in the sphere of the sinful nature but in the sphere of the Spirit, provided that the Spirit of God is in residence in you. But, assum-

ing that a person does not have Christ's Spirit, this one does not belong to Him. But, assuming that Christ is in you, on the one hand the body is dead on account of sin, but on the other hand the [human] spirit is alive on account of righteousness. And assuming that the Spirit of the One who raised up Jesus out from among the dead is in residence in you, He who raised from among the dead Christ Jesus, will also make alive your mortal bodies through the agency of the Spirit who is resident in you. So then, brethren, we are those under obligation, not to the sinful nature to live habitually under the dominion of the sinful nature. For, assuming that you are living habitually under the dominion of the sinful nature, you are on the way to dying. But, assuming that by the Spirit you are habitually putting to death the deeds of the body, you will live.

For as many as are being constantly led by God's **14-18** Spirit, these are sons of God. For you did not receive a spirit of slavery again with resulting fear, but you received the Spirit who places you as adult sons, by whom we cry out with deep emotion, Abba, [namely] Father. The Spirit himself is constantly bearing joint-testimony with our [human] spirit that we are God's children, and since children, also heirs; on the one hand, heirs of God, on the other, joint-heirs with Christ, provided that we are suffering with Him in order that we also may be glorified together, for I have come to a reasoned conclusion that the sufferings of the present season are of no weight in comparison to the glory which is about to be revealed upon us.

For the concentrated and undivided expectation of **19-25** the creation is assiduously and patiently awaiting the revelation of the sons of God; for the creation was subjected to futility, not voluntarily, but on account of the One who put it under subjection upon the basis of the hope that the creation itself also will be delivered from the bondage of corruption into the liberty of the glory of the children of God. For we know that the whole creation groans and travails together up to this moment, and not only, but we ourselves also who have the first-fruit of the Spirit, we ourselves also are groaning within

ourselves, assiduously and patiently waiting the full realization of our adult sonship at the time of the redemption of our body. For we were saved in the sphere of hope. But hope that has been seen is not hope, for that which a person sees, why does he hope for it? But if that which we do not see, we hope for, through patience we expectantly wait for it.

26, 27   And in like manner also the Spirit lends us a helping hand with reference to our weakness, for the particular thing that we should pray for according to what is necessary in the nature of the case, we do not know with an absolute knowledge; but the Spirit himself comes to our rescue by interceding with unutterable groanings. Moreover, He who is constantly searching our hearts knows what is the mind of the Spirit because, according to God, He continually makes intercession on behalf of the saints.

28-30   And we know with an absolute knowledge that for those who are loving God, all things are working together resulting in good, for those who are divinely-summoned ones according to His purpose. Because, those whom He foreordained He also marked out beforehand as those who were to be conformed to the derived image of His Son, with the result that He is firstborn among many brethren. Moreover, those whom He thus marked out beforehand, these He also summoned. And those whom He summoned, these He also justified. Moreover, those whom He justified, these He also glorified.

31-39   What then shall we say to these things? In view of the fact that God is on our behalf, who could be against us? Indeed, He who His own Son did not spare, but on behalf of us all delivered Him up, how is it possible that He shall not with Him in grace give us all things? Who shall bring a charge against God's chosen-out ones? God, the One who justifies? Who is the one who condemns? Christ Jesus, the One who died, yes, rather, who has been raised, who is on the right hand of God, who also is constantly interceding on our behalf? Who shall separate us from the love of Christ? Shall tribulation or distress or persecution or famine or naked-

ness or peril or sword? Even as it stands written, For your sake we are being put to death all the day long. We were accounted as sheep destined for slaughter. But in these things, all of them, we are coming off constantly with more than the victory through the One who loved us. For I have come through a process of persuasion to the settled conclusion that neither death nor life, nor angels, nor principalities, nor things present, nor things about to come, nor powers, nor height, nor depth, nor any other created thing will be able to separate us from the love of God which is in Christ Jesus our Lord.

Truth I speak in Christ. I am not lying, my conscience bearing joint-testimony with me in the Holy Spirit that I have a consuming grief, a great one, and intense anguish in my heart without a let-up. For I could wish that I myself were accursed from Christ on behalf of my brethren, my kindred according to the flesh, who in character are Israelites, who are possessors of the position of a son by having been placed as such, and of the glory, and of the covenants, and to whom was given the law, and who are possessors of the sacred service and the promises, of whom are the fathers, and out from whom is the Christ according to the flesh, the One who is above all, God eulogized forever. Amen. **1-5**

But the case is not such as this, that the word of God is fallen powerless; for not all who are out of Israel, these are Israel, nor because they are offspring of Abraham are all children, but: In Isaac an offspring shall be named for you. **6, 7**

That is, not the children of the flesh, these are children of God, but the children of the promise are counted for offspring; for the word of promise is this, According to this season I will come and there will be to Sarah a son. And not only, but also Rebecca, conceiving by one, Isaac, our father. For not yet having been born nor having practiced any good or evil, in order that the purpose of God dominated by an act of selecting out may abide, not out of a source of works, but out of the source of the One who calls, it was said to her, **8-13**

The older shall serve the younger; even as it stands
written, Jacob I loved, but Esau I hated.

14-18   What shall we say then? There is not unrighteousness with God, is there? Away with the thought. For to
Moses He says; I will have mercy upon whomever I will
have mercy, and I will have compassion on whomever I
will have compassion. Therefore, then, it [this being the
recipient of God's mercy] is not of the one who desires
nor even runs, but of the One who is merciful, God. For
the scripture says to Pharaoh, For this same purpose I
raised you up, in order that I may demonstrate in you
my power, and in order that there may be published
everywhere my Name in all the earth. Therefore, then,
upon whom He desires, He shows mercy; and whom
He desires to harden, He hardens.

19-21   Then you will say to me, Why does He still persist
in finding fault? For, with respect to His counsel, who
has taken a permanent stand against it? O man, nay,
surely, as for you, who are you who contradicts God?
The moldable material shall not say to the one who molds
it, Why did you make me thus, shall it? Or, does not the
potter possess authority over the clay, out of the same
lump to make, on the one hand, an instrument which is
for honorable purposes and, on the other hand, one which
is for dishonorable uses?

22-24   But if, as is the case, God desiring to demonstrate His
wrath and to make known His power, endured with much
long-suffering instruments of wrath fitted for destruction,
and in order that He might make known the wealth of
His glory upon instruments of mercy which were previously prepared for glory, even us whom He called, not
only from among Jews but also from among Gentiles.

25-29   As also in Hosea He says, I will call those, not my
people, my people, and those, not beloved, beloved. And
it shall come to be that in the place where it was said to
them, Not my people are you, there they shall be called
sons of the living God. And Isaiah cries in anguish concerning Israel, If the number of the sons of Israel be
as the sand of the sea, the remnant will be saved. For
the Lord will execute His word upon the earth, finishing

and cutting it short. And even as Isaiah said before, Except the Lord of Sabaoth had left us offspring, we would in that case have become even as Sodom and been made like Gomorrah.

What then shall we say? That Gentiles, the ones who **30-33** do not earnestly endeavor to acquire righteousness, appropriated righteousness, in fact, a righteousness which is out of a source of faith. But Israel, earnestly endeavoring to acquire a law of righteousness, did not measure up to the law. Because of what? Because, not out of a source of faith but even as out of a source of works they sought to acquire it. They stumbled up against the stone which is a stumbling stone, even as it stands written, Behold, I place in Sion a stone, a stumbling stone, and a rock of offense. And the one who places his faith upon Him will not be put to shame.

Brethren, the consuming desire of my heart and my **1-4** supplication to God on behalf of them is with a view to their salvation. For I bear testimony to them that a zeal for God they have, but not according to a full and accurate knowledge. For, being ignorant of the righteousness of God and seeking to set up their own private righteousness, to the righteousness of God they have not subjected themselves. For the termination of the law is Christ for righteousness to everyone who believes.

For Moses writes that the man who does the righteous- **5-13** ness which is of the law shall live in its sphere. But the righteousness which is out of a source of faith speaks in this manner, Do not say in your heart, Who shall ascend into heaven? This, in its implications, is to bring Christ down. Or, Who shall descend into the abyss? This, in its implications, is to bring Christ up from among those who are dead. But what does it say? Near you the word is, in your mouth and in your heart. This is the word of the Faith which we are proclaiming. If you confess with your mouth Jesus as Lord and believe in your heart that God raised Him from among the dead, you will be saved. For with the heart faith is exercised resulting in righteousness, and with the mouth confession is made resulting in salvation. For the scripture says, Everyone who

believes on Him shall not be put to shame. For there is
not a distinction between Jew and Greek. For the same
Lord is over all, constantly rich toward all those who call
upon Him. For whoever shall call upon the Name of the
Lord shall be saved.

14-17 How is it possible then that they shall call upon the
One in whom they did not believe? Moreover, how is it
possible that they will believe on the One concerning whom
they did not hear? And how is it possible that they shall
hear without one who proclaims? And how is it possible
that they shall make a proclamation except they be sent
on a mission? Even as it stands written, How beautiful
are the feet of those who bring good tidings of good
things. But not all lent an obedient ear to the good news.
For Isaiah says, Lord, who believed our message? So
then, faith is out of the source of that which is heard,
and that which is heard [the message] is through the
agency of the Word concerning Christ.

18-21 But I say, did they not hear? Most certainly. Into
all the earth their sound went out, and into the extremi-
ties of the inhabited earth, their words. But I say, Israel
did not fail to know, did it? First Moses says, I will
provoke you to jealousy by those who are no people, and
by a foolish people I will provoke you to anger. Moreover, Isaiah breaks out boldly and says, I was found by
those who are not seeking me. I was made manifest to
those who are not inquiring about me. But to Israel He
says, The whole day I stretched out my hands to a non-
persuasible and cantankerous people.

1-6 I say then, God did not repudiate His people, did He?
Far be the thought, for as for myself, I also am an
Israelite, the offspring of Abraham, of the tribe of Benjamin. God did not repudiate His people whom He foreordained. Or, do you not know absolutely in the case of
Elijah what the scripture says, how he pleads to God
against Israel? Lord, your prophets they killed. Your
altars they demolished. And as for myself, I was left
alone, and they are seeking my life. But what does the
divine answer say to him? I reserved for myself seven
thousand men who are of such a character that they did

not bow the knee to Baal. Therefore, thus also at this present season a remnant according to a choice of grace has come into being. But since it is by grace, no longer is it out of a source of works. Otherwise no longer is grace, grace.

What then? That which Israel is constantly seeking, this it did not obtain. But those chosen out obtained it. And the rest were hardened, even as it stands written, God gave them a spirit of insensibility, eyes for the purpose of not seeing, and ears for the purpose of not hearing, until this day. Even David says, Let their table become for a snare and a trap, and a stumbling block and a just retribution to them. Let their eyes be darkened in order that they may not see and in order that they may always bow down their back. **7-10**

I say then, Surely, they did not stumble so as to fall, did they? Away with the thought. But through the instrumentality of their fall salvation has come to the Gentiles with a view to provoking them [Israel] to jealousy. But since their fall is the enrichment of the world, and their defeat and loss the enrichment of the Gentiles, how much more their fulness? But to you I am speaking, the Gentiles. Inasmuch then, as for myself, as I am an apostle of Gentiles, I do my ministry honor, if by any means, possibly, I may provoke to jealousy those who are my flesh, and save some of them. **11-14**

For, in view of the fact that their repudiation results in the world's reconciliation, what will the receiving of them result in if not in life from among the dead? Now, in view of the fact that the firstfruit is holy, also the lump, and since the root is holy, also the branches. Now, since certain of the branches were broken off, and you, being a wild olive, were grafted in among them and became joint-partaker with them of the root of the fatness of the olive, stop boasting against the branches. But, assuming that you are boasting, you are not sustaining the root, but the root you. You will say then, Branches were broken off in order that I might be grafted in. Well! Because of their unbelief they were broken off. But, as for you, by faith you stand. Stop having a superiority **15-22**

complex, but be fearing; for in view of the fact that God did not spare the branches which were according to nature, neither will He spare you. Behold therefore God's benevolent kindness and His severity; on the one hand, upon those who fell, severity, and, on the other hand, upon you, God's benevolent kindness, upon the condition that you continue to remain in and abide by His benevolent kindness. Otherwise, also you will be cut out.

23-25   And, moreover, those also, if they do not remain in unbelief, will be grafted in, for God is able to again graft them in. For, as for you, in view of the fact that you were cut out of the olive tree which is wild by nature, and contrary to nature were grafted into the good olive tree, how much more will these who are according to nature be grafted into their own olive tree. For I do not desire you to be ignorant, brethren, concerning this mystery, in order that you may not be wise in yourselves, that hardening in part has come to Israel until the fulness of the Gentiles has come in.

26-32   And thus all Israel shall be saved, even as it stands written, There shall come out of Sion the Deliverer, and shall turn ungodliness from Jacob. And this to them is the covenant from me when I shall take away their sins. On the one hand, with reference to the gospel they are enemies for your sakes; on the other hand, with reference to the selected-out ones they are beloved ones for the fathers' sake; for the gifts in grace and the calling of God are with respect to a change of mind irrevocable. For, even as you formerly disbelieved God, yet now have been made recipients of mercy through the occasion of the unbelief of these, thus also these now have disbelieved in order that through the occasion of the mercy which is yours, they themselves also might now become the recipients of mercy, for God included all within the state of unbelief in order that He might have mercy upon all.

33-36   O the depth of the wealth and wisdom and knowledge of God. How unsearchable are His judgments, and how untraceable the paths He takes; for whoever knew the Lord's mind? or who became His counsellor? or who has previously given to Him and it will be recompensed to

him? Because out from Him and through Him and for Him are all things. To Him be the glory forever. Amen.

I therefore beg of you, please, brethren, through the instrumentality of the aforementioned mercies of God, by a once-for-all presentation to place your bodies at the disposal of God, a sacrifice, a living one, a holy one, well-pleasing, your rational, sacred service, [rational, in that this service is performed by the exercise of the mind]. And stop assuming an outward expression that does not come from within you and is not representative of what you are in your inner being but is patterned after this age; but change your outward expression to one that comes from within and is representative of your inner being, by the renewing of your mind, resulting in your putting to the test what is the will of God, the good and well-pleasing and complete will, and having found that it meets specifications, place your approval upon it.

1, 2

For I am saying through the grace which is given me, to everyone who is among you, not to be thinking more highly of himself, above that which the necessities in the nature of the case impose upon him to be thinking, but to be thinking with a view to a sensible appraisal of himself according as to each one God divided a measure of faith. For even as in one body we have many members but all the members do not have the same function, thus we, the many, are one body in Christ, and members severally one of another.

3-5

Having therefore gifts differing according to the grace given us, whether that of prophecy, prophesy according to the proportion of faith; or serving, exercise that gift within the sphere of service; or teaching, within the sphere of teaching; or he who exhorts, within the sphere of exhortation; the one who distributes of his earthly possessions, in the sphere of an unostentatious simplicity; the one who is placed in a position of authority, with intense eagerness and effort; the one who shows mercy, with a joyous abandon.

6-8

Love, let it be without hypocrisy. Look with loathing and horror upon that which is pernicious. Stick fast to that which is good. In the sphere of brotherly love have

9-18

a family affection for one another, vying with one another in showing honor; with respect to zeal, not lazy; fervent in the sphere of the Spirit, serving the Lord; rejoicing in the sphere of hope; patient in tribulation; with respect to prayer, persevering in it continually; with respect to the needs of the saints, being a sharer with them, eager for opportunities to show hospitality. Be constantly blessing those who are constantly persecuting you; be blessing and stop cursing. Be rejoicing with those who are rejoicing, and be weeping with those who are weeping; having the same mind towards one another, not setting your mind upon lofty things, but associating yourselves with lowly things and lowly people. Stop being those who are wise in their own opinion, requiting to no one evil in exchange for evil, taking thought in advance with regard to things that are seemly in the sight of all men. If it is possible so far as it depends upon you, with all men be living at peace.

19-21 Do not be avenging yourselves, beloved ones, but give place at once to the wrath, for it stands written, To me belongs punishment, I will repay, says the Lord. But, if your enemy is hungry, be feeding him. If he thirsts, be giving him to drink, for doing this, you will heap burning coals of fire upon his head. Stop being overcome by the evil, but be overcoming the evil by means of the good.

1-4 Let every soul put himself habitually in subjection to authorities who hold position over them, for there is not an authority except that ordained by God. Moreover, the existing authorities stand permanently ordained by God. So that the one who sets himself in array against the authority, against the ordinance of God has set himself, with the result that he is in a permanent position of antagonism against the ordinance. And those who resist shall receive for themselves judgment. For the rulers are not a terror to the good work but to the evil. Now, do you desire not to be afraid of the authority? Keep on doing the good, and you will have commendation from him, for he is God's servant to you for good. But if you are habitually doing that which is evil, be fearing, for not in vain is he wearing the sword, for he is God's ser-

vant, an executor of wrath upon the one who practices the evil.

On which account there is a necessity for putting one's self in subjection, not only because of wrath, but also because of conscience, for because of this you pay taxes; for God's public servants they are, continually giving their attention to this very thing. Deliver to all the debts due them, to the one collecting the tax, the tax; to the one collecting the custom, the custom; to the one to whom the fear is due, the fear; to the one to whom the honor is due, the honor.

5-7

Stop owing even one person even one thing, except to be loving one another; for the one who is loving another, has fulfilled the law. For this, You shall not commit adultery, you shall not kill, you shall not steal, you shall not covet, and if there is any commandment of a different nature, in this word it is summed up, in this, You shall love your neighbor as yourself. The aforementioned love does not work evil to a neighbor. Therefore, love is the fulfilling of law. And this, knowing the strategic season, that it is an hour now for you to awake out of sleep, for now our salvation is nearer to us than when we believed. The night has long been on its way, and the day has arrived. Therefore, let us at once and once for all put off the works of the darkness, and let us at once and once for all clothe ourselves with the weapons of the light.

8-12

In the same manner as in the day let us order our behavior in a seemly fashion, not in carousals and drunkenness, not in sexual intercourse and a dissolute abandon, not in strife and jealousy. But clothe yourselves with the Lord Jesus Christ and stop making provision for the sinful nature with a view to a passionate craving.

13, 14

Now, to the one who is weak with respect to his faith, be giving a cordial welcome, not with a view to a critical analysis of his inward reasonings. One, on the one hand, has confidence that he may eat all things; but the one, on the other hand, who is weak, constantly eats vegetables. The one who eats, let him not be treating with contempt the one who does not eat; and the one who

1-4

does not eat, let him not be criticising the one who eats, for God received him. As for you, who are you who are judging another's household slave? To his own personal master he stands or falls. Indeed, he shall be made to stand, for the Lord has power to make him stand.

5-9   For, on the one hand, there is he who judges a day above another day. On the other hand, there is he who subjects every day to a scrutiny. Let each one in his own mind be fully assured. The one who has formed a judgment regarding the day, with reference to the Lord he judges it. And the one who eats, with reference to the Lord he eats, for he gives thanks to God. And the one who does not eat, with reference to the Lord does not eat, and he gives thanks to God. For no one lives with reference to himself, and no one with reference to himself dies. For, whether we are living, with reference to the Lord we are living. Whether we are dying, with reference to the Lord we are dying. Therefore, whether we are living or whether we are dying, we belong to the Lord; for to this end Christ both died and lived, in order that He might exercise lordship over both dead ones and living ones.

10-13   But as for you, why are you judging your brother? Or, as for you also, why are you treating your brother with contempt? For we all shall stand before the judgment seat of God. For it stands written, As I live, says the Lord, every knee shall bow to me, and every tongue shall confess to God. Therefore, then, each one of us shall give an account concerning himself to God. Therefore, no longer let us be judging one another. But be judging this rather, not to place a stumbling block before your brother, or a snare in which he may be entrapped.

14-18   For I know with an absolute knowledge and stand persuaded in the Lord Jesus that not even one thing is unhallowed in itself except it be to the one who reasons it out to be unhallowed. To that one it is unhallowed. For, if because of food your brother is made to grieve, no longer are you conducting yourself according to love. Stop ruining by your food that one on behalf of whom Christ died. Therefore, stop allowing your good to be

spoken of in a reproachful and evil manner; for the kingdom of God is not eating and drinking, but righteousness
and peace and joy in the sphere of the Holy Spirit; for
the one who in this serves the Christ is well pleasing to
God, and because having met the specifications is approved
by men.

Accordingly, therefore, the things of peace let us be **19-21**
eagerly and earnestly seeking after, and the things which
edify, which edification is with a view to the edification
of one another. Stop on account of food ruining the work
of God. All things indeed are pure. But it is evil to the
man who eats so as to be a stumbling block. It is good
not to eat flesh, nor to drink wine, nor even anything by
which your brother stumbles.

As for you, the faith which you have, be having to **22, 23**
yourself in the sight of God. Spiritually prosperous is the
one who does not judge himself in that which he has
tested with a view to approving it should it meet specifications and, having found that it does, has placed his
approval upon it. But the one who doubts, if he eats,
stands condemned because not by faith did he eat. Moreover, everything which is not of faith is sin.

As for us, then, the strong ones, we have a moral **1-4**
obligation to be bearing the infirmities of those who are
not strong, and not to be pleasing ourselves. Each one of
us, let him be pleasing his neighbor with a view to his
good, resulting in his edification. For even the Christ did
not please himself, but even as it stands written, The re-
proaches of those who reproached you fell upon me. For
whatever things were written aforetime with a view to
our learning were written, in order that through the
patience and through the encouragement arising from the
scriptures we might be having hope.

Now, the God of the patience and the encouragement **5-7**
give to you to be thinking the same thing among one another according to Christ Jesus, in order that with one
mind and one mouth you may keep on glorifying the God
and Father of our Lord Jesus Christ. Wherefore, be
receiving one another even as also the Christ received us,
with a view to the glory of God.

8-12   For I am saying, Christ has become a servant to the circumcision on behalf of God's truth, resulting in the confirmation of the promises to the fathers and [resulting] in the Gentiles, on behalf of His mercy, glorifying God; even as it stands written, Because of this I will openly confess to you among the Gentiles and in your Name sing. And again he says, Rejoice, Gentiles, with His people. And again, Be extolling, all you Gentiles, the Lord. And let all the people extol Him. And again Isaiah says, There shall be a sprout out of the root of Jesse, even the One who arises to be a ruler of the Gentiles. Upon Him will the Gentiles place their hope.

13, 14   Now the God of the hope fill you with every joy and hope in the sphere of believing, resulting in your super-abounding in the sphere of the hope by the power of the Holy Spirit. But I have reached a settled conviction, my brethren, even I myself, concerning you, that you yourselves also are full of goodness, having been filled completely full of every knowledge with the result that you are in an abiding state of fullness, able also to be admonishing one another.

15, 16   The more boldly indeed I write to you in some measure as recalling to your mind again because of the grace which was given to me from God, resulting in my being a servant of Christ Jesus in holy things to the Gentiles, exercising a sacred ministry in the good news of God in order that the offering of the Gentiles might be well pleasing, having been sanctified by the Holy Spirit.

17-21   I have therefore my glorifying in Christ Jesus with reference to the things which pertain to God. For I will not dare to be speaking concerning anything of the things which Christ did not bring about through my agency resulting in the obedience of the Gentiles, by word and deed, by the power of attesting miracles and miracles of an extraordinary character, by the power of the Holy Spirit: so that from Jerusalem and the environs of Illyricum I have fulfilled my commission of preaching the good news of the Christ. Indeed, in this manner I have been actuated by considerations of honor to be ambitious to announce the glad tidings not where Christ was named,

in order that I would not be building upon a foundation belonging to another; but as it stands written, They shall see, those to whom there was not made an announcement concerning Him, and those who have not heard, they shall understand.

Wherefore, I also have been continually hindered by the many things in coming to you. But now no longer having opportunity in these parts, and having a passionate desire to come to you these many years, whenever I journey into Spain I am hoping to see you as I journey through, and by you to be furnished with the necessities of travel to that place, if first in part I may be fully satisfied with your fellowship.   **22-24**

But now I am going on my journey to Jerusalem, ministering to the saints. For it was the good pleasure of Macedonia and Achaia to make up a certain benefaction jointly contributed for the poor of the saints which are in Jerusalem; for it was their good pleasure, and their debtors they are. For in view of the fact that the Gentiles were fellow-partakers of their spiritual things, they are under moral obligation to minister to them in the sphere of things needed for the sustenance of the body, considering this material ministry as a sacred service. Then, having brought this to a successful termination and having secured to them this fruit, I will come through you into Spain. And I know positively that when coming to you, in the fulness of the blessing of Christ I will come.   **25-29**

But I beg of you, please, brethren, through our Lord Jesus Christ and through the love which is of the Spirit, contend vigorously with me in your prayers on my behalf to God, in order that I may be delivered from those who are non-persuasible in Judaea, and that my service which is for Jerusalem may become well pleasing to the saints, in order that in joy, having come to you through God's will, I may rest and refresh myself with you. Now, the God of the peace be with you all. Amen.   **30-33**

Now, I recommend to you, Phoebe, our sister, who is a deaconess of the assembly which is at Cenchrea, to the end that you take her to yourselves in the Lord in a   **1-5**

manner which is fitting to the saints, and that you stand by her in whatever business she may have need of you, for verily, she herself became a benefactress of many, and of me myself. Greet Prisca and Aquila, my fellow-workers in Christ Jesus, who are such that on behalf of my life they laid down their necks, to whom I not only give thanks, but also all the assemblies of the Gentiles. Also, greet the assembly which meets in their home.

5-9 Greet Epaenetus, my well-beloved, who is the first-fruit of Asia with reference to Christ. Greet Marian who is such as to have labored with wearisome effort to the point of exhaustion on your behalf with reference to many things. Greet Andronicus and Junia, my fellow countrymen and my fellow prisoners who are of excellent reputation among the apostles, who also came in Christ before I did. Greet Amplias, my beloved in the Lord. Greet Urbane, our fellow helper in Christ, and Stachys, my beloved.

10-12 Greet Apelles, the one who, having been put to the test and having been found to meet the test, is approved in Christ. Greet those belonging to Aristobulus. Greet Herodion, my fellow countryman. Greet those belonging to Narcissus, those who are in the Lord. Greet Tryphena and Tryphosa, those who labored to the point of exhaustion in the Lord.

12-16 Greet Persis, the beloved who was such that she labored to the point of exhaustion with reference to many things in the Lord. Greet Rufus, the one selected out in the Lord, and his mother and mine. Greet Asyncritus, Philegon, Hermas, Patrobas, Hermes, and the brethren with them. Greet Philologus, and Julia, Nereus and his sister, and Olympas, and all the saints with them. Greet one another with a holy kiss. There greet you all the churches of Christ.

17-20 Now, I beg of you, please, brethren, be keeping a watchful eye ever open for those who are causing the divisions and the scandals which are contrary to the teaching that you learned, and be turning away from them. For they are such as are not rendering service as bond-slaves to our Lord Christ, but to their own stomachs;

and with smooth and plausible address, which simulates goodness, and with polished eulogies, are leading astray the hearts of the innocent; for your obedience has come to the ears of all. Because of you, therefore, I am rejoicing. But I desire you to be wise ones with reference to that which is good, and pure ones with reference to that which is evil. And the God of the peace will trample Satan under your feet soon. The grace of our Lord Jesus be with you.

There greet you Timothy, my co-worker, and Lucius, **21-27** and Jason, and Sosipater, my countrymen. As for myself, I, Tertius, greet you in the Lord, the one who is putting this letter in writing. There greets you Gaius, my host and host of the whole assembly. There greet you Erastus, the manager of the city, and Quartus, the brother. Now, to the One who is of power to establish you according to my gospel, even the proclamation concerning Jesus Christ, according to the uncovering of the mystery which during eternal times has been kept in silence but now has been made known through prophetic writings according to the mandate of the eternal God, having been made known with a view to the obedience to the Faith among all nations, to God alone wise, through Jesus Christ, to Him [God alone wise] be the glory for ever and ever. Amen.

THE EXPANDED TRANSLATION OF FIRST CORINTHIANS

PREFACE TO THE CORINTHIAN LETTERS

These letters present great difficulties in translation and interpretation. Vincent in his *Word Studies in the New Testament,* when commenting on II Corinthians 10, has this to say: "Perhaps no portion of the New Testament furnishes a better illustration of the need of revision than the Authorized Version of this and succeeding chapters. It is not too much to say that, in that version, much of the matter is unintelligible to the average English reader. With the best version it requires the commentator's aid." Arthur S. Way, in his book, *The Letters of St. Paul,* speaking of the A.V. says that, conceding the dignity and charm of that translation, yet the first requisite of any translation is that it will convey with absolute clearness the meaning of the Greek text. He adds the comment that in this respect the A.V. is far from adequate in many places in Paul's letters. He presents a case in point when he says that if a student would hand in such a translation of Thucydides or Plato as the A.V. presents in its rendering of II Corinthians 10:13-16, the instructor would tell him that he did not understand his author. Dr. Way, speaking of Paul's style, says that one of its prominent features is an apparent lack of continuity of thought, almost to the point of incoherence. Again, the transition from one subject to another, from one point in an argument to the next, is not clear. The links in thought seem to be wanting. In many places where the apostle uses the word "for" the inference is not apparent. As a result, to many, Paul's letters are a collection of precious texts and inspiring passages, but to a few he is really a connected thinker, and a writer whose language is marked by sharp precision and limpid clearness of expression. The great Greek scholar, A. T. Robertson, in his *Word Pictures in the New Testament* at one point in his comments on II Corinthians remarks that he does not know what Paul means by a certain expression.

Of all Paul's writings the Corinthian letters stand out as characterized by the above translation difficulties. These difficulties this translator has had to face as he endeavored to make clear to the English reader just what Paul meant in what he wrote to the Corinthian Greeks. The expanded translation of I and II Corin-

thians as presented in this volume is designed as a commentary translation to be used alongside of the A.V. Because of the great difficulty inherent in Paul's style of writing here, it became necessary to bring in much interpretative material. When this material assumes any sizable proportions it is included in brackets. The reader is assured that this translator's work in these two letters is a careful attempt to make Paul's language clear. Where the English is somewhat awkward, the reader should understand that language idioms in translation work often result in awkward English but in a good rendering of the Greek text. The reader is warned that this expanded translation is not easy reading. It demands study, and study is required if one wishes to come to grips with the meaning of the word of God. With these prefatory remarks we will leave the reader with two of the least understood letters of Paul, with the expectation that under the blessing of the Holy Spirit he will come to a clearer understanding of these Corinthian letters.

Paul, a divinely-summoned and divinely-appointed ambassador belonging to Christ Jesus, an ambassador by reason of God's determining will, and Sosthenes our brother, to the assembly of God which is at Corinth, to those who have been set apart for the worship and service of God, this act of setting apart having been accomplished by being placed in Christ Jesus and thus being in vital union with Him, consecrated ones, this consecration having been by divine appointment and summons, with all those who are calling upon the Name of our Lord Jesus Christ in every place, their Lord and ours. Grace to you and peace from God our Father and from the Lord Jesus Christ.

I am thanking my God always concerning you, the cause of my thanksgiving being the grace of God which was given you in Christ Jesus. I mean that in everything you were made rich in Him, this wealth being in the form of every exuberant aptitude in proclaiming the Word and in the form of every kind of experiential knowledge, inasmuch as the testimony concerning the Christ was proved to be divinely-revealed truth and its reality was verified among you with the result that you are not feeling that you are trailing behind others in even one spiritual enablement for service while you are assiduously and patiently waiting for the appearance of our Lord Jesus Christ, who also will make you steadfast and constant even to the end, in character such that you cannot be called to account in the day of our Lord Jesus Christ. Faithful is God through whom you were divinely summoned into a joint-participation with His Son, Jesus Christ our Lord.

Now, I beg of you, please, brethren, my appeal to you being enforced by the Name of our Lord Jesus Christ [that Name holding within its compass all that He is in His glorious Person and wonderful salvation], I beg of you, please, that all of you be speaking the same thing, and that there be no factions among you, but that the breaches in your fellowship caused by these factions having been healed, you may remain perfectly united in the sphere of the same mind and in the sphere of the same opinion.

11-17   For it was made clear to me concerning you, my brethren, by members of Chloe's household, that there are wranglings among you. Now, what I mean is this; that each one of you is saying, As for myself, I am a follower of Paul; But as for myself, I am a follower of Apollos; But as for myself, I am a follower of Cephas; But as for myself, I am a follower of Christ. The Christ has been divided into various parts, with the present result that He lies there broken up into fragments which are distributed among you. Paul was not crucified on your behalf, was he, or, it was not into the name of Paul that you were baptized, was it? I am thankful that not even one of you did I baptize except Crispus and Gaius; lest anyone should say that into my name you were baptized. However, I also did baptize the household of Stephanas. Besides, I do not know positively whether I baptized any other person, for Christ did not send me on a mission to be a baptizer but to be a bringer of good news, not bringing this good news within the realm of philosophical discourse, lest the Cross of the Christ be emptied of its true significance and power.

18-25   For the story, that story concerning the Cross, is, on the one hand, to those who are perishing, foolishness, but to us, on the other hand, who are being saved, it is God's power. For it has been written and is at present on record, I will destroy the wisdom of those who are wise, and the discernment of those who have the ability to discern I will frustrate. Where is a philosopher, skilled in letters, cultivated, learned? Where is a man learned in the sacred scriptures? Where is a learned sophist of this age, fallacious reasoner that he is? Did not God prove foolish the wisdom of this world system? For, in view of the fact that, in the wisdom of God, the world system through its wisdom did not come to have an experiential knowledge of God, God saw fit through the aforementioned foolishness of the previously alluded-to proclamation to save those who believe, for, both, Jews are constantly demanding an attesting miracle and Greeks are constantly searching for wisdom. But as for us, we are proclaiming a Christ, one who has been crucified; to Jews, on the one hand, an offense, to Greeks,

on the other hand, folly, but to those themselves who have been divinely summoned into salvation, both Jews and Greeks, Christ, God's power and God's wisdom, because that aforementioned folly of God is wiser than men and that aforementioned weakness of God is stronger than men.

26-29

For, take a good look at your divine summons [into salvation], brethren, that not many wise men according to human standards, not many men of dignity and power, not many who are of royal or aristocratic lineage are given that divine summons [into salvation], but God selected out for himself those individuals among the world of sinners characterized by the aforementioned foolishness, in order that He might put to confusion those who are wise. And those individuals among the world of sinners, characterized by weakness, God selected out for himself, in order that He might put to confusion those who are characterized by strength. And those individuals among the world of sinners, who are not of royal or noble ancestry but belong to the common people and those who are utterly despised, God selected out for himself, the aforementioned classes of individuals looked upon as nonentities, in order that He might deprive of force, influence, and power those who think themselves to be somewhat, to the end that humanity may not in a single instance boast in His presence.

30,31

But as for you, out from Him as a source are you in Christ Jesus who became wisdom for us from God, both righteousness and sanctification and redemption, in order that even as it stands written, He who boasts, in the Lord let him be boasting.

1-5

And as for myself, having come to you, brethren, I came, not having my message dominated by a transcendent rhetorical display or by philosophical subtlety when I was announcing to you the testimony of God, for, after weighing the issues, I did not decide to know anything among you except Jesus Christ and this very One as crucified. And as for myself, when I faced you, I fell into a state of weakness and fear and much trembling. And my message and my preaching were not couched in

specious words of philosophy but were dependent for their efficacy upon a demonstration of the Spirit and of power, in order that your faith should not be resting in human philosophy but in God's power.

6-8   There is a wisdom, however, which we are in the habit of speaking among those who are spiritually mature, but not a wisdom of this present age or even a wisdom of the rulers of this age who are in the process of being liquidated. But we speak God's wisdom in the form of a mystery long hidden but now revealed and understandable, that wisdom which has been kept secret which God foreordained before the ages with a view to our glory, which wisdom not one of the rulers of this age has known in an experiential way, for had they known it, in that case they would not have crucified the Lord of the glory.

9-11   But even as it stands written, The things which eye did not see nor ear hear and which did not arise within an individual's heart, so many things as God prepared for those who love Him, for to us God the Father revealed them through the intermediate agency of His Spirit. For the Spirit is constantly exploring all things, even the deep things of God. For who is there of men who knows the things of the individual person except the [human] spirit of that aforementioned individual person which is in him? In the same manner also the things of God no one has known except the Spirit of God.

12, 13   But as for us, not the spirit of the world system did we receive but the Spirit who is of God in order that we might come to know the things which by God have been in grace bestowed upon us, which things also we put into words, not in words taught by human philosophy but in words taught by the Spirit, fitly joining together Spirit-revealed truths with Spirit-taught words.

14-16   But the unregenerate man of the highest intellectual attainments does not grant access to the things of the Spirit of God, for to him they are folly, and he is not able to come to know them because they are investigated in a spiritual realm. But the spiritual man investigates indeed all things, but he himself is not being probed by

anyone. For who has come to know experientially the Lord's mind, he who will instruct Him? But as for us, Christ's mind we have.

As for myself, I also, brethren, was not able to speak to you as I would to those dominated by the Holy Spirit, but as I would to those dominated by the evil nature, as I would to those in Christ who are still immature spiritually. Milk I fed you, not solid food, for not yet were you able to assimilate the latter. In fact, not even yet at the present time are you able to do so. For, in so far as there are among you jealousy and strife, are you not those dominated by the evil nature, and are you not ordering your manner of life as an unsaved man would do? For whenever someone says, As for myself, I indeed am a follower of Paul, but another of a different character says, As for myself, I am a follower of Apollos, are you not mere men? What then is Apollos? And what is Paul? We are ministering servants through whose intermediate agency you believed, servants in each case in the manner as the Lord gave to each of us. As for myself, I planted, Apollos watered, but God has been causing that which was sown to grow. So that he who plants is not anything, nor he who waters, but God who causes things to grow.

Now, the one who plants and the one who waters are one. But each one of us will receive his specific pay appropriate to his specific work, for we are God's fellow workers. You are God's land under cultivation, God's edifice. According to the grace of God which was given to me, I as a skillful architect laid a foundation, but another builds upon it. But let each one be taking heed how he builds upon it, for an alternative foundation no one is able to lay alongside of the one which is being laid, which foundation is a person, Jesus Christ.

Now, assuming that anyone builds upon the aforementioned foundation gold, silver, precious stones, wood, hay, stubble, the work of each person will become apparent, for the day will make it known, because it [the day] will be made clear as to its identity by means of one of its attributes, namely, fire. And the fire itself will put

1-7

8-11

12-15

each person's work to the test for the purpose of approving it should it meet the required specifications, the test being to determine what sort of work it is as to quality. Assuming that the work of anyone which he has built upon it [the foundation, Christ] endures in that it has met these specifications, he shall receive a reward. Assuming that the work of anyone will be burned up, he will incur a loss, but he himself shall be saved, but being saved thus, it will be as escaping destruction in the midst of the fire which burns up his works.

16, 17   Do you not all know that all of you are God's inner sanctuary and that the Spirit of God is making His home in you? If, as is the case, anyone morally corrupts the inner sanctuary of God, this person God will bring to the place of ruin, for the inner sanctuary of God is holy, of which holy character you are.

18-23   Let no one continue to be deceiving himself. If, as is the case, anyone among you thinks himself to be wise in the sphere of the things of this age, let him become a fool [in the estimation of this age] in order that he may become wise, for the wisdom of this world system is foolishness as God looks at it. For it has been written and is at present on record, He catches those who are wise in their false wisdom, and again, The Lord knows the reasonings of those who are wise, that they are futile reasonings. Wherefore, let no one continue to be boasting in men, for all things are yours, whether Paul or Apollos or Cephas or the existing order of material things or life or death or present things or things about to come, all belong to you, and as for you, you belong to Christ and Christ belongs to God.

1-5   In this manner let a man measure and classify us, as servants of Christ and as those who have been entrusted with the mysteries of God and their disposition. Under these circumstances it is further sought in stewards that a man be found to be faithful. But with me it is a very small thing that I am being put on trial by you or by the judicial day of mankind. In fact, I do not even put myself on trial, for I am conscious of not even one thing against myself, but not by this means do I

stand justified. Indeed, He who puts me on trial is the Lord. Wherefore, stop exercising censorious judgment with reference to anything before the epochal, strategic season, until that time whenever the Lord may come, who will both turn the light on the hidden things of the darkness and bring out into the open the counsels of the hearts. And then to each one there shall come his praise from God.

And these things, brethren, I referred to myself and Apollos, things true of the whole class [of servants of the Lord Jesus] to which we belong, doing this for your sakes, in order that you may learn from our example not to go beyond the things that stand written, to the end that you do not bear yourselves loftily, one on behalf of one individual [teacher] as against another of a different character. For who makes a distinction between you and others? And what do you have which you did not receive? But since also you received it, why are you boasting as though you did not receive it? Already have you become completely satiated with the result that your state of complete satisfaction persists through present time? Already did you become wealthy? Without us did you enter that new state of being in which you reign as kings? However, I wish indeed that you did reign as kings, in order that, as for us also, we might reign as kings with you, for it seems to me that God exhibited us, the apostles, as those who in the eyes of men are the most inferior in the scale of human existence, as men doomed to die, because we were exhibited as a spectacle to be gazed at and made sport of by the universe, both by angels and by men. As for us, fools are we on account of Christ. But as for you, you are members of the intelligentsia in your union with Christ. As for us, we are those who are frail and infirm. But as for all of you, you are those who are mighty. As for all of you, you are those who are illustrious, honorable, held in esteem by others. But as for us, we are those whom no one respects. To this very hour we are hungry and thirsty and scantily clothed and maltreated and, going from place to place, we have no fixed home, and we labor to the point of exhaustion, working at our trade [that of

6-13

tent making] with our own hands. When insulting abuse is being heaped upon us, we invoke blessings upon those who are mistreating us. When we are being persecuted, we patiently bear it. When we are publicly slandered, we pleadingly admonish — I beg of you, please. We have become in the estimation of the world as the filth discarded by humanity as the result of cleansing one's self, dirt scraped off of all things, to this very moment.

14-21   Not as shaming you am I writing these things, but as my children, beloved ones, I am warning and admonishing you, for if you may be having ten thousand tutors in Christ, yet not many fathers do you have, for in Christ Jesus through the gospel, as for myself, I begot you. I beg of you, please, therefore, be becoming imitators of me. For this very reason I sent to you Timothy, who is my child, a beloved one, and one in the Lord, who is trustworthy and can be depended upon, who will bring to your remembrance my ways which are in Christ Jesus, even as in every assembly everywhere I am teaching. Now, on the supposition that I am not coming to you, certain ones have an inflated ego. But I will come to you shortly if the Lord wills, and I will take cognizance, not of the speech of those with an inflated ego but of their power, for the kingdom of God is not in the sphere of speech but in that of power. What are you desiring? With a stick shall I come to you or in a love that has as its impelling motive the benefit of the one loved, the exercise of which love demands self-sacrifice, and in the spirit of meekness?

1-8   There is actually fornication reported to be among you, and this fornication of such a nature that it does not exist even among the Gentiles, that a certain person is possessing the wife of his father. And as for you, you have been guilty of an inflated ego and are at present in the same state. And have you not rather gone into mourning, to the end that the one who has done this deed might be taken out of your midst? For, as for myself, I indeed, being absent in body but present in spirit, already handed down my sentence, and this sentence stands as though I were present concerning this one who thus did this thing. In the Name of the Lord Jesus, when

you are gathered together, and my spirit, with the power
of our Lord Jesus, my sentence is that you deliver such a
one to Satan for the subjugation of the flesh [the evil
nature], in order that the spirit might be saved in the
day of the Lord. Your boasting [in the state of the local
assembly] is not seemly or fitting. Do you not know with
a positive assurance that a little yeast permeates and
affects the entire bread dough with itself? Cleanse out
completely, at once and once for all, the old yeast which
is part of a world which has passed away for you and
out from which you were saved, in order that you may
be a fresh aggregation of individuals, even as you are
without yeast. For, indeed, our Passover was slain,
Christ. Wherefore, let us be keeping the feast, not with
the yeast which has been relegated to a time that is past
when we lived a life not for us today, neither with the
yeast of malice and perniciousness, but with cakes per-
meated and affected by the yeast of an unadulterated life,
having no admixture of evil in them, and having in them
the yeast of truth.

I wrote to you in my letter not to be mingling in a   9-13
close and habitual intimacy with those who indulge in
unlawful sexual intercourse. I did not altogether forbid
you having dealings with the fornicators who are members of this world system [of evil] or with those who
are covetous and rapacious, or with idolaters, since then
you would be obliged to go out of the world of mankind.
But now I am writing to you to urge you not to be
mingling in a close and habitual intimacy — should anyone who is called a brother [Christian] be a fornicator or
a covetous person or an idolater or a reviler or a drunk-
ard or rapacious — with such a person not even to be eating. For what responsibility of mine is it to pass judgment upon those who are outside [the Church]? Indeed,
those who are outside will God judge. Expel at once the
pernicious person from among yourselves.

Is anyone of you who has a case against another dar-   1-8
ing to be going to law before those who are unrighteous
and not before the saints? Or, do you not all know that
the saints shall judge the world system [of evil]? And
in view of the fact that the world system is being judged

by you, are you those who are unfit to sit on the tribunal of a judge where trifling affairs are judged [forming courts yourselves to settle matters among yourselves]? Do you not know that we shall sit in judgment upon angels, to say nothing at all of judging the affairs of this life? Therefore, if you may be having courts [for the adjudication of your private matters], those who are least esteemed and of the most humble station in the local assembly, seat these on the judge's bench. I am saying this to you with a view to arousing your sense of shame. Is it thus, that you do not have one among you who is wise, who will be able to arbitrate between brother and brother? But brother goes to law with brother, and this before unbelievers. Nay! It is already a total [moral] defeat for you, having lawsuits with one another. Why do you not permit yourselves rather to be wronged? Why do you not permit yourselves rather to be defrauded? But, as for yourselves, you are committing wrong, and you are defrauding, and doing this to brethren.

9-11   Or do you not know that unrighteous individuals will not inherit God's kingdom? Stop being deceived; neither fornicators nor idolaters nor adulterers nor those who are of a voluptuous nature, given to the gratification of sensual, immoral appetites, neither men who are guilty of sexual intercourse with members of their own sex, nor thieves, nor those who are always greedy to have more than they possess, nor drunkards, nor revilers, nor extortioners, shall inherit God's kingdom. And these things you were, certain ones of you. But you bathed yourselves clean [from sin in the fountain filled with blood drawn from Immanuel's veins], but you were set apart for God, but you were made righteous in the Name of the Lord Jesus and by the Spirit of our God.

12-20   All [good] things are under my power of choice to be doing, but all things are not profitable. All things are under my power of choice, but I will not be brought under the power of any one of them. The various kinds of food are for the stomach, and the stomach is for these various kinds of food. But God will abolish both it and them. But the body is not for fornication but for the Lord, and the Lord is for the body. And God raised up

the Lord and will also raise us up through His power. Do you not know that your bodies are members of Christ? Having taken away then the members of Christ, shall I make them members of a harlot? Let not such a thing take place. Or, do you not know that he who joins himself with his harlot is one body [with her]? For they shall become, He says, these two, one flesh. But he who joins himself to the Lord is one spirit [with Him]. Be fleeing from fornication. Every act of sin which a man may do is outside of his body, but he who commits fornication is sinning against his own body. Or do you not know that your body is an inner sanctuary of the Holy Spirit, whom you have from God, and that you are not your own? For you were purchased at a price. Now therefore, glorify God in your body.

Now, with reference to the things concerning which **1-7** you wrote. It is perfectly proper, honorable, morally befitting for a man to live in strict celibacy. But because of the fornications, let each man be having his own wife, and let each woman be having her own husband. Let the husband be rendering to his wife that which is due her, and also let the wife render to her husband that which is due him. The wife does not have authority over her own body, but her husband does. Likewise also the husband does not have authority over his own body, but the wife does. Do not continue to rob each other [by withholding yourselves from one another] except it be by mutual consent for a time in order that you may give yourselves to prayer, and that you may be united again, in order that Satan may not solicit you to sin because of your lack of self-control. But this I am saying by way of a concession [in view of your circumstances], not by way of an injunction. But I wish that all men were even as also I myself. But each one has his own spiritual gift from God, one, on the one hand, in one way, and the other, on the other hand, in another way.

I say then to the unmarried men and to the widows **8-14** that it is a right procedure for them if they remain as I also am. But assuming that they are not able to exercise self-control in the realm of the continent life, let them marry, for it is more advantageous to marry than to

continue to burn [with the heat of sexual passion]. But to those who have married I command, not I, but the Lord, that the wife should not depart from her husband, but and if she depart, let her also remain unmarried or let her be reconciled to her husband. And the husband, let him not be putting away his wife. And to the rest I myself speak, not the Lord. Assuming that a certain brother has a wife who is an unbeliever and she herself is content to live with him, let him not be putting her away. And the wife who is such that she has an unbelieving husband, and this husband is content to live with her, let her not be putting her husband away, for the husband who is an unbeliever has been sanctified by virtue of his association with his wife in her position as a saved individual [this sanctification being in the marriage relation, that marriage being declared holy by reason of the Christian standing of the wife]. And the unbelieving wife has been sanctified by virtue of her association with her husband. Otherwise your children would be unclean. But now they are holy.

15-24   But assuming that the unbelieving husband departs, let him be departing. A [Christian] brother or [Christian] sister is not in the position of a slave, namely, bound to the unbelieving husband or unbelieving wife in an indissoluble union in cases such as these; but God has called us [to live] in peace. For how do you know positively, O wife, whether you will save your husband, or, how do you know, husband, whether you will save your wife? Only, as the Lord has assigned to each one his lot [in life], as God has called each one, in that way let him be ordering his manner of life. And so in all the assemblies I am giving orders. Was any certain person divinely summoned [into salvation] when he was in a state of circumcision? Let him not have the marks of circumcision effaced. Has any certain person been divinely summoned [into salvation] when he was uncircumcised? Let him not be circumcised. This thing called circumcision is not anything, and this thing called uncircumcision is not anything, but keeping the commandments of God [is what counts]. Each one, in the circumstance in which he was divinely summoned [into salvation], in

this let him be remaining. Were you divinely summoned when you were a slave? Let not that be a concern to you. But on the assumption also that you are able to become a free man, the rather take advantage of the opportunity, for the slave who was divinely summoned by the Lord is the Lord's freedman. Likewise, he who was divinely summoned when he was a freedman, is Christ's slave. At a price you were purchased. Do not go on becoming those who are subservient to men. Each one in the sphere in which he was divinely summoned, brethren, in this let him be remaining in the presence of God.

Now, concerning the virgins [unmarried women], an **25-28** injunction from the Lord I do not possess. But I am giving my reasoned judgment as one who is trustworthy by reason of the mercy shown him by the Lord. I consider therefore this to be salutary because of the necessity imposed by the present circumstances, that it is good for an individual to be just as he is. Have you been bound to a wife? Stop seeking to be loosed. Have you been loosed from a wife? Stop seeking a wife. But and if you marry, you did not sin. And if the virgin marry, she did not sin. However, such as these shall have tribulation in the sphere of one's physical existence [on earth]. But, as for myself, I would be sparing you.

But this I am saying, brethren, The strategic, epochal **29-31** period of time [in which we are living] has been shortened, that henceforth both those who have wives be as though not having wives, and those who are weeping be as though they are not weeping, and those who are rejoicing as though not rejoicing, and those who are purchasing in the market place as though they did not possess anything, and those who are making use of this world [the things of human existence] as not making excessive use of the same, for the temporary fashion of this world is passing away.

But I desire you to be without anxious cares. He **32-40** who is unmarried seeks to promote the interests of the things of the Lord, how he may please the Lord. But he who is married is concerned with the things of the world,

how he may please his wife, and is distracted. Both the
unmarried woman and the virgin seek to promote the
interests of the things of the Lord in order that they may
be set-apart ones to God and His service both with respect to the body and the spirit. But the woman who is
married is concerned with the things of the world, how
she may please her husband. But this I am saying for
your own profit, not in order that I may throw a noose
over you [that is, constrain you to obey my commands],
but I am saying this in order that in a seemly manner
you may assiduously serve the Lord without distraction.
But, assuming that a certain man thinks that he is acting
in an unseemly manner in the case of his virgin daughter,
if she be past the bloom of youth, and it [a marriage]
thus ought to take place, whatever he desires, let him
be doing. He is not sinning. Let them [the daughter and
the man she loves] marry. But he who stands firm in
his heart, having no constraint upon him, but has authority concerning his own private desire, and has come to
a settled decision to be keeping his own daughter in a
state of virginity, shall do well. So that also he who
gives his own virgin daughter in marriage is doing well,
and he who does not do so will do better. A wife is
bound as long as her husband may live. But if her husband dies, she is free to marry whomever she desires,
only in the Lord. But she is in a state more conducive
to her well-being if she remains as she is, in my judgment. However, I think, as for myself, I also have God's
Spirit [in this, as well as my own judgment].

1-7   Now, concerning things sacrificed to idols, We know,
[do you say?], because all of us are possessers of knowledge. The aforementioned knowledge inflates the ego,
but the love [God's love produced in the heart] builds up
[the Christian life]. Assuming that anyone thinks that
he has come to know anything, not yet has he come to
know in a manner in which it is a necessity in the nature
of the case to know. Now, assuming that anyone loves
God, this person is known by God. Therefore, concerning
the act of eating things that have been sacrificed to idols,
we know positively that an idol is a nonentity in the
world and that there is no God but one. For, indeed,

assuming that there are so-called gods, whether in heaven
or on earth, even as there are gods many and lords
many, yet to us there is one God, the Father, out from
whom as a source are all things and we for Him, and
one Lord Jesus Christ, through whose intermediate
agency all things exist and we through Him. But not
in all men is this knowledge. Now, certain ones by reason of their long association with the idol until the
present moment, eat the things that had been previously
sacrificed to the idol, as an idol-sacrifice, and their conscience, being weak, is polluted.

But food will not provide for us an entree to God.   8-13
Neither if we do not eat do we fall short. Neither if
we eat do we exceed [others]. But be taking heed that
this right of yours does not possibly become a stumbling
block to those who are weak. For if a certain one sees
you, the one who has knowledge, reclining at a sacrificial
banquet in the idol's temple, will not the conscience of
the one who is weak be built up to the place where he
will be eating the things sacrificed to idols? For the one
who is weak, through your knowledge is being ruined
[in his Christian life], your brother on account of whom
Christ died. Moreover, sinning in this manner against
your brethren and inflicting a blow on their conscience
when it is weak, against Christ you are sinning; because
of which very fact, since food makes my brother stumble,
I will in no case eat animal flesh forever, in order that
I may not make my brother stumble.

Am I not free? Am I not an apostle? Have I not   1-3
seen the Lord with a discerning eye and at present have
Him in my mind's eye? Are not you all my work in the
Lord? Assuming that to others I am not an apostle,
yet at least I am to you, for as for you all, you by virtue
of your position in the Lord and your vital union with
Him, are the seal which confirms and proves and authen-
ticates my apostleship. This is my defense to those who
are investigating me.

We [Paul] do not have the right to eat and drink   4-10
[as guests of the local church], do we? [Your answer in
the negative, which I expect, is ridiculous]. We do not

151

have a right to be supporting a wife who is a [Christian] sister [believer] as also the rest of the apostles and the brethren of the Lord and Cephas, have we? [Your negative answer again is wrong]. Or, as for myself only and Barnabas, do we not have a right not to be working? Who makes a military expedition at any time at his own private expense? Who plants a vineyard and does not eat its fruit? Or, who shepherds a flock and does not partake of the milk of his flock? I am not saying these things in accordance with the reasoning of mankind, am I? Or, the law, does it not say these things? for in Moses' law it has been written and is at present on record, You shall not muzzle an ox when he is threshing out the grain. Oxen are not a concern to God, are they? Or, on account of us is He assuredly saying it? For on our account it was written, that he who is ploughing ought to be ploughing in hope of partaking, and he who is threshing ought to be threshing in hope of partaking.

11-14   As for us, since we sowed spiritual things for you, is it a great thing if we shall reap from you the things which are needful to sustain our physical existence? Since others partake of this claim upon you, do not we the more? Nevertheless, we did not make use of this right of ours, but are putting up with all things in order that we may not cut off the onward progress of the good news concerning the Christ. Do you not know positively that those who are engaged in the work relative to the sacred things of the temple derive their sustenance from the things that come out of the temple, that those who are in constant attendance at the altar have a share with the altar [in the sacrifice placed upon it]? In the same manner also the Lord ordained that those who are proclaiming the good news should be deriving their living from the good news.

15-17   But as for myself, I have not made use of these things in even one instance, and at present continue the same policy. Moreover, I am not writing these things [concerning privileges] in order that in this manner it should be done in my case, for it were good for me rather to die than — no one shall nullify my boasting. For if I am preaching the good news, there is nothing for me

to boast about, for a necessary compulsion is pressing
down upon me, for woe to me if I do not proclaim the
good news. For, assuming that I am doing this of my
own volition, I have a recompense; but doing it without my own volition, a responsibility of administering
[the propagation of the good news] has been entrusted
to me and at present is the impelling motive that makes
it impossible not to proclaim it.

What then is my remuneration? namely, that when   **18-23**
I am proclaiming the good news I may give out the good
news without charge, with the end in view of not making
full use of my right [to be supported financially by those
to whom I minister] in the [proclaiming of the] good
news. For, being free from all [not obligated to anyone
because of not holding a salaried position] I made myself a slave to all in order that I may win the more [souls
to the Lord Jesus]. And I became to the Jews as a Jew
in order that I may win Jews; to those under law, as one
under law, not being myself under law, in order that I
may win those under law; to those who are without law
[the Gentiles], as being without law, not being an out-
law with respect to God, but within the sphere of Christ's
law, in order that I may win those who are without law.
To those who are weak, I became as one who is weak,
in order that I may win those who are weak. To all men
I have become all things in order that I may by all means
save some. And I am doing all things for the sake of
the good news in order that I may become a joint-partici-
pant with others in it.

Do you not know that those who are running in a   **24-27**
race are indeed all running, but one receives the victor's
award? Be running in such a manner as the one who
won the race, in order that you may obtain the victor's
award. Everyone who participates in the athletic games
exercises constant self-control in all things, those, to be
sure, in order that they may receive a perishable victor's
garland of wild olive leaves to be worn as a crown of
victory, but as for us [we engage in Christian service,
exercising constant self-control to obtain] a victor's garland which is imperishable. As for myself, therefore, I
so run, in no uncertain manner. I so swing my fists, not

as one who, when fighting, misses his opponent, merely beating the air and not striking a straight blow which finds its target. But I beat my body black and blue and make it my abject slave lest somehow, when I have preached to others, I myself should be disqualified [from further Christian service].

1-5   For I do not desire you to be ignorant, brethren, that our fathers, all of them, were under the [Shekinah] cloud and all went through the sea. And all had themselves immersed, surrounded by the cloud [above] and the sea [on both sides], thus shut up to Moses [as their leader]. And all ate the same spiritual food and all drank the same spiritual drink, for they were drinking from a spiritual Rock that followed them, and the aforementioned Rock was the Christ. But not with the greater part of them was God pleased, for they [their dead bodies] were strewn along the ground in the uninhabited region.

6-13   Now, these things have been made examples for us to the end that we should not be those who have a passionate craving for evil things as also those had a passionate craving. Stop becoming idolaters as some of them were, even as it stands written, The people sat down to eat and drink and rose up to be giving way to hilarity. Neither let us be committing fornication even as certain of them committed fornication, and there fell in one day twenty-three thousand. Neither let us be putting the Lord to an all-out test, trying Him to the utmost, even as certain of them tried Him and by means of snakes were perishing day after day. Stop grumbling, discontentedly complaining, even as certain of them grumbled and kept on being destroyed one after another by the destroyer. Now, these things were happening to them from time to time by way of examples, and they were written for our admonition to whom the ends of the ages have come. So that he who thinks he stands, let him be taking heed lest he fall. A testing time or a temptation has not laid hold of you with the result that these have you in their grip, except those to which mankind is continually subject. But God is faithful who will not permit you to be tested nor tempted above that with which you are able to cope, but will, along with the testing

time or temptation, also make a way out in order that you may be able to bear up under it.

Wherefore, my beloved ones, be fleeing from the idolatry. I am speaking as to men of good sense. As for you, you be judges of what I am saying. **14, 15**

The cup of the blessing [which our Lord consecrated by giving thanks] which we consecrate with prayer, is it not a symbol of our joint-participation in the blood of the Christ? The bread which we break, is it not a symbol of our joint-participation in the body of Christ? Seeing that there is one loaf of bread, we, the many, are one body, for we all share with one another in eating from the one aforementioned loaf of bread. Be looking at Israel, the nation. Are not those who are eating the sacrifices joint-participants in the altar? Therefore, what am I asserting? That that which is sacrificed to idols is anything? Or that an idol is anything? What I am saying is that the things they sacrifice, to demons and not to a god they sacrifice. And I do not desire you to become joint-participants in offering sacrifices to demons. You are not able to be drinking the Lord's cup and the demons' cup. You are not able to be partaking together at the Lord's table and the demons' table. Or, are we provoking the Lord to anger? We are not stronger than He, are we? **16-22**

All things are permissible but not all things are profitable or expedient. All things are permissible, but not all things promote growth in Christian character. Let no person be seeking his own good but that of the other person. Everything which is being sold in the meat market be eating, asking not even one question [whether the meat offered for sale is the residue of heathen sacrifices], doing this for the sake of your conscience, for the earth belongs to the Lord, and its fulness. On the assumption that anyone of those who are unbelievers invites you to be his guest, and you desire to be going, everything which is set before you be eating, asking not even one question for the sake of your conscience. But if anyone says to you, This has been offered in sacrifice to idols, stop eating of it in consideration for that one who **23-30**

pointed it out to you and for the sake of his conscience.
I mean by conscience, not his own but that of the other
person, for to what [good] purpose is my liberty being
censured by another's conscience? As for myself, assuming that I partake with thankfulness, why am I being
evil spoken of unjustly because of that for which I am
giving thanks?

31-XI 1   Whether, therefore, you are eating or drinking or
whatever you are doing, be doing all to the glory of God.
Be becoming those who do not cause others to sin by your
mode of life, giving no occasion of stumbling both to
Jews and Gentiles and also the Church of God, even as
I also in all things accommodate myself to all, not seeking my own profit but the profit of the many, in order
that they might be saved. Become imitators of me, even
as I also am an imitator of Christ.

2-10   Now, I am praising you because [as you say] you
have kept me in your remembrance in all things and at
present still do have me in your thinking, even as also
you are holding fast to those things which were delivered to me to be handed down to you, which I also delivered to you to be passed on to succeeding generations.
Moreover, I desire you to know that the head of every
man is the Christ, and the woman's head is the man, and
the head of the Christ is God the Father. Every man
while praying or prophesying [giving out the word of
God in the public assembly, which word he received by
divine revelation] having a shawl hanging down over his
head [a Jewish and Roman custom] dishonors his head.
But every woman while praying or prophesying with
her head uncovered dishonors her head, for this would
be one and the same thing as if she had her head shaved.
For, assuming that a woman is uncovered, let her also
cut her hair close. But since it is dishonorable for a
woman to be shaven or have her hair cropped close, let
her put a shawl down over her head. For, indeed, a male
individual is morally obligated not to cover his head in
that manner since he is so constituted as to be the derived image and glory of God. But the woman is the
glory of a man. For a man is not out of a woman as a
source, but a woman out of a man. Assuredly, a man

was not created for the sake of the woman, but a woman for the sake of the man. On this account the woman is under moral obligation to be having a sign of [the man's] authority [over her] on her head because of the angels.

11-16 Nevertheless, neither is a woman [complete] apart from a man, nor a man [complete] apart from a woman in the Lord, for even as the woman came out of the man as a source, thus also does the man owe his existence to the intermediate agency of the woman. But all things are out of God as a source. Come to a decision among yourselves. Is it seemly or fitting for a woman to be engaged in prayer to God not wearing the shawl hanging down over her head? Does not the innate sense of propriety itself based upon the objective difference in the constitution of things [the difference between the male and the female] teach you that if indeed a man allows his hair to grow long, it is a disgrace to him, but if a woman allows her hair to grow long, it is her glory? because her head of hair has been given to her for a permanent covering [answering in character to but not a substitute for the shawl]. If, as is the case, anyone presumes to be cantankerous [about the moral obligation of a woman to wear a head covering when engaged in public prayer in the assembly], as for us, we do not have such a custom [namely, that of a woman praying with uncovered head], neither do the assemblies of God.

17-22 Moreover, when giving you this charge, I am not praising you, because you are not coming together [in the local assembly] for the better but for the worse. For indeed, first of all, when you come together in the assembly, I am hearing that divisions have their regular place among you, and I partly believe it, for it is a necessity in the nature of the case also for factions to be among you, in order that also those who have been put to the test and have met the specifications and have been approved might become identified as such among you. Therefore, when you come together to the same place, it is not possible to eat a supper the character of which is that it could be a supper designated as belonging to the Lord. For each one in the eating [of the supper]

takes his own private supper beforehand. And one indeed is hungry and another is intoxicated. Do you not have houses for the eating and the drinking? Or, the Church of God are you despising, and are you making those ashamed who do not have the means [by which to buy food]? What shall I say to you? Shall I praise you? In this I am not praising you.

23-34   For, as for myself, I received by direct revelation from the presence of the Lord that which also I in turn passed on to you, that the Lord Jesus on the night during which He was being betrayed took bread, and having given thanks, He broke it and said, This is my body which is [given] on your behalf. This be doing with a view to remembering me. In like manner also He took the cup after the partaking of the food, saying, This cup is the covenant new in its nature, a covenant which is within the sphere of my blood. This be doing as often as you are drinking it, with a view to remembering me. For as often as you are eating this bread and drinking this cup, the death of the Lord you are proclaiming until that time whenever He may come. So that, whoever is eating the bread or drinking the cup of the Lord in an unworthy manner shall be guilty of the body and the blood of the Lord. But let an individual be putting himself to the test for the purpose of approving himself and finding that he meets the prescribed specifications, let him thus be eating of the bread and drinking of the cup. For the one who eats and drinks is eating and drinking so as to bring judgment upon himself if he does not properly evaluate the body. Because of this, among you are many who have infirmities and are in continued ill health, and a considerable number are sleeping [dead]. Now, if we properly evaluated and formed a right estimate of ourselves, in that case we would not be judged. But when we are being judged by the Lord, we are the subjects of a disciplinary judgment in order that we may not be condemned with the world. So that, my brethren, when you are coming together for the purpose of eating, be waiting for one another. In the event that anyone is hungry, let him be eating at home in order that you do not come together with the result that you will be judged.

And the other matters which remain I will dispose of whenever I come.

Now, concerning the spiritual gifts, brethren, I do not desire you to be ignorant. You all know that when you were Gentiles you were led astray to the idols, which do not have the faculty of speech, as on different occasions you would be led. Wherefore, I make known to you that no individual speaking by means of God's Spirit says, Jesus is anathema [accursed], and no person is able to say, Jesus is Lord, except by means of the Holy Spirit. Now, there are different distributions of spiritual gifts, these gifts being diverse from one another, but there is the same Spirit. And there are different distributions of various kinds of ministries, but the same Lord. And there are different distributions of divine energy motivating these gifts in their operation, but the same God who by His divine energy operates them all in their sphere. But to each one there is constantly being given the clearly seen operations of the Spirit with a view to the profit [of all].

1-7

For to one is given through the intermediate agency of the Spirit a word of wisdom, and to another a word of knowledge according to the same Spirit, to another faith by the same Spirit, and to another gifts of healing by the one Spirit, and to another the working of miracles, and to another the giving forth of divine revelations, and to another the correct evaluation of those individuals who give forth divine revelations, and to another various kinds of languages, and to another the interpretation of languages. But all these the one and same Spirit is by divine energy putting into operation, dividing to each one separately even as He desires.

8-11

For even as the body is one and has many members, and all the members of the body being many, are one body, thus also is the Christ, for indeed by means of one Spirit we all were placed into one body, whether Jews or Gentiles, whether slaves or free men. And we all were imbued with one Spirit. For, indeed, the body is not one but many members. If the foot should say, Because I am not a hand, I am not of the body; it is not there-

12-17

fore not of the body? And if the ear should say, Because I am not an eye, I am not of the body; it is not therefore not of the body? If the whole body were an eye, where would the hearing be? If the whole body were the hearing, where would the sense of smell be?

18-27   But now God placed the members, each one of them, in the body even as He desired. But if all were one member, where would the body be? But now, indeed, they are many members, but one body. And the eye is not able to say to the hand, I do not have need of you, or again, the head to say to the feet, I do not have need of you. No, much rather, the members of the body which seem to be more feeble, are necessary. And the members of the body which seem to be less honorable, upon these we bestow more abundant honor. And our uncomely members have more abundant comeliness. And our comely members have no need. But God compounded the body together, having given more abundant honor to the part which lacked, in order that there may not be division, but that the members should have the same solicitous concern about the welfare of one another. And whether one member suffers, all the members suffer with it, or one member is honored, all the members rejoice with it. And as for you, you are Christ's body and members individually.

28-31   And God indeed placed some for His own use in the Church, first apostles; second, prophets; third, teachers; then workers of miracles; then gifts of healing; also those whose ministry it is to help others; and administrators; and different languages. All are not apostles, are they? All are not prophets, are they? All are not teachers, are they? All are not workers of miracles, are they? All do not have gifts of healing, do they? All do not speak in languages, do they? All do not interpret, do they? But be constantly zealous after the greater spiritual gifts. And yet I point out a superexcellent way.

1-3   If in the languages of men I speak and the languages of the angels but do not have love [Greek word here used of God's love produced in the heart of the yielded saint by the Holy Spirit, a love that impels one to deny him-

self for the sake of the loved one], I have already become and at present am sounding brass or a clanging cymbal. And if I have the gift of uttering divine revelations and know all the mysteries and all the knowledge, and if I have all the faith so that I am able to keep on removing mountain after mountain, but am not possessing love, I am nothing. And if I use all my possessions to feed the poor, and if I deliver up my body [as a martyr] in order that I may glory, but do not have love, I am being profited in not even one thing.

Love meekly and patiently bears ill treatment from others. Love is kind, gentle, benign, pervading and pene-trating the whole nature, mellowing all which would have been harsh and austere; is not envious. Love does not brag, nor does it show itself off, is not ostentatious, does not have an inflated ego, does not act unbecomingly, does not seek after the things which are its own, is not irritated, provoked, exasperated, aroused to anger, does not take into account the evil [which it suffers], does not rejoice at the iniquity but rejoices with the truth, endures all things, believes all things, hopes all things, bears up under all things, not losing heart nor courage. Love never fails.

4-8

But whether there are utterances given by a person consisting of divine revelations he has received, they shall cease; whether languages, they shall stop, whether knowl-edge, it shall be done away; for we know in a partial, fragmentary, incomplete way, and we utter divine revela-tions in the same way. But whenever that which is com-plete comes, that which is incomplete and fragmentary will be done away. When I was a child I was accustomed to speak as a child. I used to understand as a child. I was accustomed to reason as a child. When I have become a man and have the status of an adult, I have permanently put away the things of a child, for we are seeing now by means of a mirror obscurely, but then, face to face. Now I know only in a fragmentary fashion, but then I shall fully know even as also I was known. But now there remains faith, hope, love; these three. But the greatest of these is this previously mentioned love.

8-13

1-10   Be constantly pursuing this love, earnestly endeavoring to acquire it. Moreover, be earnestly desiring the spiritual gifts, and do this in order that you might more efficiently impart to others the divine revelations you have received. For the one who is uttering words in a tongue [a language not understood except through an interpreter] is not speaking to men but to God, for no one hears him so as to understand what he is saying. And he utters with his human spirit [as energized by the Holy Spirit] divine revelations not explained. But he who imparts divine revelations to men is speaking with the result of upbuilding the Christian life, and exhortation, and consolation. The one who utters words in a tongue builds himself up in his Christian life. But he who imparts divine revelations to others builds up the local assembly. Now I desire that all of you be speaking in tongues, but I prefer that you impart divine revelations to others which you have received. Moreover, greater is the one who imparts divine revelations to others than he who speaks in tongues, with this exception — that he interpret, in order that the local assembly might receive upbuilding.

6-11   But now, brethren, if I come to you speaking in tongues, what will it profit you unless I speak to you either in the form of a disclosure of the truth or in that of experiential knowledge or in that of an impartation of a divine revelation, or in that of teaching? Yet even in the case of lifeless things which give out a sound, whether it be a wind instrument or a harp, if it does not make a difference in the sounds, how will the music which is played by the wind instrument or the harp be understood? For if a military trumpet gives an indistinct sound, who shall put himself in readiness for war? Thus also in your case, if by means of the tongue you do not give a word which is clear and definite, how will that which is being spoken be understood? For you will [otherwise] be speaking into the air. So many kinds of voices [languages], it may be, exist in the world, and not one is without its particular significance. Therefore, if I do not know the meaning of the voice, I shall be to the one who is speaking a person who utters confused

and unintelligible sounds, mere jargon, and the one who is speaking will be to me just such a person too.

Thus also, as for yourselves, since you are those who are most eagerly desirous of spirits [spiritual powers], be desiring them in order that you may abound in them with a view to the building up of the local assembly. Therefore, let the one who speaks in a tongue be praying that he may be unfolding the meaning of what he is saying, for if I am praying in a tongue, my spirit [the human spirit as moved by the Holy Spirit] is praying, but my intellect confers no benefits upon others. How, therefore, does the matter stand? I will pray by means of my spirit. But I will pray also with the aid of my intellect. I will sing by means of my spirit. But I also will sing with the aid of my intellect. Else if you are uttering eulogies and praises [to God] by means of your spirit, how is it possible for the one who occupies the position of the unlearned to say the Amen to your act of giving thanks since he does not know what you are saying? For you indeed give thanks in an admirable way, but the other one is not built up in his Christian life.

12-17

I thank my God that I speak in tongues more than you all, but in the church assembly I would rather speak five words with my understanding in order that I might instruct others than ten thousand words in a tongue. Brethren, stop becoming little children who need instruction in reasoning, but be infants in the sphere of malice, and in the sphere of the reasoning process be becoming those who are mature. In the law it stands written, By means of tongues of a different nature and by means of the lips of a foreigner I will speak to this people, and not even thus will they listen to me, says the Lord. So that the aforementioned tongues are for an attesting miracle, not to those who believe but to unbelievers. But the impartation of divine revelations on the part of those who receive them is not for the unbelievers but for those who believe.

18-22

If, therefore, the entire local assembly comes together in one place, and all are speaking in tongues, and there

23-25

enter the unlearned or the unbelievers, will they not say that you are raving mad? But if all impart divine revelations to others, and someone comes in who is an unbeliever or an unlearned person, he is brought under conviction [as to his sins] by all. He is put on trial and is the subject of an examination and a scrutiny by all. The secrets of his heart become evident, and thus, having fallen upon his face, he will worship God, proclaiming that God is among you indeed.

26-33 How, therefore, does the matter stand, brethren? Whenever you come together, each one has a song or psalm, has something he wishes to teach, has a divine revelation, has a tongue, has an interpretation. Let all things be done with a view to building up [the assembly]. Whether anyone speaks in a tongue, let it be two, or at the most three [at any single meeting], and one after another, in turn, and let one person be interpreting. But if there is no interpreter present, let him be maintaining his silence in the assembly and let him be speaking to himself and to God. Let those who impart to others the divine revelations they received, speak, two or three of them, and let the others evaluate their discourse. And if anything is revealed to another who is seated, let the first one be keeping silence, for you all can function thus as a prophet one by one in order that all may be learning and all may be encouraged. And the [human] spirits of those giving out a divine revelation are subject to the control of these prophets, for God is not a God of disorder but of harmony.

33-40 As in all the local assemblies of the saints, let the women be keeping silent, for they are not permitted to be speaking, but let them be putting themselves in the place of subjection and obedience, even as also the law says. Now, assuming that they are desirous of learning something, let them be asking their own husbands at home, for it is a disgrace for a woman to be speaking in the local assembly. Or is it from you that the word of God went forth? Or to you only did it reach? Assuming that anyone thinks that he is a prophet or spiritual, let him recognize that the things which I am writing to you are the Lord's commandment. But assuming that he is

ignorant [of the fact that Paul is inspired], he is being disregarded. So that, my brethren, be desiring earnestly to be imparting to others divine revelations, and stop forbidding the speaking in tongues. But let all things be done in a seemly manner and in a right order.

Now, I am making known to you, brethren, the good **1-11** news which I brought as glad tidings to you, which also you took to yourselves, in which also you have taken a stand, through which you are being saved, in what word I announced it to you as glad tidings, assuming that you are holding it fast unless you believed in vain; for I delivered to you among the first things that which also I received, that Christ died on behalf of our sins according to the scriptures, and that He was entombed, and that He has been raised on the third day according to the scriptures, and that He appeared to Cephas, then to the Twelve. After that He appeared to more than five hundred brethren at one time, of whom the majority are remaining to the present time, but certain ones fell asleep. After that He appeared to James, then to all the apostles, and in the last of all His appearances, He appeared also to me, an unperfected, stillborn embryo. For, as for myself, I am the least of the apostles. I am not fit to be called an apostle because I persecuted the Church of God. But by the grace of God I am what I am. And His grace to me did not turn out in vain, but I labored to the point of exhaustion more abundantly than all of them; however, not I myself, but the grace of God which labored with me. Therefore, whether it were I or they, thus are we preaching and thus did you believe.

Now, in view of the fact that Christ is being preached **12-19** that He arose from among the dead, how are certain saying that there is not a resurrection of dead people? Now, assuming that there is no resurrection of dead people, neither has Christ been raised. And assuming that Christ has not been raised, then it follows that our preaching is futile, and futile also is your faith. Moreover, we shall also be discovered to be false witnesses of God because we testified with respect to God that He raised up His Christ, whom He did not raise up, assuming then that dead people are not being raised up. For assuming that

dead people are not being raised up, neither has Christ
been raised up. And assuming that Christ has not been
raised, your faith is futile. You are still in your sins.
Then also those who fell asleep in Christ perished. Assuming that in this life we have hoped only, we are of
all men those who are most miserable and most to be
pitied.

20-28   But now Christ has been raised out from among the
dead, a firstfruit of those who have fallen asleep. For
since through the agency of man death came, also through
the agency of man comes a resurrection of the dead. For
even as in Adam all die, so also in the Christ all shall be
made alive, but each one in his proper rank, Christ, a first-
fruit, afterwards those who belong to the Christ in His
coming. Then comes the end, whenever He yields up
the kingdom to God, even the Father, whenever He shall
abolish all rule and authority and power. For it is a
necessity in the nature of the case for Him to be ruling
as King until that time when He will put all His enemies
under His feet. As a last enemy, death is being abolished,
for all things He put in subjection under His feet. But
when He says that all things He has put in subjection,
it is clear that He is excluded who put all things in subjection to Himself. But whenever all things are put under
subjection to Him, then also the Son himself shall be in
subjection to Him who subjected all things under Him
in order that God the Father may be all in all.

29-34   Otherwise, what shall those do who are being baptized for the sake of those who are dead? Assuming that
the dead are not actually raised up, why then are we being
baptized for their sake? And as for us, why are we constantly in danger every hour? I am daily in danger of
death by my glorying over you, brethren, which I have
in Christ Jesus our Lord. If, as is the case, in the manner of men I fought with wild beasts at Ephesus, what
profit comes to me? Assuming that dead people are not
raised, let us eat and let us drink, for tomorrow we die.
Stop being led astray. Evil companionships corrupt good
morals. Return to soberness of mind in a righteous fashion and stop sinning, for certain ones possess an ignorance of God. I say this to your shame.

But a certain one will say, How are the dead raised **35-38**
up, and with what kind of a body do they come? Stupid
one, as for you, that which you sow is not made alive
unless it dies. And that which you sow, not the body
which shall come into being do you sow, but mere seed,
it may be of wheat or any of the rest of the seeds. But
God gives to it a body in accordance with that procedure
which He originally purposed, and to each of the seeds
its own peculiar body.

All flesh is not the same flesh, but there is indeed one **39-41**
flesh of men, and another of beasts, yet another of birds,
still another of fish. There are bodies for heavenly be-
ings and bodies for those who dwell on the earth. But
indeed, the glory of the heavenly bodies is one thing, and
the glory of the earthly bodies is of a different kind.
There is one kind of glory of the sun, and another glory
of the moon, and another glory of the stars, for star
differs from star in glory.

Thus also is the resurrection of those who are dead. **42-50**
It [the body] is sown in corruption. It is raised in incorruption. It is sown in dishonor. It is raised in glory.
It is sown in weakness. It is raised in power. It is sown
a body which is a fit instrument by which the individual
can live a life in which the interests and activities of the
soul-life predominate. It is raised a body which is a fit
instrument by which the individual can live a life in
which the interests and activities of the human spirit
predominate. Since there is a soulical body, there is also
a spiritual body. And thus it stands written, The first
man Adam came into existence a living soul. The last
Adam became a life-giving spirit. But not first is the
spiritual, but the soulical, afterward the spiritual. The
first man is out of the earth as a source, made of earth.
The second Man is out of heaven as a source. As is the
dust of the earth in character, such are those who are of
earthly origin, and as is that which is heavenly in character, such also are those who are of heavenly origin.
And even as we bore the derived image of that which is
earthly, we shall also bear the derived image of that which
is heavenly. Now, this I am saying, brethren, that flesh

and blood are not able to inherit God's kingdom, neither will corruption inherit incorruption.

51-58 Behold, I am imparting to you a mystery. All shall not sleep, but all shall be changed. In an instant of time so small that it cannot be divided into smaller units, in the blink of an eye, at the last trumpet, for a trumpet will sound, and the dead shall be raised incorruptible, and as for us, we shall be changed, for it is a necessity in the nature of the case for that which is corruptible to invest itself with incorruption, and that which is mortal to clothe itself with immortality. Now, whenever that which is corruptible shall invest itself with incorruption, and that which is mortal shall clothe itself with immortality, then will be brought to pass the word which stands written, Death has been swallowed up with the result that victory has been attained. Where, O death, is your victory? Where, O death, is your sting? The sting of death is sin, and the power of sin is the law. But thanks be to God who gives to us the victory through our Lord Jesus Christ. So that, my brethren beloved, keep on becoming steadfast, unmovable, always abounding in the work of the Lord, knowing that your fatiguing labor is not unproductive of results, as this labor is done in the Lord.

1-4 Now, concerning the collection of money which is for the saints, even as I gave orders to the local assemblies of Galatia, thus also as for you, you do the same. On every first day of the week let each one of you have the habit of putting aside at home whatever he may be prospered in, accumulating and keeping it in reserve, in order that when I may come, then there may not be any collections. And whenever I come, whomever you will approve after having put him to the test, these I will send to carry your bounty to Jerusalem. And if it [the gift] be sufficiently large so as to warrant me also going, they shall go with me.

5-9 Now, I shall come to you whenever I pass through Macedonia, for I am passing through Macedonia. And it may be that with you I will remain or even spend the winter, in order that as for you, you may furnish me with the requirements of travel wherever I may be going,

for I do not desire to see you now while passing by on my journey, for I hope to remain with you a certain length of time, if the Lord permits me. However, I remain at Ephesus until Pentecost, for a door is opened to me, great and effectual, and there are many who are entrenched against me.

10-12 Now, if Timothy comes, be seeing to it that he is with you without fear, for he carries on the Lord's work as also I do. Therefore, let no one treat him as of no account, setting him at naught, but send him on his way in peace, seeing to it that he has the requisites for travel in order that he may come to me, for I am awaiting him with the brethren. Now, concerning Apollos our brother, I begged him much to come to you with the brethren, but it was not at all his desire to come at present, but he will come whenever he deems the opportunity auspicious.

13-18 Be keeping a watchful eye ever open. Be standing fast in the Faith. Be showing yourselves to be men. Be mighty in strength. All that you are doing, let it be done in love. Now, I exhort you, brethren, you know the household of Stephanas, that it is a firstfruit of Achaia, and that they took upon themselves the responsibility of a ministering service to the saints, that you yourselves also put yourselves under the leadership of such as these and everyone who works with us and labors to the point of exhaustion. Now I rejoice at the coming of Stephanas and Fortunatus and Achaicus, because that which was lacking on your part, these filled up, for they refreshed my spirit and yours. Recognize, therefore, such as these for what they are.

19-24 The local assemblies of Asia send greeting. Aquila and Priscilla send cordial greetings in the Lord together with the assembly that meets in their home. All the brethren send greetings to you all. Greet one another with a holy kiss. The greeting with my own hand — Paul. If anyone is not fond of the Lord, let him be anathema [a man accursed, devoted to the direst woes]. Maranatha [Our Lord comes]. The grace of the Lord Jesus be with you. My love be with you all in Christ Jesus.

THE EXPANDED TRANSLATION OF SECOND
CORINTHIANS

Paul, an ambassador belonging to Christ Jesus through the desire of God, and Timothy our brother, to the local assembly of God, the one which is in Corinth, together with the saints, all of them, who are in the whole of Achaia. Grace be to you and peace from God our Father and from the Lord Jesus Christ. **1, 2**

Eulogized be the God and Father of our Lord Jesus Christ, the Father of compassionate mercies and a God of every consolation and encouragement, who consoles and encourages us in our every affliction and tribulation in order that we may be able to console and encourage those who are in any affliction or tribulation by means of the consolation and encouragement with which we ourselves are being consoled and encouraged by God. Because even as the sufferings of Christ [for righteousness' sake endured in the opposition of sinners to His ministry on earth] overflow to us, thus our consolation and encouragement [given to others] overflow through Christ. And if we are being hard pressed by reason of affliction, it is for the sake of your consolation, encouragement, deliverance, and preservation. If we are being consoled and encouraged, it is for the sake of your consolation and encouragement, which consolation and encouragement are operative in the patient enduring of the same sufferings which we also are suffering. And our hope for you is unshaken and constant, knowing that as you are joint-participants of the sufferings, thus also you shall be of the consolation and encouragement. **3-7**

For we do not desire you to be ignorant, brethren, concerning our affliction which came to us in Asia, that we were weighed down beyond our power so that we despaired even of living. But we ourselves have had the answer of death in ourselves and at this time still have that experience, in order that we should not be trusting in ourselves but in the God who raises the dead; who delivered us out of so great a death and will deliver us, on whom we have placed our hope and right now still maintain that attitude of hope that also He will yet deliver us, you also helping together on our behalf by your supplication, in order that thanksgiving may be given **8-11**

for the gracious mercy shown to us by reason of the many [who prayed for us].

12-14   For our glorying is this, the testimony of our conscience, that in the holiness, purity, and unsullied character of God, not in human wisdom but by God's grace we ordered our behavior in the world, and this was more abundantly evident to you. For, no other things are we writing to you but those things which you are reading or even acknowledge to be what they really are, and which I hope you will acknowledge to the end, as also certain ones of you acknowledged us for what we really are, that we are even as that in which you glory, and you are that in which we glory in the day of our Lord Jesus.

15-20   And having become fully persuaded of this I, after mature consideration, desired to come to you first, in order that you may be having a second bestowment of grace [by reason of my second visit to you], and to go through you [your city] into Macedonia, and again from Macedonia to come to you and be sent on my way to Judaea with the travel requisites for the journey. Therefore, having this desire, under these circumstances I did not exhibit fickleness of mind, did I? Or, the things which I purpose, do I purpose them in a merely human capacity, that there should be with me the yes, yes [today] and the no, no [tomorrow]? But as God is faithful, our word to you is not a yes and a no, for the Son of God, Christ Jesus, who among you was proclaimed by us, through me and Silvanus and Timothy, did not become yes and no, but in Him yes has become yes and remains so. For as many promises as are promises of God have become in Him yes and are a yes at present. Wherefore also through Him is the Amen to the glory of God through us.

21-24   Now, He who is constantly confirming us more firmly in our position in and union with Christ [in conforming us to His likeness] and who anointed us is God, who also placed His seal upon us and gave us the token payment guaranteeing the payment in full of our salvation, which token payment is the Spirit in our hearts. Moreover, as for myself, I call God as a witness against my

soul [if I am speaking falsely] that to spare you, I did not come as yet to Corinth, not that we have lordship over your faith, but that we are co-workers in producing your joy; for by faith you stand.

But I decided this in my own interest and for my own sake, not to come again to you in grief. For, as for myself, if, as is the case, I cause you grief, who then is he who makes me joyful except the one who was made to grieve by me? And I wrote this very thing, lest, when I came, I should have grief from those whom it was a necessity in the nature of the case to be making to rejoice, having confidence in you all that my joy is the joy of all of you, for out of a source of much affliction and anguish of heart I wrote to you through many tears, not in order that you may be made to grieve, but in order that you may come to know experientially the sacrificial love which I have so abundantly for you. Now, if, as is the case, anyone has caused grief, he has not grieved me, but to some extent he has caused grief to you all, in order that I may not be exerting too much pressure upon you all. Sufficient to such a one is this punishment which was inflicted by the majority, so that on the contrary you should rather graciously grant forgiveness and encourage and strengthen him lest, possibly, such a person may be swallowed up with his excessive grief. Wherefore, I beg of you, please, that you confirm publicly and solemnly by a judicial decision your love for him.

For with this end in view I wrote in order that I may come to know by experience your approved character, this approval based upon the fact that you met the specifications laid down, whether you are those who are obedient in all things. Now, to whom you forgive anything, I also forgive, for also that which I myself have forgiven, if I have forgiven anything, for your sakes I have forgiven it in the presence of Christ, in order that no advantage may be gained over us by Satan, for we are not ignorant of his purposes. Now, having come to Troas for the purpose of preaching the good news of the Christ, and a door having been opened for me by the Lord, I have had no relaxation in my spirit because I did not find

Titus, my brother, but having bidden them farewell, I
went off to Macedonia. Now, thanks be to God who
always leads us in triumph in the Christ and makes known
the aroma of the experiential knowledge of himself
through us in every place, because a fragrance of Christ
we are to God among those who are being saved and
among those who are perishing, to the one, an odor
proceeding from death resulting in death, and to the other,
an aroma proceeding from life resulting in life. And
who is sufficient for these things? For we are not as the
many who are adulterating the word of God, but as
of an unadulterated, unsullied purity of character, but
as from God we are speaking in the sight of God in
Christ.

1-3   Are we beginning again to be commending ourselves?
Or, we do not need, as some, commendatory letters to
you or commendatory letters from you, do we? As for
you, you are our letter which has been permanently engraved in our hearts, and which is being known and read
by all men. You are those who are openly shown to be
a letter which exhibits Christ, this letter having been
ministered [written] by us, not having been written with
ink but by the Spirit of the living God, not on stone
tablets but on tablets that are human hearts.

4-9   And such confidence are we having through the Christ
towards God. Not that we are sufficient in ourselves to
evaluate anything, this evaluation originating from ourselves, but our sufficiency has its source in God who also
made us sufficient as those who minister a testament, new
in quality, not of the letter [of the law] but of the Spirit,
for the letter [of the law]kills, but the Spirit makes alive.
Now, since the ministration of death which has been
engraved by means of letters on stones was surrounded
with glory so that the sons of Israel were not able to fix
their gaze upon the face of Moses because of the glory
of his face, which glory was of a transient nature, how
shall not rather the ministration of the Spirit be surrounded with glory? For in view of the fact that the
ministration of condemnation was glorious, by so much
more will the ministration of righteousness superabound
in the sphere of the glorious.

For even that which has been made glorious [the   **10-18**
ministration of death] has not [really] been made glorious in this respect, namely, on account of the glory [of
the ministration of righteousness], which glory super-
abounds. For, since that which is passing away was with
glory, by so much more that which remains is within the
sphere of glory. Having therefore such a hope, we use
great freedom and boldness of speech, and not even as
Moses put a covering over his face to the end that the
sons of Israel should not fix their gaze upon the termination of that which is passing away. But their minds
were hardened, for to this very day the same covering
remains at the reading of the testament whose usefulness
is over, it not being revealed that it [the covering] is
being done away in Christ. But even today, whenever
Moses is being read, a covering lies upon their heart.
However, whenever it [Israel] shall turn to the Lord, the
covering is being taken away [by the one who turns to
the Lord]. But the Lord is the Spirit and where the
Spirit of the Lord is there is liberty. Now, as for us,
we all, with uncovered face, reflecting as in a mirror the
glory of the Lord, are having our outward expressions
changed into the same image from one degree of glory
to another according as this change of expression pro-
ceeds from the Lord, the Spirit, this outward expression
coming from and being truly representative of our Lord.

Because of this, having this ministry [of the new   **1-6**
testament] even as we were made the objects of mercy
[in its bestowal], we do not lose courage, but we have
renounced the hidden things of shame, not ordering the
manner of our lives in the sphere of craftiness, nor even
adulterating the word of God [by an admixture of
error], but by means of an open declaration of the truth
commending ourselves to every variety of the conscience
of men in the sight of God. But if also, as is the case,
our gospel has been covered, in the case of those who
are perishing it has been covered, in whom the god of
this age blinded the minds of the unbelievers to the end
that the light of the good news of the glory of the Christ
who is the derived image of God should not dawn upon
them, for we do not proclaim ourselves but Christ Jesus

as Lord; but we proclaim ourselves as your slaves for the sake of Jesus, because the God who said, Out of darkness light shall shine, shined in our hearts, resulting in an illumination being given of the knowledge of the glory of God in the face of Christ.

7-15   But we have this treasure [the reflection of the light of the knowledge of the glory of God in the face of Christ] in earthenware containers, in order that the super-excellence of the power might be from God as a source and not from us. We are being hard pressed from every side, but we are not hemmed in. We are bewildered, not knowing which way to turn, but not utterly destitute of possible measures or resources. We are being persecuted, but not left in the lurch, not abandoned, not let down. We are being knocked down, but not destroyed, always bearing about in our body the dying of the Lord Jesus in order that the life of Jesus might be clearly and openly shown in our body, for, as for us, we who are living are perpetually being delivered over to death for Jesus' sake in order that the life of Jesus might be clearly and openly shown in our mortal body. So that death is operative in us but the life is operative in you. But we have the same Spirit of faith [as the Psalmist] according as it has been written and is at present on record, I believed, wherefore I spoke. And as for us, we are believing, wherefore also we are speaking, knowing that He who raised up the Lord Jesus shall also raise us with Jesus and shall present us with you, for all things are for your sake in order that the grace having been multiplied through the intermediate agency of the many [in their prayers for me] may cause the thanksgiving to super-abound, resulting in the glory of God.

16-18   Wherefore, we are not losing courage. But and if, as is the case, our outward self is progressively decaying, yet our inward self is being changed into a new kind of life [fit for the new spiritual existence into which we have been ushered in salvation, and constantly being conformed to the image of the Lord Jesus] day by day. For our momentary light burden of affliction is working out for us more and more surpassingly an eternal, heavy weight of glory while we are not contemplating the things

that are seen but the things which are not seen, for the things which are seen are temporary, but the things which are not seen are eternal.

For we know that if our house of this present tent-life on earth be taken down, a building from God we have, a house not made with hands, eternal in the heavens. For indeed, in this [tent] we are groaning, longing to be clothed in addition with our house which is from heaven, seeing that also, having been clothed, we shall not be found naked [a disembodied spirit]. For indeed, we being in this tent, are groaning, being weighed down, because we do not desire to be unclothed [divested of our mortal body] but clothed upon [invested with our heavenly body], in order that that which is mortal may be swallowed up by the life.

Now, He who by His working in us made us fit for this very thing [the change from mortality to life] is God, He who gave us the Spirit as a token payment in kind, guaranteeing to us the rest of our salvation. Being therefore always confident, and knowing that while we are in our natural home [for this earthly existence] in our body, we are living abroad, absent from [that home in heaven] the Lord, for through faith we are ordering our manner of life, not by something seen. Now, we are of good courage and well pleased rather to be away from our body as our home, and at home face to face with the Lord. Wherefore, we make it our aim, whether at home or living abroad, to be well pleasing to Him, for it is necessary in the nature of the case for all of us to be openly shown as to our true character before the judgment seat of Christ, in order that each one may receive [a recompense with respect to] the things which were practiced through the agency of our body, whether they were good or bad.

Knowing therefore the fear of the Lord, we are persuading men [of our sincerity and integrity], but to God we have been openly shown [as to our character], and I am hoping that we have been openly shown to be what we are in your consciences. We are not again commending ourselves to you, but [are writing these things] as

1-4

5-10

11-17

giving you a base of operations from which to glory about us, in order that you may be having this matter of glorying with which to answer those who are glorying in outward appearance and not in the heart [the inner man]. For, whether we were out of our mind, it was with respect to God; whether we are of sober mind, it is with respect to you. For the love which Christ has [for me] presses on me from all sides, holding me to one end and prohibiting me from considering any other, wrapping itself around me in tenderness, giving me an impelling motive, having brought me to this conclusion, namely, that One died on behalf of all, therefore all died, and that He also died on behalf of all in order that those who are living no longer are living for themselves but for the One who died on their behalf and instead of them, and was raised. So that, as for us, from this particular time onward, not even one individual do we know as judged upon the basis of human standards. Even though we [Paul in his unsaved state] have known Christ as judged by human standards, yet now no longer do we know Him as such. So that, assuming that anyone is in Christ, he is a creation new in quality. The antiquated, out-of-date things [which do not belong to the new life in Christ Jesus] have passed away. Behold, all things have become new in quality.

18-21   But the aforementioned all things are from God as a source, the One who reconciled us to himself through the intermediate agency of Christ and gave to us the ministry whose work is that of proclaiming the message of this reconciliation, namely, that absolute deity in Christ was reconciling the world [of sinners] to himself, not putting down on the liability side of their ledger their trespasses, and lodged in us the story of the reconciliation. Therefore, on behalf of Christ and in His place we are acting as ambassadors, as though God were saying, I beg of you, please, through us as His intermediate agents. We beg you in Christ's stead, Be reconciled at once to God. He who did not know sin in an experiential way, on behalf of us and instead of us, was made [the representative of] sin, in order that, as for us, we might become a righteousness of God in Him.

Moreover also, we, working together with God, beg of you not to receive the grace of God without any salutary results, for He says, In an epochal, strategic season, propitious in character, I hearkened to you, and in a day of salvation I ran to your cry and brought you aid. Behold, now is a propitious, epochal season, behold, now is a day of salvation. We are giving no occasion of stumbling to anyone in order that our ministering service may not be found with blot or blemish and thus be censored but in all things recommending ourselves as God's ministering servants should do: in much patience under trials, bearing up and not losing heart or courage; in afflictions, in calamity and straits, in distressing situations, in stripes inflicted by a beating with rods, in imprisonments, in the midst of political instability, in labors to the point of exhaustion, in sleeplessness at night, in hunger, in pureness, in knowledge, in long-suffering patience under ill treatment, in kindness marked by gentleness and graciousness, in the Holy Spirit, in a love devoid of hypocrisy, in the word of truth, in God's power, by means of the weapons of the righteousness [offensive weapons] on the right hand and [defensive weapons] on the left, by glory and dishonor, by slanderous report and good report, as those who are disseminating deceit and yet true, as being a nonentity, obscure, without proper credentials and yet fully recognized, as dying and behold we are living, as chastened yet not put to death, as sorrowful yet always rejoicing, as poor yet making many wealthy, as having not even one thing, yet possessing all things.

Our mouth stands open to you [we speak freely to you, we keep nothing back]. O Corinthians, our heart is broadened and enlarged [widened in its sympathy towards you]. You are not compressed nor narrowed down in us [you have ample space in our heart; we hold you within a great love], but you are compressed and narrowed down in your affections [you have tightened up in your affection for me]. Now, as a return in kind for my affections toward you, as to children I am speaking to you, you also be enlarged [make a large place in your heart for me].

14-VII 1   Stop being joined as with a yoke to unbelievers in a common state or endeavor which latter are of a character different from and diametrically opposed to the state of a child of God and any endeavor in which he may properly engage, for what partnership does righteousness have with lawlessness? Or, what does light have in common with darkness? And what harmony does Christ have with Belial? Or, what part does a believer have with an unbeliever? And what agreement does the inner sanctuary of God have with idols? For, as for us, we are an inner sanctuary of the living God, even as God said, I will dwell in them in fellowship with them as in a home and I will live my life in and through them. And I will be their God and they themselves will be my people. Wherefore, come out at once from their midst and separate yourselves at once, says the Lord, and stop touching that which is unclean. And, as for myself, I will receive you kindly and treat you with favor. And I will be to you a Father. And as for you, you will be to me sons and daughters, says the Lord Almighty. Having therefore these promises, beloved ones, let us cleanse ourselves from all contamination which may defile the flesh [the human body] and the [human] spirit, progressively accomplishing holiness in the fear of the Lord.

2-16   Make room in your hearts for us. We wronged no man. We corrupted no man. We took advantage of no man for the sake of gain. I am not saying this in the spirit of condemnation, for I have said before that you are in our hearts, to die together and to live together. Great is my boldness of speech toward you. Great is my glorying on your behalf. I have been completely filled with the encouragement. I am being caused to superabound with joy in all our tribulation, for even after we came into Macedonia our frail humanity experienced no relaxing from the oppression and tension of tribulation, but I was having pressure brought to bear upon me from every side, on the outside, contentions [with adversaries], within, fears. Nevertheless, He who encourages those who are downcast, encouraged us, our God, in the coming and personal presence of Titus, and not only in his coming and personal presence but also by the encouragement with which he was encouraged over you, bring-

ing back tidings to us of your longing [to see me], your mourning [at the rebuke I sent you], your zeal on my behalf, so that I rejoiced yet more; for though I caused you grief by my letter, I do not regret it, though I did regret it, for I see that that letter caused you to grieve, though but for a season; I now am rejoicing, not because you were made to grieve but because you were made to grieve resulting in your repentance, for you were made to grieve in accordance with the will of God, in order that in not even one thing would you sustain injury or damage by reason of us, for the grief which is according to the will of God achieves a repentance which leads to salvation, a repentance which has no regret. But the grief which is exercised by the world in its outworking results in death. For, look. This very same thing, this being made to grieve in accordance with God's will, to what extent it produced earnestness in you, yes, verbal defense of yourselves, in fact, indignation, yes, fear, in fact, longing, yes, zeal, in fact, the meting out of disciplinary punishment. In everything you showed yourselves to be immaculate in the aforementioned matter. [They had cleared themselves from the guilt of connivance with the case of incest by disciplining the guilty brother.] Therefore also I wrote to you, not on account of the one who committed the wrong [the incestuous son] nor even on account of the one who was wronged [his father], but that your earnestness which was on our behalf might be openly shown among you in the sight of God. On this account we have been encouraged and comforted. And in addition to this encouragement and comfort of ours we rejoiced the more exceedingly at the joy of Titus because his spirit has been refreshed by all of you, for if, as is the case, I have boasted to him about you, I was not caused any disappointment, but as all things in the sphere of truth we spoke to you, thus also our boasting before Titus turned out to be truth. And his heart is more abundantly toward you while he recalls to himself the obedience of you all, as with fear and trembling you received him. I rejoice that in everything I am of good courage concerning you.

Moreover, we make known to you, brethren, the **1-7** grace of God which has been given among the churches

of Macedonia, that in the midst of a severe testing which was in the form of afflictions, the test being for the purpose of approving them in their reaction to trials, the superabundance of their joy and their poverty which went down to the depths, superabounded with the result of the plenitude of their liberality; because in the measure of their ability, I testify, and beyond their ability, voluntarily, with much exhortation they begged us as a favor that they might participate in the ministry to the saints, and not even as we expected but they gave themselves first to the Lord and to us by the will of God with the result that we exhorted Titus that, even as he made a beginning on a previous occasion, thus also he would complete in you this grace also. Moreover, even as in everything you superabound, in the realm of faith and a ready exposition [of the Word] and in knowledge, and in every earnestness, and in the divine and self-sacrificial love which, proceeding from you, has us as its object, in this grace [of giving] also be superabounding.

8-12 I am not speaking by way of commandment, but through the instrumentality of others I am putting to the test the genuineness of your own love with the intent that it will meet my specifications and have my approval put upon it. For you know by experience the grace of our Lord Jesus Christ, that He being wealthy, for your sakes became poor, in order that, as for you, by means of His poverty you might be made wealthy. And in this I am giving my judgment, for this is profitable for you, being such that you were the first to make a beginning, not only to so do, but also to be desirous of doing a year ago. And now complete the doing also, in order that, according as there was the eagerness to be desirous, thus also there may be the completion in accordance with your ability; for, assuming that the eagerness is present, it is acceptable according to that which a person might have, not according to that which he does not have.

13-15 For the collection [of money] is not being made in order that to others there might be relief from stress and strain and that pressure might be brought to bear upon you. But, out of fairness to all, at the present season your superfluity may be a supply for that which they

lack, in order that their superfluity may become a supply for your lack, so that there might be an equitable arrangement in this matter, even as it stands written, He who gathered much had nothing over, and he who gathered the little, did not lack.

But thanks be to God who is constantly putting into the heart of Titus the same earnest solicitude for you, because he indeed embraced our exhortation, and being more than ordinarily earnest, of his own accord went to you. And we sent together with him the brother whose praise in the [proclamation of the] good news is spread throughout all the assemblies, and not that only, but who also was chosen by the assemblies as our travel companion in the matter of this grace [their financial contributions for the poor saints at Jerusalem] which is being administered by us [this arrangement whereby two are responsible for the distribution of the money] with a view to the glory of the same Lord and our eagerness, arranging this for ourselves lest anyone find fault with us in this great liberality which is being ministered by us. For we take forethought to provide things, in their external appearance as well as in their intrinsic value, honest not only in the sight of the Lord but also in the sight of men. And we sent with them our brother whom we often proved to be earnest in many things, having put him to the test for that purpose, namely, to put our stamp of approval upon him, but now much more earnest by reason of his great confidence which he has in you. Whether you are asking concerning Titus, he is my colleague and fellow-worker with respect to you; whether concerning our brethren, they are missionaries of the assemblies, the glory of Christ. Wherefore, be demonstrating to them in the presence of the assemblies the evidence of your divine and self-sacrificial love and of our boasting concerning you.

16-24

For indeed, concerning the ministering to the saints, it is superfluous for me to be writing to you, for I know positively of your earnestness concerning which I boast of you to the Macedonians, that Achaia has been prepared since a year ago; and your zeal stimulated the majority of them. But I am sending the brethren in order

1-4

that our boasting which is concerning you may not be rendered futile in this respect [in the collecting of the money] so that, just as I was saying, you may be prepared lest by any means, if there come with me any of Macedonia and they find you unprepared, we — we do not say you — should be put to shame in this confidence.

5-9

Therefore I deemed it necessary to exhort the brethren that they should go before to you and make ready your liberal gift which was previously promised, that this might be ready beforehand, thus as a matter of generosity and not as a gift which a covetous spirit would withhold but gives grudgingly under pressure. But [although I am not pressing you to give] this [is true] — he who sows sparingly shall also reap sparingly, and he who sows in a beneficent, generous spirit, with a view to the blessing of the recipient, shall also reap blessings given in a beneficent, generous manner. Let each one give according as he has purposed in his heart, not out of an annoyed and troubled heart, nor because of necessity, for God loves a cheerful, ready giver. Moreover, God is powerful to make every grace superabound to you in order that, having always an all-sufficiency in all things, you may superabound to every good work, even as it stands written, He [the liberal person] scattered abroad, he gave to those who are poor, his righteousness abides forever.

10-15

Now, He, who supplies seed to the sower and bread for food, shall also supply and multiply your seed [your means of giving] and increase the fruits of your righteousness, you being enriched in everything resulting in all liberality which is of such a nature as to achieve through us thanksgiving to God, because the ministration of this sacred service is not only filling up the things which the saints are lacking, but also is superabounding in many thanksgivings to God, inasmuch as they [the saints in Judaea] through your approved character, which approval finds its basis in this ministration, are glorifying God for the obedience of your confession with respect to the good news regarding the Christ and the liberality of your contribution to them and to all, while they also, with petitions on your behalf, are longing after you be-

cause of the grace of God upon you which cannot be measured. Thanks be to God for His ineffable gift.

Now, I myself, Paul, beg of you, please, through the meekness and sweet reasonableness of the Christ, who indeed in personal appearance am [as some of you say by way of reproach] grovelling, slavish, mean-spirited [the pagan attitude towards the Christian grace of humility] among you, but being absent, am of good courage toward you, [however that may be], I beg of you, please, that when I am present, I may not be courageous with the confidence with which I am counting on myself to be bold toward certain who take account of us as ordering our behavior in accordance with mere human considerations. For, though we are ordering our behavior in the sphere of human experience, not in accordance with mere human considerations are we waging warfare [against evil], for the weapons of our warfare are not human but mighty in God's sight, resulting in the demolition of fortresses, demolishing reasonings and every haughty mental elevation which lifts itself up against the experiential knowledge [which we believers have] of God, and leading captive every thought into the obedience to the Christ, and being in readiness to discipline every careless, apathetic hearing of and disobedience to the Word [if there remain any still disobedient] when your obedience [to me and my apostolic authority] shall be fulfilled. You are in the habit of looking at external appearance. If, as is the case, anyone has fully persuaded himself that he is Christ's [belongs to a special party of which he has placed Christ at the head], let him be considering this again with himself, that just as he himself belongs to Christ, so also do we. For, even if I should boast somewhat more abundantly concerning our authority which the Lord gave me for your building up and not for your casting down, I shall not be put to shame, in order that I may not seem as if I would make you afraid by my letters, Because his letters, indeed, they say, are weighty and powerful, but his bodily presence is weak and his discourse of no account. Let such a one [who makes comments such as the above] take into account this fact that the kind of person we are in our discourse through our letters when we are absent, such are we also

in action when we are present. For we are not daring to judge ourselves worthy to be among nor compare ourselves with certain ones of those who are commending themselves. But they themselves, measuring and comparing themselves with themselves, are without understanding.

13-18   But, as for us, we will not boast without a proper standard of measurement but in accordance with the measure of the measuring rule which God apportioned to us as a measuring unit, one that reaches even up to you [Paul's divinely appointed field of service]. For we did not extend ourselves beyond the prescribed limit as though we did not reach as far as to you, for we came as far as to you in announcing the good news about the Christ, not boasting without a proper standard of measurement, namely, not in other men's labors, but having hope that as your faith grows, we may be increased [in our apostolic efficiency] among you in accordance with our measuring rule [apportioned to us in our apostolic labors], resulting in a superabundance [of fruit in service], with a view to proclaiming the good news in the regions beyond you, not boasting ourselves in another's field of activity with reference to the things made ready [in advance by others, namely, the Christian assemblies already founded by others]. But he who boasts, let him be boasting in the Lord, for not he who recommends himself, that one is accepted after having been put to the test, but he whom the Lord recommends, that one has His stamp of approval placed upon him, that approval being based upon the fact that the approved one has met the test satisfactorily.

1-6   Would that you would be patiently tolerant of me in a little foolishness [ironically of his enforced self-vindication and boasting]. But you are really patiently tolerant of me. For I am jealous over you with a godly jealousy, for I gave you in marriage to one husband that I might present you as a pure virgin to the Christ. But I fear, lest by any means, as the snake deceived Eve in his craftiness, your minds should be corrupted from your simplicity [single-hearted loyalty] and purity [uprightness of life] which you express towards Christ. For, in-

deed, if, as is the case, he who comes proclaims another person as Jesus than the one whom we proclaimed, or you receive a spirit different in nature from the one you received, or a message of good news different in character from that message you received, you are most beautifully tolerant of him. For I account myself as not being in even one thing inferior to these superfine apostles. But even if, as is the case, I am not a professional orator in the realm of discourse, yet I am not unlearned nor unskilled in the realm of knowledge, but in everything we made it [our knowledge of God's word] plain among all with a view to your benefit.

7-9 Or, did I commit a sin in humbling myself [in supporting myself making tents] in order that you might be exalted [in spiritual privileges] because I preached the good news of God to you without charge? I robbed other assemblies, having taken wages from them, accepting from them more than their share of my support in order to minister to you. And when I was present with you and was in want, I was not a burden to anyone, for that which I lacked, the brethren, having come from Macedonia, supplied. And in all things I kept myself from being a burden to you and will continue to keep myself thus.

10-15 As the truth concerning Christ is in me, this boasting [in my independence of financial support] shall not be stopped so far as it pertains to me in the regions of Achaia. Wherefore? Because I do not love you? God knows. Moreover, that which I do [refusing to accept financial help from you] I will also continue to do, in order that I may cut off the particular occasion [the opportunity for attacking me should I accept help] from those who desire an occasion, that in the matter of their boast [namely, that since they had apostolic rank they possessed the right to be financially supported] they may be found even as also we are. For such men as these are false apostles, crafty workers, changing their outward expression to one which does not come from within and is not representative of their inner character but is assumed from without, masquerading as Christ's apostles. And no marvel, for Satan himself changes his outward

expression from one that comes from his inner nature and is representative of it, to one that is assumed from without and not representative of his inner being, masquerading as a messenger of light. Therefore it is no great thing if also, as is the case, his servants change their outward expression from one that comes from their inner nature and is representative of their inner character, to one that is assumed from without and not representative of their inner being, masquerading as servants of righteousness, whose end shall be according to their works.

16-20   I say again, let no man think me to be foolish. But even if you do, as is the case, yet receive me as foolish in order that I also [as well as they] may boast a little. That which I am saying, not after the pattern of the Lord am I speaking, but as in foolishness, in this confidence of boasting. Seeing that many are boasting in accordance with human standards and in human attainments, I also will boast, for you gladly tolerate those who are foolish, being wise yourselves. For you tolerate a man, if, as is the case, he brings you to the point of abject slavery; if a man strips you of your possessions [by greedily demanding maintenance]; if a man takes you captive; if a man exalts himself; if a man slaps you in the face.

21-28   I am speaking by way of disparagement [humbly of myself], as though, as for ourselves, we have been weak. And yet, whereinsoever a man is bold, I am speaking in foolishness, as for myself, I am bold also. Hebrews are they? I also. Israelites are they? I also. Offspring of Abraham are they? I also. Servants of Christ are they? I am speaking as one who is beside himself, I more [in a higher degree than they], in labors to the point of exhaustion more abundantly than they, in prisons more abundantly than they, in stripes inflicted by being whipped, beyond measure, in danger of death, often. From the Jews five times I received forty stripes less one. Three times I was beaten with rods. Once I was stoned. Three times I was shipwrecked. I have spent a night and a day in the sea. In journeyings often, in perils of rivers, in

perils of robbers, in perils from those of my own race, in perils from the Gentiles, in perils in the city, in perils in an uninhabited region, in perils in the sea, in perils among false brethren, in labor and travail, in sleepless nights often, in hunger and thirst, in need of food often, in cold and in lack of sufficient clothing; apart from the things I just enumerated is this, the pressure, day after day, namely, my anxiety for all the assemblies.

29-33

Who is weak, and I am not weak? Who is being made to stumble, and I am not indignant? Since it is a necessity in the nature of the case for me to boast, I will boast of the things that concern my weakness. The God and Father of our Lord Jesus knows, He who is the Eulogized One forever, that I am not lying. In Damascus the ethnarch under Aretas the king kept a constant guard over the city of the Damascenes in an effort to apprehend me, and through a window I was let down in a rope basket through [a window in] the wall and escaped out of his hands.

1-5

It is a necessity in the nature of the case for me to be boasting, though it is not expedient [my opponents force me to do so], but I will come to visions and revelations of the Lord. I know a man in Christ, fourteen years ago, whether in the body I do not know positively, or out of the body I do not know positively — God knows — this man being of such a character that he was caught up to the third heaven. And I know such a man, whether in the body or apart from the body, I do not know — God knows — that he was caught up into Paradise and heard unspeakable words which it is not lawful for a man to utter. Concerning such a man as this I will boast, but concerning myself I will not boast except in my weaknesses.

6-10

For, if I should desire to boast, I shall not be foolish, for I shall speak the truth. But I am abstaining [from boasting] lest any man consider me above that which he sees me to be or above that which he hears from me. And with respect to the superabundance of the revelations, in order that I may not be exalted over-

much, there was given to me a thorn in the flesh, a messenger of Satan, to the end that he might constantly maltreat me lest I be exalted overmuch. Concerning this three times I begged the Lord that he might depart from me. And He has said to me, and His declaration still stands, My grace is enough for you, for power is moment by moment coming to its full energy and complete operation in the sphere of weakness. Therefore, most gladly will I the rather boast in my weaknesses in order that the power of the Christ [like the Shekinah Glory in the Holy of Holies of the Tent of Meeting] may take up its residence in me [working within me and giving me help]. Wherefore I am well content in weaknesses, in insults, in necessities, in persecutions, and in circumstances under which I am subject to extreme pressure on behalf of Christ, for when I am weak, then I am filled with ability and power.

11, 12   I have become foolish and am so now [boasting thus]. As for you, you drove me to it. For as for myself, I ought to have been by you commended, which obligation on your part you have not fulfilled. [Had you done so, you would have saved me from boasting], for in not even one particular was I behind the superfine apostles, although I am nothing. Indeed, the miracles of the apostle, the purpose of which is to furnish credentials of that office, were fully performed among you in all patience, both by means of attesting miracles and miracles of a startling, imposing, amazement-wakening character, and miracles that demonstrate God's power.

13-18   For what is there in which you were treated in an inferior manner to the rest of the assemblies except that, as for myself, I myself did not burden you? Forgive me this wrong. Look! This is a third time I am ready to come to you, and I will not be a burden to you, for I am not seeking your possessions but you. For the children are under no moral obligation to be accumulating material resources for the parents, but the parents for the children. But as for myself, I will most gladly spend and be wholly spent for the sake of your souls. Assuming for the moment that I love you more abundantly [than I love other assemblies I have founded], am I being

loved less [than I am being loved by other assemblies]?
[Is that the way you are requiting my love?] But let
it be so. [Let the former matter be dismissed.] As for
myself, I did not saddle you with a burden. Nevertheless, [you say that] being crafty, I caught you [for my
own enrichment from the collection for the poor saints]
by means of a tricky bait. Of those whom I have sent
to you, there was not one through whom I took advantage
of you, was there? I exhorted Titus, and with him I
sent the brother. Titus did not take advantage of you in
anything, did he? Did we not order our behavior by
means of the same Spirit, and in the same footsteps?

For a long time you are thinking that it is to you I am   **19-21**
presenting my verbal defense. In the sight of God in
Christ are we speaking. But all the things, beloved ones,
[which we are speaking] are for your upbuilding. For
I fear lest by any means, having come, I will find you
such as I desire you not to be, and as for myself, I will
be found by you such as you do not desire me to be [in-
dignant to the point of severity at your backsliding], lest
by any means there should be strife, jealousy, outbursts
of boiling rage, factions, defamation of character, secret
slanders, inflated egos, disorders, lest, having come again,
my God should humiliate me before you, and I should
grieve for many of those who have sinned previously and
did not repent of their uncleanness, and fornication, and
unbridled passionate craving which they committed.

This is a third time I am coming to you. Upon the   **1-4**
basis of the mouth of two witnesses or three shall every
word be established. I have said previously, and I do
say beforehand, as when I was present the second time,
so now being absent, to those who sinned heretofore and
to all the rest, that if I come again I will not spare you,
since you are seeking a proof that Christ speaks in me,
He who is not weak in relation to you [as you think me
to be], but is powerful in your midst, for though He was
crucified in [the] weakness [of His humanity], yet He
lives by means of God's power. And as for ourselves,
we are weak [in company] with Him [as partaking of
frail humanity], but we shall live with respect to you together with Him through God's power.

5, 6   Be putting yourselves to the test whether you are in the Faith. Be putting yourselves to the test for the purpose of approving yourselves, and finding that you meet the specifications, put your approval upon yourselves. Or, do you yourselves not recognize that Jesus Christ is in you, unless you are those who are disapproved? But I hope that you shall come to know that, as for us, we are not disapproved.

7-10   Now, we are praying to God that you do not even one bit of evil, not, as for us, in order that we may appear as approved, but in order that, as for you, you may be doing that which is honorable, but as for us, in order that we may be as those who are disapproved, for we are not able to do anything against the truth, but for the truth. For, as for us, we rejoice when we are weak, but as for you, when you are strong. And for this we also pray, for your spiritual equipment. On this account I am writing these things when I am absent, in order that I may not deal sharply [with you] in accordance with the authority which the Lord gave me for building up and not for casting down.

11-13   Finally, brethren, be rejoicing. See to it that you are being spiritually equipped and adjusted. Be encouraged. Be of the same mind. Be living at peace. And the God of love and peace shall be with you. Greet one another with a holy kiss. All the saints send greeting to you.

14   The grace of the Lord Jesus Christ and the love of God and the partnership of the Holy Spirit be with you all.

THE EXPANDED TRANSLATION OF
GALATIANS

PREFACE TO PAUL'S LETTER TO THE
GALATIANS

This is another of Paul's letters of a highly doctrinal nature and therefore demands a meticulously accurate rendering of the Greek text, for doctrine is the foundation and cornerstone of the Christian system of belief. And what is more, it deals with a heresy, namely, justification by faith plus works. And this must be clearly defined.

After his introductory words the great apostle says: "I marvel that ye are so soon removed from him that called you into the grace of Christ unto another gospel which is not another" (1: 6, 7). An observant student sees that at the very outset Paul contradicts himself (A.V.). He brands the gospel which these Galatians had embraced, "another gospel," and before he finishes the sentence he says that it is "not another gospel." The two Greek words translated in their order are *heteros* and *allos*. Both have the meaning of "another," but the first means "another of a different kind," whereas the second means "another of the same kind." Now, a standard translation is unable to bring out the distinction between these synonyms because it is held down to a minimum number of words, whereas an expanded translation using as many words as it desires, offers the following; "to a message of good news diametrically opposed to the gospel, which message is not an alternative gospel." The Judaizer's message was both different from the message Paul preached and also diametrically opposed to it. This is brought out by the first Greek word. It was not an alternative message, fit to take the place of the gospel Paul preached. This is brought out by the second Greek word.

When Paul wrote, "When it pleased God . . . to reveal His Son in me that I might preach Him among the heathen" (1:14, 15), did he mean "reveal Him through me as I preached," or "reveal Him to me in my inner being?" The answer is found in the Greek word translated "reveal," (*apokaluptō*) which means "to uncover something which had been previously hidden." Our Lord had already been preached at the time Paul began His

197

ministry and therefore was not hidden. Paul meant "to reveal His Son to Paul by an inward revelation." The expanded translation offers "to give me an inward revelation of His Son."

We will look at an instance where a standard translation, because it does not handle a Greek idiom, makes an incorrect statement. An idiom in a language is a way of saying something which is peculiar to that language and not therefore found in the language into which the translation is being made. The statement is as follows; "Before faith came, we [Jews] were kept under the law, shut up unto the faith which should afterwards be revealed" (3:23). This means that faith was not exercised for salvation until the Christian era. But Paul had just written, "Abraham believed God, and it was accounted to him for righteousness" (3:6). Here he says that Abraham exercised faith for salvation. Again a careful student of the Word discovers a contradiction. The solution to the difficulty is found in the presence of the Greek definite article before the first use of the word "faith." It is, "before the faith came." The syntactical use of the article here is that it points back to a previously mentioned faith which is defined in its context, the faith spoken of in verse 22. This is faith in the Lord Jesus as Saviour. Faith in Old Testament times was in the God who would some day offer a sacrifice for sin. This is a prophetic faith, looking forward to a sacrifice that would pay for the sinner's sin. Faith in the Lord Jesus in this Age of Grace is an historic faith, looking back upon an historic sacrifice that paid for sin. It was before this aforementioned faith came to be exercised that the Jewish nation was kept under the law. The expanded translation offers "but before the aforementioned faith came," pointing back to the faith defined in verse 22.

An instance where a standard translation cannot bring out the full force of a Greek word is found in 4:19 where Paul writes: "My little children, of whom I travail in birth again until Christ be formed in you" (A.V.). What did Paul mean by saying "until Christ be formed in you?" The English verb "form" means "to give form or shape to, to frame, construct, to fashion, to mold." The verb here is in the passive voice. To translate according to Webster's Unabridged Dictionary from which this definition is taken would result in the following; "until Christ be given shape or form, constructed, fashioned, molded." But in what sense this is to be done the English reader is at a loss to know. The Greek word is *morphoomai,* a philosophical term referring to the act of

giving outward expression of one's inner nature, that expression coming from and being truly representative of that nature. The expanded translation reads, "until Christ be outwardly expressed in you." Paul was speaking of the outward expression of the indwelling Christ which the Galatian Christians had lost because they had put themselves under the Mosaic law where there was no provision of an indwelling Holy Spirit for purposes of sanctification, one of whose ministeries was to express the Lord Jesus outwardly through the believer. These Galatian saints had fallen out of sanctifying grace, and Paul prays that this outward expression of the indwelling Lord Jesus might be restored by their act of discarding law as a method of living their Christian lives and again coming under the sweet exhortations and powerful enablements of grace. This tremendous truth the expositor will not find in the standard English translation no matter how long he searches. The expanded translation gives it to him at first glance. This casts a flood of light upon the entire section (chapters 4 and 5) dealing with sanctification.

Paul in his closing words says, "Ye see how large a letter I have written unto you with mine own hand" (6:11). The Greek text will never agree to this rendering. Paul wrote, "You see with what large letters I write to you with my own hand." Paul had contracted an oriental eye disease on his first missionary journey as he was passing through Pamphylia where it was prevalent. When he reached Pisidian Antioch, the first of the Galatian cities in which he preached, he had become totally incapacitated. He speaks of this in 4:13-15. This disease, called ophthalmia, resulted in almost total blindness. Paul was in the habit of dictating his letters as in the case of Romans where Tertius was his secretary (Rom. 16:22). But in the case of the writing of Galatians, the need was so urgent, that, having no secretary available or because he wanted to impart a most personal touch to the letter in view of the delicate situation of heresy in these churches, he wrote the letter himself. To accommodate his dim vision he had to write in the large inch-high Greek capital letters. The words "have written" (A.V.) are the translation of the Greek aorist indicative, which normally is translated by a past tense in English. But here it is what is called "an epistolary aorist," a device by which a Greek letter writer does the recipient of his letter the courtesy of looking at his act of writing as the reader would look at it when he received the letter, namely, as a

past event, even though it is a present occurrence to him as the writer of the letter. The A.V. translates it as a past event. The expanded translation uses the present tense. The epistolary aorist refers to the entire letter as having been written in these large letters and settles the question whether Paul wrote only the final part of the letter or the entire letter in large letters. From the above examples the English reader can readily understand how much additional truth he will find as he studies this expanded translation of Galatians.

Paul, an apostle, not from men nor even through
the intermediate agency of man, but through Jesus Christ
and God the Father who raised Him from among the
dead, and all the brethren with me, to the assemblies of
Galatia. Grace to you and peace from God our Father
and from the Lord Jesus Christ who gave himself in
behalf of our sins so that He might rescue us out from
this present pernicious age according to the will of our
God and Father, to whom be the glory for ever and ever.
Amen.

1-5

I am marvelling that in such a manner suddenly you
are becoming of another mind and deserting from Him
who called you in the sphere of Christ's grace to a message of good news diametrically opposed to the gospel,
which message is not an alternative gospel. Only, there
are certain ones who are troubling your minds and are
desiring to pervert the gospel of Christ. In fact, even if
we or a messenger from heaven should preach a gospel
to you which goes beyond that which we preached to you
as good news, let him be accursed. Even as we have
said on a previous occasion, indeed, now again I am saying, If, as is the case, anyone preaches a gospel to you
which goes beyond that which you took so eagerly and
hospitably to your hearts, let him be accursed. For, am
I at this present moment seeking to win the favor of
men rather than the approval of God? Or, am I making
it my business to be constantly pleasing men? If I still
were pleasing men, in that case Christ's bondslave I
would not be.

6-10

For I make known to you, brethren, the message
which was announced as good news by me, that it is not
as to its nature, human. For, as for myself, neither did
I receive it directly from man, nor was I taught it, but
I received it through a revelation given me by Jesus
Christ.

11, 12

For you heard of my manner of life aforetime in
Judaism, that beyond measure I kept on continually
persecuting the Church of God and continually bringing
destruction upon it, and I was constantly blazing a
pioneer path, outstripping in Judaism many of my own

13, 14

age in my race, being more exceedingly zealous of my ancestral traditions.

15-17   But when it was the good pleasure of the One who set me apart before I was born and called me by His grace to give me an inward revelation of His Son in order that I might proclaim Him as glad tidings among the Gentiles, immediately I did not put myself in communication with flesh and blood for the purpose of consultation; neither did I go up to Jerusalem to those who were apostles before me, but I went away into Arabia, and again returned to Damascus.

18-24   Then, after three years, I went up to Jerusalem to become acquainted with Cephas, and remained with him fifteen days. But another of the apostles I did not see except James the brother of our Lord. But the things which I am writing to you, behold, in the sight of God, I am not lying. Then I went into the regions of Syria and Cilicia, but remained personally unknown to the assemblies of Judaea which are in Christ. Indeed, they only kept on hearing, The one who used to persecute us at one time now is announcing the glad tidings of the Faith which at one time he was ravaging. And they were continually glorifying God [for that which they found] in me.

1-10   Then, after the space of fourteen years, again I went up to Jerusalem, accompanied by Barnabas, having taken along also Titus. And I went up in accordance with a revelation. And I laid before them for their consideration the gospel which I am preaching among the Gentiles, but privately to those of recognized eminence, lest by any means I should be running or had run in vain. But not even Titus who was with me, although he was a Gentile, was compelled to be circumcised. Now it was because of the false brethren who had been surreptitiously brought in, those of such a character that they sneaked in for the purpose of spying out our liberty which we are having in Christ Jesus, with the expectation of reducing us to abject slavery; to whom not even for an hour did we yield with reference to the particular voluntary submission demanded, in order that the truth of the gospel

might abide for you. But to be something at the hands of those who were of repute, whatever they were aforetime, is of no importance to me. God accepts not man's person. For those who were of repute imposed nothing on me. But on the contrary, when they saw that I had been entrusted with [the responsibility of preaching] the gospel to the uncircumcised as Peter with [the responsibility of preaching] the gospel to the circumcised — for He who worked effectively for Peter with respect to his apostolate to the circumcision also worked effectively for me with respect to the Gentiles — and having come to perceive the grace which was given to me, James, and Cephas, and John, those who in reputation were looked upon as pillars, gave to me and Barnabas the right hand of fellowship, to the end that we should preach the gospel to the Gentiles and they themselves to the circumcision; only, that we should keep on remembering the poor, which very thing I have made a diligent and eager effort to do.

But when Cephas came to Antioch, to his face I **11-21** opposed him, because he stood condemned. For before certain from James came, with the Gentiles it was his habit to eat meals. But when they came he began gradually to draw himself back, and began slowly to effect a final separation, fearing those of the circumcision. And the rest of the Jews also played the hypocrite jointly with him, so that even Barnabas was swept along with their hypocrisy. But when I saw that they were not pursuing a straight-forward course in relation to the truth of the gospel, I said to Cephas in the presence of everybody, If you, being a Jew, habitually are living after the manner of the Gentiles, and not after that of the Jews, how is it that you are compelling the Gentiles to live after the Jewish manner? As for us, we are Jews by nature, and not sinners of Gentile origin; and knowing that a man is not justified by law works but only through faith in Christ Jesus, we also placed our trust in Christ Jesus, in order that we might be justified by faith in Christ and not by law works, because by law works there shall no flesh be justified. But if, as is the case, while seeking to be justified in Christ, we [Jews] ourselves also were

found to be sinners, is Christ therefore a promoter of sin? Away with the thought; for if the things I tear down, these again I build up, I exhibit myself as a transgressor; for, as for myself, I through the intermediate agency of the law died to the law, in order that I might live with respect to God. With Christ I have been crucified, and it is no longer I who live, but there lives in me Christ. And that life which now I live in the sphere of the flesh, by faith I live it, which faith is in the Son of God who loved me and gave himself on my behalf. I do not thwart the efficacy of the grace of God. For if through law comes righteousness, then Christ died without a cause.

1-9 O, unreflecting Galatians, who bewitched you, before whose eyes Jesus Christ was placarded publicly as the crucified One? This only am I desiring to learn from you. By means of law works did you receive the Spirit or by means of the message which proclaims faith? Are you so unreflecting? Having begun by means of the Spirit, now are you being brought to spiritual maturity by the flesh? So many things did you suffer in vain? If indeed they really were in vain? Therefore, the One who is constantly supplying the Spirit to you in bountiful measure, and constantly working miracles among you, by means of law works is He doing these things, or by means of the message which proclaims faith?

Just as Abraham believed God, and his act of faith was credited to him, resulting in his righteousness. You perceive, therefore, that those who are of faith, these are sons of Abraham. And the scripture, forseeing that on a basis of faith God justifies the Gentiles, announced the good news beforehand to Abraham, namely, All the Gentiles shall be blessed in you. So that those who are believing ones are being blessed in company with believing Abraham.

10-14 For as many as are of the works of the law are under curse, for it stands written, Cursed is every one who is not remaining constantly in all things which stand written in the book of the law in order to do them. But that in a sphere of law no one is being justified in the sight of God is clear, because, The righteous man shall

live by means of faith. And the law is not of faith; but the one who has done them shall live in them. Christ delivered us by the payment of ransom from the curse of the law by becoming a curse in behalf of us, because it stands written, Accursed is everyone who is suspended upon a tree, in order that to the Gentiles the blessing of Abraham might come in Jesus Christ, to the end that the promise of the Spirit we [Jew and Gentile] might receive through faith.

Brethren, what I have to say is in accordance with **15-18** common human practice. Even though it be a man's covenant, when it has finally been ratified, no man annuls it nor adds stipulations to it. Now to Abraham were made the promises, and to his Descendant. He does not say, And to the descendants, as in respect to many descendants, but in respect to one Descendant, and to your Descendant, who is Christ. This now is what I mean. A covenant previously established by God, the law which came after four hundred and thirty years does not render void with the result that the promise becomes inoperative, for if the inheritance is from law [as a method of divine dealing], no longer is it from promise [as a method of divine dealing]. But to Abraham, through the intermediate instrumentality of promise, God has in grace freely bestowed it.

What is then the significance of the law? For the **19-23** sake of transgressions it was added until there should come the Descendant to whom the promise was made, having been promulgated by angels through the instrumentality of the hand of a mediator. Now, the mediator is not a go-between representing the interests of one individual, but God is one individual. Is therefore the law against the promises of God? God forbid. For if a law had been given which was able to impart life, righteousness in that case would have been from the law. But the scripture shut up all under sin in order that the promise on the ground of faith in Jesus Christ might be given to those who believe. But before the aforementioned faith came, under law we were constantly being guarded, being shut up with a view to the faith about to be revealed.

24-29   So that the law became our guardian until Christ, in order that on the grounds of faith we might be justified; but this faith having come, no longer are we under the guardian, for all of you are God's sons through faith in Christ Jesus, for as many as were introduced into union with Christ, put on Christ. There is neither Jew nor Greek, there is neither slave nor free, there is neither male nor female. For you are all one in Christ Jesus. And since you are Christ's, then are you Abraham's descendants, heirs according to the promise.

1-7   Now I say, that as long as the heir is in his minority, he does not differ one bit from a slave, even though he is owner of all, but is under guardians and stewards until the time previously fixed by his father. In like manner, we also, when we were in our minority, were in a permanent state of servitude under the rudimentary first principles of mankind. But when there came the fulness of the time, God sent off His Son, woman-born, made subject to law, in order that He might deliver those under law to the end that we might be placed as adult sons. And because you are sons, God sent forth the Spirit of His Son into your hearts crying, Abba [namely], my Father. So that no longer are you a slave but a son, and since you are a son, you are also an heir through God.

8-11   But at that time, in fact, not knowing God, you were in a slave's bondage to the gods which are not gods by nature. But now having come to know God, indeed, rather having become known by God, how is it possible that you are turning back again to the weak and beggarly rudimentary principles to which you are again bent on being in bondage? Days you are scrupulously and religiously observing, and months, and seasons, and years. I am afraid about you lest perhaps in vain I have labored to the point of exhaustion for you.

12-20   Become as I am, because I also became as you were, brethren; I am beseeching you. You had done me no wrong. But you know that because of an infirmity of the flesh I preached the gospel to you on the occasion of my first visit. And the test to which you were subjected and which was in my flesh, you did not loathe nor

utterly despise, but as a messenger of God you received me, as Christ Jesus. Where is therefore your spiritually prosperous state? For I bear witness to you that if it had been possible, you would have dug out your own eyes and given them to me. So then I have become your enemy because I am telling you the truth? They are zealously paying you court, but not honestly, desiring to isolate you in order that you might be paying court to them. But it is good to be zealously courted in a good thing at all times, and not only when I am present with you, my born ones, concerning whom I am again striving with intense effort and anguish until Christ be outwardly expressed in you. Moreover, I was wishing that I were present with you at this very moment and could thus change my tone, because I am perplexed about you.

Be telling me, you that are bent upon being under **21-31** law, are you not hearing the law? For it stands written, Abraham had two sons, one from the maidservant and one from the freewoman. But, on the one hand, the son of the maidservant was one born in the ordinary course of nature. On the other hand, the son of the freewoman was one born through the promise, which class of things is allegorical. For these are two covenants, one from Mount Sinai, begetting bondage, which is as to its nature classed as Hagar. Now this Hagar is Mount Sinai in Arabia, and corresponds to the Jerusalem which now is, for she is in bondage with her children. But the Jerusalem which is above is free, which is our Mother. For it stands written, Rejoice, barren woman who does not bear. Break forth and cry, you who do not travail, because more are the children of the desolate than of the one who has a husband. And, as for you, brethren, after the manner of Isaac are you children of promise. But just as then, he who was born according to the flesh was constantly persecuting him who was born according to the Spirit, so also now. But what does the scripture say? Throw out the maidservant and her son. For the son of the maidservant shall by no means inherit with the son of the freewoman. Therefore, brethren, we are children, not of a maidservant, but of the freewoman.

1-12   For this aforementioned freedom Christ set you free. Keep on standing firm therefore and stop being held in again by a yoke of bondage. Behold, I, Paul, am saying to you that if you persist in being circumcised, Christ will be advantageous to you in not even one thing, and I solemnly affirm again to every man who receives circumcision, that he is under obligation to do the whole law. You are without effect from Christ, such of you as in the sphere of the law are seeking your justification. You have lost your hold upon [sanctifying] grace. For, as for us, through the agency of the Spirit, on the ground of faith, a hoped-for righteousness we are eagerly awaiting, for in Christ Jesus neither circumcision is of any power nor uncircumcision, but faith coming to effective expression through love. You were running well. Who cut in on you and thus hindered you from obeying the truth? This persuasion is not from the One who calls you. A little yeast is permeating the whole lump. As for myself, I have come to a settled persuasion in the Lord with respect to you, namely, that you will take no other view than this. But the one who troubles you shall bear his judgment, whoever he is. And I, brethren, if I am still preaching circumcision, why am I in spite of this fact still being persecuted? Then the stumbling block of the Cross has been done away. I would that they who are upsetting you would even have themselves mutilated.

13-15   For, as for you, upon the basis of freedom you were called, brethren. Only do not turn your liberty into a base of operations for the evil nature, but through love keep on constantly serving one another, for the whole law in one utterance stands fully obeyed, namely, in this, Love your neighbor as you do yourself. But if, as is the case, you are biting and devouring one another, take heed lest you be consumed by one another.

16-21   But I say, Through the instrumentality of the Spirit habitually order your manner of life, and you will in no wise execute the passionate desire of the evil nature, for the evil nature constantly has a strong desire to suppress the Spirit, and the Spirit constantly has a strong desire to suppress the evil nature. And these are entrenched in

an attitude of mutual opposition to one another so that you may not do the things that you desire to do. But if you are being led by the Spirit you are not under law. Now the works of the evil nature are well known, works of such a nature as, for example, fornication, uncleanness, wantonness, idolatry, witchcraft, enmities, strife, jealousy, angers, self-seekings, divisions, factions, envyings, drunkenness, carousings, and the things of such a nature which are like these things, respecting which things I am telling you beforehand even as I told you in advance, that those who are in the habit of practicing things of that nature shall not inherit the kingdom of God.

22-26

But the fruit of the Spirit is love, joy, peace, longsuffering, kindness, goodness, faithfulness, meekness, self-control. Against such things as these there is no law. And they who belong to Christ Jesus crucified the evil nature with its dispositions and cravings once for all. In view of the fact that we are being sustained in spiritual life by the Spirit, by means of the Spirit let us go on ordering our conduct. Let us stop becoming vain-glorious, provoking one another, envying one another.

1-5

Brethren, if, however, a man be overtaken in a sin, as for you who are the spiritual ones, be restoring such a one in a spirit of meekness, taking heed to yourself lest you also be tempted. One another's burdens be constantly bearing, and thus you will fully satisfy the requirements of the law of the Christ. For if anyone thinks himself to be something when he is nothing, he is deceiving himself. But his own work let each one put to the test and thus approve, and then with respect to himself alone will he have a ground for glorying, and not with respect to the other one [with whom he had compared himself], for each shall bear his own private burden.

6-10

Moreover, let the one who is being taught the Word constantly be holding fellowship with the one who is teaching in all good things. Stop leading yourselves astray. God is not being outwitted and evaded. For whatever a man is in the habit of sowing, this also will he reap; because the one who sows with a view to his

own evil nature, from his evil nature as a source shall reap corruption. But the one who sows with a view to the Spirit, from the Spirit as a source shall reap life eternal. Let us not slacken our exertions by reason of the weariness that comes with prolonged effort in habitually doing that which is good. For in a season which in its character is appropriate, we shall reap if we do not become enfeebled through exhaustion and faint. So then, in like manner, let us be having opportunity, let us be working that which is good to all, but especially to those of the household of the Faith.

11-18   You see with what large letters I am writing to you with my own hand. As many as desire to make a good outward appearance in the sphere of the flesh, these are trying to compel you to receive circumcision, their only motive being that they might not be persecuted by reason of the cross of Christ, for not even those who are circumcised are themselves keeping the law, but they desire you to be circumcised in order that in your flesh they may glory. For, as for me, far be it from me to be glorying except in the cross of our Lord Jesus Christ, through whom to me the world stands crucified and I to the world. For neither circumcision is anything, nor uncircumcision, but a new creation. And as many as by this rule are ordering their conduct, peace be upon them, and mercy, even upon the Israel of God. Henceforth, let no man furnish me trouble, for I bear branded the marks of the Lord Jesus in my body. The grace of our Lord Jesus Christ be with your spirit, brethren. Amen.

THE EXPANDED TRANSLATION OF PAUL'S
LETTER TO THE EPHESIANS

PREFACE TO PAUL'S LETTER TO THE
EPHESIANS

This letter, containing the deepest church truth, is a treasure house of rich spiritual food, highly doctrinal in character. It contains the longest sentence in print, commencing at chapter 1, verse 3, and extending through verse 14. Such words of a highly doctrinal content as "chosen, predestinated, adoption, dispensation, earnest, purchased possession," are in this expanded translation clearly rendered.

Paul prays that "Christ may dwell in your hearts" (3:17, A.V.) which becomes in the expanded translation, "in order that Christ may finally settle down and feel completely at home in your hearts," a beautiful concept that one cannot get out of the word "dwell." In the A.V. of (4:11) there are five individuals mentioned. A rule of Greek syntax allows but four, the words "pastors and teachers" being in a construction which requires us to understand that one person is referred to by the two designations, namely, a teaching pastor, or a pastor who also is a teacher. The punctuation of the A.V. in 4:12 makes the teaching pastor responsible for all the work in the local church, whereas the expanded translation offers this; "He gave teaching pastors for the equipping of the saints for ministering work with a view to the building up of the Body of Christ," making the teaching pastor a specialist in training members of his congregation to engage in Christian service. Instead of the A.V. rendering, "Be filled with the Spirit" (5:18), the expanded translation offers, "Be constantly controlled by the Spirit," which makes this truth clear. The A.V. has "Husbands, love your wives" (5:25). The expanded translation defines that particular word for "love" in the words, "The husbands, be loving your wives with a love self-sacrificial in its nature." And so one could go on enumerating the treasures found in this letter. But we will leave the letter now for the reader to discover more of these treasures for himself.

Paul, an ambassador of Christ Jesus through the will of God, to the saints, the ones who are [in Ephesus], namely, believing ones in Christ Jesus. Grace to you and peace from God our Father and the Lord Jesus Christ.   **1, 2**

May the God and Father of our Lord Jesus Christ be eulogized, the One who conferred benefactions upon us in the sphere of every spiritual blessing in the heavenly places in Christ, even as He selected us out for himself in Him before the foundations of the universe were laid, to be holy ones and without blemish before His searching, penetrating gaze; in love having previously marked us out to be placed as adult sons through the intermediate agency of Jesus Christ for himself according to that which seemed good in His heart's desire, resulting in praise of the glory of His grace which He freely bestowed upon us in the Beloved, in whom we are having our redemption through His blood, the putting away of our trespasses according to the wealth of His grace which He caused to superabound to us in the sphere of every wisdom and understanding, having made known to us the mystery of His will according to that which seemed good to Him, which good thing He purposed in himself, with respect to an administration of the completion of the epochs of time to bring back again to their original state all things in the Christ, the things in the heavens and the things on the earth, in Him, in whom also we were made an inheritance, having been previously marked out according to the purpose of the One who operates all things according to the counsel of His will, with a view to our being to the praise of His glory who had previously placed our hope in the Christ, in whom also, as for you, having heard the word of the truth, the good news of your salvation, in whom also having believed, you were sealed with the Spirit of the promise, the Holy Spirit, who is the token payment of our inheritance guaranteeing the full payment of all, looking forward to the redemption of the possession which is being preserved with a view to the praise of His glory.   **3-14**

On account of this, I also, having heard of the faith in the Lord Jesus which is among you and of your love   **15-23**

to all the saints, do not cease giving thanks for you as I constantly make mention of you in my prayers, that the God of our Lord Jesus Christ, the Father of the glory, might give to you a spirit of wisdom and revelation in the sphere of a full knowledge of Him, the eyes of your heart being in an enlightened state with a view to your knowing what is the hope of His calling, what is the wealth of the glory of His inheritance in the saints, and what is the superabounding greatness of His inherent power to us who are believing ones as measured by the operative energy of the manifested strength of His might, which might was operative in the Christ when He raised Him from among the dead and seated Him at His right hand in the heavenly places, over and above every government and authority and power and lordship and every name that is constantly being named, not only in this age, but also in the one about to come. And all things He put in subjection under His feet, and Him He gave as Head over all things to the Church, which is of such a nature as to be His body, the fulness of the One who constantly is filling all things with all things.

1-10   And you being dead with reference to your trespasses and sins, He made alive; in the sphere of which trespasses and sins at one time you ordered your behavior as dominated by the spirit of the age in this world system, as dominated by the leader of the authority of the lower atmosphere, the source also of the spirit that is now operating in the sons of the disobedience among whom also we all ordered our behavior in the sphere of the cravings of our evil nature, continually practicing the desires of our evil nature and of our thoughts, and were continually children of wrath by nature, as also the rest. But God, being wealthy in the sphere of mercy, because of His great love with which He loved us, and we, being dead with respect to our trespasses, made us alive together with the Christ; by grace have you been saved completely in past time, with the present result that you are in a state of salvation which persists through present time, and raised us with Him and seated us with Him in the heavenly places in Christ Jesus, in order that He might exhibit for His own glory in the ages that will pile

themselves one upon another in continuous succession, the surpassing wealth of His grace in kindness to us in Christ Jesus. For by the grace have you been saved in time past completely, through faith, with the result that your salvation persists through present time; and this [salvation] is not from you as a source; of God it is the gift, not from a source of works, in order that no one might boast; for we are His handiwork, created in Christ Jesus with a view to good works which God prepared beforehand in order that within their sphere we may order our behavior.

On this account be remembering that at one time, **11-18** you, the Gentiles in the flesh, the ones habitually called uncircumcision by that which is called circumcision in the flesh made by hand, that you were at that time without a Messiah, alienated from the commonwealth of the Israel and strangers from the covenants of the promise, not having hope and without God in the world. But now in Christ Jesus you, who at one time were far off, have become near by the blood of the Christ. For He himself is our peace, the One who made the both one, having broken down the middle wall of the partition, the enmity, in His flesh having rendered inoperative the law of the commandments in ordinances, in order that the two He might create in himself, resulting in one new man, making peace, and in order that He might reconcile the both in one body to God through the Cross, having put to death the enmity by it, and having come, He proclaimed glad tidings of peace to you who were far off, and to you who were near, because through Him we have our entree, the both of us, by one Spirit into the presence of the Father.

Now then, no longer are you aliens and foreign so- **19-22** journers, but you are fellow citizens of the saints and householders of God, having been built up upon the foundation of the apostles and prophets, there being a chief cornerstone, Jesus Christ himself, in whom the whole building closely joined together grows into a holy inner sanctuary in the Lord, in whom also you are being built together into a permanent dwelling place of God by the Spirit.

1-7   On this account I, Paul, the prisoner of the Messiah, Jesus, on behalf of you, the Gentiles, assuming that you heard of the administration of the grace of God which was given to me for you, that by revelation there was made known to me the mystery even as I wrote above in brief, in accordance with which you are able when you read to understand my insight into the mystery of the Christ which in other and different generations was not made known to the sons of men as now it has been revealed to His holy apostles and prophets by the Spirit, that the Gentiles are fellow heirs, and belong jointly to the same body, and are fellow partakers of His promise in Christ Jesus, revealed through the good news of which I became one who ministers according to the gift of the grace of God, which grace was given to me according to the operative energy of His power.

8-12   To me, the one who is less than the least of all saints, there was given this grace, to the Gentiles to proclaim the good news of the incomprehensible wealth belonging to the Christ, and to bring to light what is the administration of the mystery which has been kept covered up from the beginning of the ages in the God who created all things, in order that there might be made known now to the principalities and powers in the heavenly places through the intermediate agency of the Church the much-variegated wisdom of God, according to the eternal purpose which He carried into effect in the Christ, Jesus our Lord, in whom we are having our freedom of speech and entree in perfect confidence through faith in Him.

13-19   Wherefore, I am asking in my own interest, that you do not lose heart by reason of my tribulations on your behalf which are of such a nature as to be your glory. On this account I bow my knees to the Father from whom every family in heaven and on earth is named, that He would grant to you according to the wealth of His glory, with power to be strengthened through the Spirit in the inward man, that the Christ might finally settle down and feel completely at home in your hearts through your faith; in love having been firmly rooted and grounded in order that you may be able to grasp with all the saints what is the breadth and width and height and depth, and

to know experientially the love of the Christ which sur-
passes experiential knowledge in order that you may be
filled up to the measure of all the fulness of God.

Now to the One who is able to do beyond all things, **20, 21**
superabundantly beyond and over and above those things
that we are asking for ourselves and considering, in the
measure of the power which is operative in us, to Him
be the glory in the Church and in Christ Jesus into all
the generations of the age of the ages. Amen.

I beg of you, please, therefore, I, the prisoner in the **1-6**
Lord, order your behavior in a manner worthy of the
divine summons with which you were called, with every
lowliness and meekness, with longsuffering, bearing with
one another in love, doing your best to safeguard the
unanimity of the Spirit in the bond of peace. There is
one Body and one Spirit, even as also you were called in
one hope of your calling, one Lord, one Faith, one placing into [the Body of Christ by the Holy Spirit], one
God and Father of all, the One above all and through
all and in all.

But to each one of us there was given the grace in the **7-16**
measure of the gift of the Christ. Wherefore He says,
Having ascended on high, He led away captive those
taken captive and gave gifts to men. Now, the fact that
He ascended, what is it except that also He descended
into the nether parts of the earth? The One who descended himself is also the One who ascended above all
the heavens, in order that He might fill all things. And
He himself gave some, on the one hand, as apostles, and,
on the other hand, as prophets, and still again some as
bringers of good news, and finally, some as pastors who
are also teachers, for the equipping of the saints for
ministering work with a view to the building up of the
Body of Christ, until we all attain to the unity of the
Faith and of the experiential, full, and precise knowledge
of the Son of God, to a spiritually mature man, to the
measure of the stature of the fulness of the Christ, in
order that we no longer may be immature ones, tossed
to and fro and carried around in circles by every wind of
teaching in the cunning adroitness of men, in craftiness

which furthers the scheming deceitful art of error, but
speaking the truth in love, may grow up into Him in
all things, who is the Head, Christ, from whom all the
Body constantly being joined closely together and constantly being knit together through every joint of supply according to the operative energy put forth to the
capacity of each part, makes for increased growth of the
Body resulting in the building up of itself in the sphere
of love.

17-19   This, therefore, I am saying and solemnly declaring
in the Lord, that no longer are you to be ordering your
behavior as the Gentiles order their behavior in the
futility of their mind, being those who have their understanding darkened, who have been alienated from the life
of God through the ignorance which is in them, through
the hardening of their hearts, who, being of such a nature as to have become callous, abandoned themslves to
wantonness, resulting in a performing of every uncleanness in the sphere of greediness.

20-24   But as for you, not in this manner did you learn the
Christ, since, indeed, as is the case, you heard and in Him
were taught just as truth is in Jesus, that you have put
off once for all with reference to your former manner
of life the old self who is being corrupted according to
the passionate desires of deceit; moreover, that you are
being constantly renewed with reference to the spirit of
your mind; and that you have put on once for all the
new self who after God was created in righteousness and
holiness of truth.

25-32   Wherefore, having put off the lie once for all, be
speaking truth each with his neighbor, because we are
members belonging to one another. Be constantly angry
with a righteous indignation, and stop sinning. Do not
allow the sun to go down upon your irritated, exasperated,
embittered anger. And stop giving an occasion for acting
[opportunity] to the devil. The one who is stealing, let
him no longer be stealing, but rather let him be laboring,
working with his own hands that which is good, in order
that he may be having that wherewith to be sharing with
the one who is having need. Every word that is rotten

and unfit for use, out of your mouth let it not be proceeding, but whatever is good, suitable for edification with respect to the need, in order that it may impart grace to the hearers. And stop grieving the Spirit, the Holy Spirit of God, with whom you were sealed with a view to the day of redemption. All manner of harshness and violent outbreaks of wrath and anger and brawling and slanderous speech, let it be put away from you together with all manner of malice. And be becoming kind to one another, tenderhearted, forgiving each other even as and just as also God in Christ forgave you.

Be becoming therefore imitators of God, as children **1-6** beloved, and be ordering your behavior within the sphere of love, even as Christ also loved you and gave himself up in our behalf and in our stead as an offering and a sacrifice to God for an aroma of a sweet smell. But fornication and uncleanness, every kind of it, or covetousness, let it not be even named among you, just as it is befitting to saints, and obscenity and foolish talking or ribaldry, which things have not been seemly or fitting, but rather giving of thanks, for this you know absolutely and experientially, that every whoremonger or unclean person or covetous person, who is an idolator, does not have an inheritance in the kingdom of the Christ and of God. Let no one keep on deceiving you by means of empty words, for because of these things there comes the wrath of God upon the sons of the disobedience.

Stop therefore becoming joint-participants with them; **7-12** for you were at one time darkness, but now you are light in the Lord. As children of light be habitually conducting yourselves; for the fruit of this light is in the sphere of every beneficence and righteousness and truth, putting to the test and then approving what is well pleasing to the Lord. And stop having fellowship with the unfruitful works of this darkness, but rather be rebuking them so as to bring out confession and conviction, for concerning the things done in secret by them it is shameful to be speaking.

But all the aforementioned things, when they are re- **13-21** proved by the light, are made visibly plain, for everything that is being made plain is light. Wherefore He says, Be

waking up, he who is sleeping, and arise from the dead, and there shall shine upon you the Christ. Be constantly taking heed therefore how accurately you are conducting yourselves, not as unwise ones but as wise ones, buying up for yourselves the opportune time, because the days are pernicious. On this account stop becoming those who are without reflection or intelligence, but be understanding what the will of the Lord is. And stop being intoxicated with wine, in which state of intoxication there is profligacy. But be constantly controlled by the Spirit, speaking to one another in psalms and hymns and spiritual songs, singing and making melody in your hearts to the Lord, giving thanks always concerning all things in the Name of our Lord Jesus Christ to God, even the Father, putting yourselves in subjection to one another in the fear of Christ.

22-33   The wives, be putting yourselves in subjection with implicit obedience to your own husbands as to the Lord, because a husband is head of the wife as the Christ is Head of the Church, He himself being the Saviour of the Body. Nevertheless, as the Church subjects itself in obedience to the Christ, in this manner also the wives should subject themselves in obedience to their husbands in all things. The husbands, be loving your wives with a love self-sacrificial in its nature, in the manner in which Christ also loved the Church and gave himself on behalf of it, in order that He might sanctify it, having cleansed it by the bath of water in the sphere of the Word, in order that He might himself present to himself the Church glorious, not having spot nor wrinkle nor any of such things, but in order that it might be holy and unblamable. In this manner ought also the husbands to love their wives as their own bodies. The one who loves his own wife loves himself, for no one ever yet hated his own flesh, but nourishes and cherishes it, even as the Christ, the Church, because members are we of His Body. Because of this a man shall leave behind his father and his mother and shall be joined to his wife, and the two shall become one flesh. This mystery is great. However, I am speaking with regard to Christ and the Church. Nevertheless, also as for you, let each one in this

manner be loving his own wife as himself, and the wife, let her be continually treating her husband with deference and reverential obedience.

The children, be always obedient to your parents in the Lord, for this is a righteous thing. Be always honoring your father and your mother, which is a commandment of such a nature as to be the first commandment with a promise, in order that it may be well with you, and in order that you may live long upon the earth. And the fathers, stop provoking your children to anger, but be rearing them in the discipline and admonition of the Lord. The slaves, be constantly obedient to those who, according to the flesh, are your masters, with fear and trembling, in singleness of your heart as to the Christ, not in the way of eye service as men-pleasers, but as Christ's bondslaves, doing the will of God from the soul, with good will rendering a slave's service as to the Lord and not as to men, knowing that each one, whatever good he may do, this he will receive from the presence of the Lord, whether he is a slave or whether he is free. And the masters, be practicing the same things toward them, giving up your threatening, knowing that also their Master and yours is in heaven, and there is not partiality with Him.

1-9

Finally, be constantly strengthened in the Lord and in the active efficacy of the might that is inherent in Him. Clothe yourselves with the full armor of God to the end that you will be able to hold your ground against the strategems of the devil, because our wrestling is not against blood and flesh, but against the principalities, against the authorities, against the world rulers of this darkness, against spirit forces of perniciousness in the heavenly places. On this account, take to yourself, at once and once for all, the complete armor of God in order that you may be able to resist in the day, the pernicious day, and having achieved all things, to stand. Stand therefore, having girded your loins in the sphere of truth, and having clothed yourself with the breastplate of righteousness, and having sandalled your feet with a firm foundation of the good news of peace; in addition to all these, taking to yourselves the shield of faith by

10-20

means of which you will be able to quench all the fiery arrows of the pernicious one, and take the helmet of salvation, and the sword of the Spirit which is the word of God; through the instrumentality of every prayer and supplication for need, praying at every season by means of the Spirit, and maintaining a constant alertness in the same with every kind of unremitting care and supplication for all the saints, and on behalf of me, in order that there might be given me utterance in the opening of my mouth, in every fearless, confident freedom of speaking, to make known the mystery of the good news on behalf of which I am an ambassador in a chain, in order that in it I may speak with every fearless and confident freedom as it is necessary in the nature of the case for me to speak.

21-24   But in order that you also might come to know my circumstances, what I am doing, all things to you, Tychicus, the beloved brother and faithful ministering servant in the Lord, will make known, whom I am sending to you for this same purpose in order that you might come to know our circumstances and in order that he might encourage your hearts. Peace to the brethren and love with faith from God the Father and the Lord Jesus Christ. The grace be with all those who are loving our Lord Jesus Christ in sincerity.

Definition of Terms

DEFINITION OF TERMS

In order to bring out in some instances the approximate total of the Greek text even in an expanded translation it sometimes becomes necessary to use words which are not in one's daily vocabulary. Some readers may need to consult a dictionary for their meaning. A handy dictionary containing words of this kind used in this expanded translation is included. While readers who have had the benefit of education on the higher levels will read this translation with ease, others may at times find it necessary to consult the definition of a word. The word "entree" is an example. The translator could have used the simpler word "access," but in doing so would have left behind in the Greek text some precious nugget of truth which the word "entree" carries with it and the word "access" does not include. Take for instance Romans 5:2, "By whom [the Lord Jesus] also we have access by faith into this grace wherein we stand" (A.V.). Webster defines "access" as "admittance, admission." But the Greek word means more than that. The word was used of a person who procured for his friend an audience with a king, provided him with the correct attire to enter the king's presence, and brought him into favor with the king. That is more than mere admittance into the presence of the king. The word "entree" is from the French and has a meaning very similar to the Greek word. To bring our illustration up to date, "access" is what is granted a person when the brass-buttoned, scarlet-liveried doorman grants you admittance to the public entrance of a fashionable apartment hotel. "Entree" is what is given this same person when the family who is entertaining him as a guest opens its arms wide in a hearty welcome, making him one of the family. A believing sinner is not only granted admittance into God's grace, but upon entering into the enjoyment of its blessings finds the open arms of an affectionate heavenly Father ready to embrace His new child as His own. That is *entree*. Our Lord died for our sins in order that He might provide for us an entree into the presence of God (I Peter 3:18).

Take the word "pretermission." The A.V. translates Romans 3:25, "whom God hath set forth to be a propitiation through faith in His blood, to declare His righteousness for the remission

of sins that are past, through the forbearance of God." The word "remission" means "an act of remitting or forgiving or pardoning, a cancellation." But God did do that before the Cross. The Greek word for "remission" is *aphesis,* which means "to put off" or "to put away." Sin was not put away until our Lord died at Calvary. The Greek word here is *paresis* which Trench defines as "the passing by of sins for the present, leaving it open in the future either to entirely *remit,* or else adequately to punish them, as may seem good to Him who has the power and right to do the one or the other." Webster defines "pretermission" as "omission," the verb "pretermit" as "to let pass by without mention, notice, or attention, to pass by or over." The correct translation of this scripture therefore demands such a word as this which the reader does not use in daily conversation.

The word "imbalance," describing the mental state of those who saw the miracles performed by our Lord and His apostles and who listened to their words, refers to a lack of proper balance, and is the best English word which will translate the Greek word.

The word "fulcrum" is not ordinarily used in everyday language but admirably translates the Greek word. Webster defines the word as a "prop or support" and refers the reader to the definition of a lever, "a bar used to pry loose or dislodge something firmly fixed." The A.V. of Romans 7:8 has, "But sin, taking occasion by the commandment, wrought in me all manner of concupiscence." The expanded translation reads, "But the sinful nature using the commandment as a fulcrum brought about in me every kind of evil craving." The sinful nature used God's commandments as a fulcrum to pry out sinful acts in the sense that when the sinful nature is faced with God's law, it rebels against it and brings out sin in the life all the more. The more commandments that are given, the more sin is committed.

And so one could go on giving examples of the need of using unfamiliar words not commonly used in ordinary conversation. The English reader is urged to make use of this dictionary appendage when he comes to a word with which he may not be familiar. This expanded translation demands study, and is thought-provoking. It is impossible drowsily to peruse its pages or gallop over its surface in a rapid, superficial reading and expect to come to grips with what the Bible writers meant to convey.

A

ACTUATE — to put into action or motion, to move or incite to action, to stir or inspire to activity, to arouse.

ADJUDICATE — to hear or try and determine, as a court of law, to settle by judicial decree, to come to a judicial decision, to act as a judge.

ADMIRABLE — wonderful, marvellous, having qualities to excite wonder united with approbation, deserving the highest esteem, excellent.

ADMIXTURE — act of mixing, or the compound formed by mixing different substances together, that which is added to anything by mixing.

ADROITNESS — skill and readiness, dexterity, address.

ADULTERATE — to corrupt, debase, or make impure by an admixture of a foreign or a baser substance; figuratively, to make corrupt or impure by adding new, strange, or foreign elements.

AGGREGATION — collection or union into a mass or sum.

ALLEGORY — a description of one thing under the image of another.

ANTIQUATED — grown old, bygone, fallen into disuse, old-fashioned.

APATHETIC — void of feeling, not susceptible of deep emotion, unemotional, indifferent.

APTITUDE — readiness in learning, general fitness or suitableness, appropriateness, natural disposition or tendency to a particular action or effect.

ARBITRATOR — a person chosen by parties who have a controversy to settle their differences.

AROMA — a distinctive, agreeable fragrance or odor, figuratively, a characteristic and suggestive quality, flavor, as: the subtle aroma of genius.

ARROGANT — making or having the disposition to make exorbitant claims of rank or estimation, giving oneself an undue degree of importance, presumptuously haughty.

229

ARTEMIS — an Olympian goddess by the Romans identified with Diana.

ARTISAN — one who practices or professes some liberal art, an artist, one trained to manual dexterity in some mechanic art or trade, a handicraftsman.

ASSIDUOUS — performed with constant diligence and attention, unremitting, persistent, constant in application or attention, devoted, attentive.

ASSIMILATE — to appropriate and transform or incorporate into the substance of an assimilating body, to absorb or appropriate, as nourishment.

ATTEST — to bear witness to, to certify, to affirm to be true or genuine, to authenticate, to be or stand as proof.

AUGMENT — to enlarge or increase in size, amount, or degree, to make bigger.

AUSPICIOUS — favoring or conducive to success, fortunate, prosperous, auguring or predicting good.

B

BENEFACTOR — one who does good to one.

BOUNTY — liberality in bestowing gifts, gracious or liberal giving, generosity, munificence.

C

CANTANKEROUS — exhibiting ill nature, perverse, contentious, crossgrained, malicious.

CELIBACY — state of being unmarried, single life.

CENTURION — a commander of a hundred soldiers.

CENSORIOUS — severe in making remarks on others, or on their writings or manners.

CHILIARCH — a commander of a thousand soldiers.

CHRONOLOGICAL — containing an account of events in the order of time, according to the order of time.

COAGULATE — to clot, congeal, as of blood.

COALITION — a temporary alliance of persons for a joint action or purpose.

COGNIZANCE — apprehension by the understanding, conscious recognition.

COHORT — in the Roman army, one of the ten divisions of a legion, having at first 300, later 500 to 600 soldiers.

COLONNADE — a series or range of columns placed at regular intervals sometimes with adjuncts such as a pavement.

CONCESSION — act of conceding or yielding, usually implying a demand, claim, or request, the admitting of a point in an argument, the voluntary yielding of a disputable point as not necessary to the main contention or by way of grounding a fresh argument in its place.

CONCISE — expressing much in few words, brief and compact.

CONJURATION — a constraining of spirits or demons by invocation of a sacred name or by a spell.

CONNIVANCE — intentional failure or forbearing to discover a wrongdoing, voluntary oversight, passive consent or cooperation.

CONSECRATE — to make or declare sacred or holy, to set apart, dedicate, devote to the service or worship of God.

CONSUMMATION — completion, perfection, end, goal.

CONTINENT — exercising restraint as to the indulgence of desires or passions, temperate, moderate; specifically, exercising continence or self-restraint, sexually chaste.

COPE — to enter or maintain a hostile contest, to struggle, to combat, to strive or contend on equal terms or with a measure of success, to match, to equal, to encounter.

CORRAL — to surround and enclose, to coop up, to confine in as in a corral.

COUCH — to put in some form of language, to express, phrase.

CREDENTIAL — that which gives a title to credit or confidence, testimonials, showing that a person is entitled to credit, or has a right to exercise official power.

D

DEFAMATION — a bringing into disrepute, dishonor, disgrace, injuring another's reputation by any slanderous communication.

DEFERENCE — courteous or complaisant regard for another's wishes, consideration, regard.

DELEGATE — to send with a commission, to depute, to send one to act for another.

DEMOLISH — to throw or pull down, to raze, to destroy, to pull to pieces, to ruin.

DEVIATION — a wandering from the way, variation from the common way, from an established rule, a standard or position.

DIAMETRICAL — as remote as possible, entirely or directly adverse.

DISPARAGE — to dishonor by a comparison with what is inferior, to lower in rank or estimation by actions or words, to speak slightingly of, to depreciate, undervalue.

DISPOSITION — the administering of anything, management, the ordering or arranging of anything.

DISQUALIFY — to deprive of some power, right, or privilege as by positive restriction.

DISSEMINATE — to sow broadcast, to scatter.

DISSOLUTE — loosed from restraint, unrestrained, loose in morals and conduct, wanton, lewd, debauched.

DIVEST — to unclothe, to strip, to put off; lay aside, as of clothes, arms, equipage.

DURESS — hardness, harshness, cruelty, affliction, constraint, pressure, compulsion.

E

EDIFICE — a building, a structure, a large or massive building as a palace or a church.

EGO — the entire man considered as union of soul and body, the self, whether considered as an organization or system of mental states, or as the consciousness of the individual's distinction from other selves.

ENTREE — freedom of access, permission or right to enter, as to have the entree of a house. The French word of which "entree" is the English spelling was used of the permission to enter the throne-room of a king. The word "entree" means more than a mechanical entrance into an enclosed space, but includes a welcome into the affections and favor of others.

ENVIRONS — the suburbs or districts around a place, surroundings.

EPICUREANISM — the philosophy that pleasure is the only good and the end of all morality; given to luxury or to sensual gratification, adapted to luxurious tastes.

EPOCHAL — a point of time determined by some significant event, any event or point of time marking the beginning of a relatively new development, a period of time characterized by a distinctive development or a memorable series of events.

EQUITABLE — according to natural right or natural justice, just, right, honest, upright, impartial.

ETHNARCH — the governor of a province or a people.

EULOGIZE — to speak or write in strong commendation of, to praise.

EVALUATE — to ascertain the value or amount of, to appraise carefully.

EXPERIENTIAL — derived from, based on, or pertinent to experience.

EXTOL — to place on high, to elevate, exalt.

EXUBERANT — characterized by abundance or super-abundance, plenteous, luxuriant; carried, maintained, or experienced to an extreme degree, effusive, lavish.

F

FACTIOUS — addicted to forming parties or factions and raising dissensions, seditious.

FACTUAL — relating to or containing facts, restricted to or involving fact as opposed to theory.

FALLACIOUS — embodying a fallacy, misleading, delusive, deceitful.

FLABBERGAST — to astonish, strike with wonder.

FORUM — the market place or public place of a city, the center of judicial and public business; where public discussions were held.

FULCRUM — a prop or support, a bar used to pry loose or dislodge something firmly fixed.

FUTILE — answering to no useful end, ineffectual, worthless.

G

GRATUITOUS — given freely or without recompense, granted without pay or without claim or merit.

H

HEBREW — a Jew who opposed Hellenism and held firmly to all the principles and regulations of the law.

HELLENIST — a Jew who took a Greek name, accepted a school of Greek philosophy in addition to his Jewish faith, and tried to combine the wisdom of Greece with the faith of Israel.

HERMES — an Olympian god, son of Zeus and Maia, identified by the Romans as Mercury, the herald and messenger of the Greek gods.

I

IMBALANCE — lack of balance.

IMBUE — to saturate, to tinge deeply, to impregnate, permeate.

IMMACULATE — without stain or blemish, spotless, undefiled, pure.

IMPLICATION — involvement, close connection or combination; involved in the nature or being of something though not shown, expressed, or developed.

INCANTATION — to chant a magic formula over one, the use of spells or verbal charms, sorcery, enchantment.

INDISSOLUBLE — incapable of being annulled, perpetually binding or obligatory, firm, stable.

INDUBITABLE — not doubtful, too evident for doubt, unquestionable.

INEFFABLE — incapable of being expressed in words, unutterable, indescribable.

INFLATE — to swell or distend with air or gas, to puff up, elate, as to inflate one with pride or vanity.

INGRATIATE — to introduce or commend to favor, to bring into favor, to win one's way into favor.

INSTIGATE — to goad or urge forward, to provoke, incite.

INTELLIGENTSIA — informed intellectual people collectively, the educated, professional group, class, or party.

INTERMEDIATE — to come between, to interpose, to act as an intermediate agent.

INVALIDATE — to weaken or lessen the force of, to destroy the authority of, to render of no force or effect.

INVEST — to envelop as with a garment, to clothe, dress, or array, to surround or endue as with something extrinsic.

IRREVOCABLE — incapable of being recalled or revoked, past recall, unalterable.

ISOLATE — to place in a detached situation, to place by itself or alone, to insulate.

J

JEOPARDIZE — to expose to loss or injury, to risk, hazard, endanger, imperil.

JUDICIAL — of or pertaining to the administration of justice or courts of justice.

L

LASSO — a rope or long thong of leather with a running noose, used for catching horses, cattle. The verb means "to catch with a lasso."

LICTOR — an officer who attended the chief magistrates when they appeared in public to cause due respect to be paid them, also to apprehend and punish criminals.

LINEAGE — descent in a line from a common progenitor, race, family, descending line of offspring.

LIQUIDATE — figuratively, to clear up and dispose of, bring to an end or consummation.

M

MALTREAT — to abuse, to treat roughly.

MARSHAL — to dispose in order, especially a military or ceremonious order, to usher, direct, guide, or lead.

MOTIVATE — to move, impel, induce, incite.

N

NETHER — situated down or below, lying beneath or in the lower part.

NORM — a rule or authoritative standard, model, type, pattern.

NULLIFY — to make legally void, to render invalid, to render of no value, consequence, or efficacy.

O

OBLITERATE — to erase or blot out, efface, to remove or destroy utterly.

OSTENTATION — act of making an ambitious display, unnecessary show, pretentious parade.

P

PARTIALITY — inclination to favor one party, partisanship, a predilection or inclination to one thing.

PARTICULARIZE — to state in detail, to make separate in conception or reality, to individualize, to limit to a particular class.

PERNICIOUS — highly injurious or destructive in character, deadly, fatal, intending or doing evil, wicked, villainous.

PHARISEES — the straitest religious sect of the Jews, emphasizing the strictest conformity to the Mosaic law, believing in immortality, the resurrection of the body, the existence of spirits, punishment and reward in the future life.

PHILOSOPHICAL — of or pertaining to philosophy, which latter word is defined as the love of wisdom, the science which investi-

gates the most general facts and principles of reality and of human nature and conduct.

PLAGIARIST — one guilty of literary or artistic theft, publishing as his own the literary productions of another.

PLENITUDE — completeness, plentiful, fullness.

POIGNANT — as affecting sense, one's feelings penetratingly sharp or keen, piercingly effective, acute, cutting, pungent.

PORTENT — usually an event, situation or the like which presages evil, a forewarning.

PRENATAL — before birth.

PRETERMISSION — the passing by of sins for the present, leaving it open in the future either entirely to remit, or else adequately to punish them, as may seem good to Him who has the power and right to do the one or the other.

PRISTINE — belonging to the earliest period or state, original, primitive, hence, uncorrupted by civilization or the world.

PROCONSUL — a governor or military commander in a province, an administrative officer in a colony or conquered territory.

PROFLIGACY — dissolute character or conduct, continuous dissipation.

PROGENITOR — an ancestor in the direct line, a forefather.

PROMULGATION — publication, open declaration, an official proclamation.

PROPITIOUS — favorably disposed, graciously inclined, benevolent, favorable, auspicious.

PROPRIETY — quality or status of being proper or fitting, suitability, fitness, correctness.

PROSELYTE — a new convert, especially to some religion or religious sect, a convert to Judaism who performs all the religious duties required of the Jews and enjoys all the privileges.

PUNCTILIOUS — scrupulously exact in details or forms.

Q

QUADRUPED — an animal having four feet.

R

RELEGATE — to assign as to a class or sphere, to consign by classifying or appraising.

REMUNERATION — recompense, pay.

REQUISITE — something indispensable or essential.

RESIDUE — that which remains after a part is taken, separated, removed or designated; remainder.

RHETORIC — the art of expressive speech or discourse, especially of literary composition; as cultivated by the Greeks, the study of the principles and technical resources of oratory, including both composition and delivery.

RUDIMENTARY — consisting of first principles, elementary.

S

SADDUCEES — a Jewish party, opponents of the Pharisees, held to the sacred text itself, rejected the traditions of the elders, denied the resurrection of the body and future retribution, asserting that the soul dies with the body, denied the existence of angels or spirits.

SALUTARY — promoting health, curative, restorative, conducive to salvation, promoting or conducive to a beneficial or satisfying outcome.

SANHEDRIN — the highest Jewish assembly for government in the time of our Lord.

SATIATE — to feed or satisfy to the full, as an appetite or desire, to indulge to the extent of desire, to fill beyond natural desire, to gratify to repletion or loathing, to surfeit, glut, to saturate.

SCRUPULOUS — careful or strict in doing what is right or proper, exact, punctilious.

SCRUTINIZE — to examine closely, to inspect or examine with critical attention.

SEQUENCE — a series having continuity and connection; that which follows later or as a consequence.

SIMULATE — to assume or have the mere appearance of without the reality, to counterfeit, feign, imitate.

SOLICITOUS — full of concern or fears, apprehensive, troubled concerned, full of desire, eager, anxiously willing, meticulously careful or attentive.

SOPHIST — a thinker, a philosopher, now usually a captious or fallacious reasoner.

SOULICAL — of or pertaining to the soul. The spirit of man gives him God-consciousness and makes him a moral free agent with a religious nature. The soul gives him self-consciousness and world-consciousness. The spirit has to do with the things of God, salvation, worship, service to God. The soul has to do

with the affairs of everyday life, the material universe, fellowship with others, the secular part of life.

SPECIFICATION — the act of determining by a mark or limit, notation of limits, a designation of particulars.

SPECIOUS — apparently right, superficially fair, just, or correct, but not so in reality, appearing well at first view, plausible.

SPHERE — circuit or range of action, knowledge, or influence, compass, province.

STABILIZE — to make steadfast or firm.

STIPULATION — a contracting or agreement, that which is agreed upon, an agreement, covenant, contract.

STOICISM — the philosophy which teaches indifference to pleasure or pain; impassiveness, repression of feeling.

STRATEGY — the use of artifice, planning, or intrigue, as in "a strategic point," any point in the theatre of operations affording a far-reaching advantage to its possessor.

SUBSERVIENT — useful in an inferior capacity, subordinate, serving to promote some end, servile, truckling.

SUBSISTENCE — means of support, provisions, livelihood.

SUBSTANTIATE — to establish the existence or truth of by proof or competent evidence, to verify.

SUBTLETY — the quality of being intangible, indefinable, abstruse, a finely-drawn or delicate distinction, something difficult to perceive or trace, mental acuteness or penetrativeness.

SUPERFLUOUS — in excess of what is sufficient, necessary, normal, or desirable; superabundant, not needed, nonessential.

SURREPTITIOUS — to withdraw privately; done, made, acquired, or enjoyed by stealth, or without proper authority, clandestine.

T

THWART — to oppose or baffle, as a purpose, to run counter to, to contravene, hence to frustrate or defeat, obstruct, block.

TOLERANCE — the act or practice of or capacity for bearing suffering or hardship, endurance; the disposition to allow the existence of beliefs, practices, or habits differing from one's own without acceptance of them; intellectual forbearance with reference to views, opinions, or actions with which one is not in full sympathy.

TRANSCEND — to rise above or beyond the limits or powers of, to overpass, to exceed, to surpass. The adjective "transcendent" means, superior, surpassing, extraordinary.

TRANSIENT — passing quickly from existence, of short or uncertain duration, transitory, short-lived, not settled or established.

TRIBUNAL — the seat of a judge, the bench on which a judge sits when administering justice, a court or forum of justice, a person or body of persons having authority to hear and decide disputes so as to bind the disputants.

TUTELARY — having the guardianship or charge of protecting a person or thing, as a tutelary goddess.

TUTOR — a guard or keeper, one who has charge of the instruction of another.

TYPHOON — a tropical cyclone, a great wind.

U

UNANIMITY — being of one mind, agreeing in opinion, design, or determination.

UNINHIBITED — lack of self-restraint, failure to check or hold back.

V

VACILLATE — to sway through lack of equilibrium, to waver, totter, fluctuate, oscillate, to waver in mind, will, or feeling, to hesitate in choice of opinions, courses.

VALET — a manservant who attends a man, taking care of his clothes and caring for his physical needs.

VERACIOUS — habitually speaking truth, truthful.

VOID — to make to be of no validity or effect, to annul, nullify.

VOLITION — act of willing or choosing, act of deciding, as on a course of action or an end to be striven for; the exercise of the will, the power of willing or choosing.

VOLUPTUOUS — ministering to, pertaining to, inclining to, or arising from sensuous or sensual gratification, luxurious, sensuous, given to or spent in enjoyments of luxury, pleasure or sensual gratification.

W

WARDEN — one who keeps guard, a watchman, a guardian.

WRANGLING — to dispute angrily, to quarrel peevishly and noisily, to brawl.

Z

ZEUS — the chief of the Olympian gods, identified by the Romans with Jupiter.

BIBLIOGRAPHY

In preparing this translation of the Greek New Testament, Volume II, Acts through Ephesians, the translator has used the following Greek authorities in his research work and acknowledges with deep gratefulness the help he has received from them.

GREEK COMMENTARIES

Expositor's Greek Testament edited by W. Robertson Nicoll; *Acts* by R. J. Knowling; *Romans* by James Denney; *I Corinthians* by G. G. Findlay; *II Corinthians* by J. H. Bernard; *Galatians* by Frederic Rendall; *Ephesians* by S. D. F. Salmond; *Word Studies in the New Testament* by Marvin R. Vincent; *Alford's Greek Testament* by Henry Alford; *Word Pictures in the New Testament* by A. T. Robertson.

LEXICONS

Greek-English Lexicon by Joseph H. Thayer; *Vocabulary of the Greek Testament* by Moulton and Milligan; *Biblico-Theological Lexicon of New Testament Greek* by Hermann Cremer; *Greek-English Lexicon* by Liddell and Scott; *New Testament Synonyms* by Archbishop Trench.

Index

INDEX

ACTS

		PAGE
I		**17-19**
1 - 5		17
6 - 8		17
9 - 11		17
12 - 14		18
15 - 17		18
18 - 20		18
21 - 26		18, 19
II		**19-22**
1 - 4		19
5 - 11		19, 20
12, 13		20
14 - 18		20
19 - 21		20
22 - 24		20, 21
25 - 28		21
29 - 36		21, 22
37 - 41		22
42 - 47		22
III		**23, 24**
1 - 11		23
12 - 16		23, 24
17 - 21		24
22 - 26		24
IV		**25-27**
1 - 4		25
5 - 14		25, 26
15 - 18		26
19 - 22		26
23 - 31		26, 27
32 - 37		27
V		**27-30**
1 - 6		27, 28
7 - 11		28

		PAGE
12 - 16		28
17 - 25		29
26 - 28		29
29 - 32		29, 30
33 - 36		30
37 - 42		30
VI		**30-32**
1 - 7		30, 31
8 - 15		31, 32
VII		**32-36**
1 - 7		32
8 - 10		32
11 - 16		33
17 - 21		33
22 - 29		33, 34
30 - 41		34, 35
42, 43		35
44 - 47		35
48 - 53		35
54 - VIII :1		35, 36
VIII		**36-39**
1, 2		36
3 - 8		36
9 - 11		36, 37
12, 13		37
14 - 17		37
18 - 25		37, 38
26, 27		38
27 - 33		38
34 - 40		38, 39
IX		**39-42**
1, 2		39
3 - 9		39
10 - 14		39, 40
15 - 19		40

		PAGE
19 - 21		40
22 - 25		40, 41
26 - 31		41
32 - 35		41
36, 37		41, 42
38 - 43		42
X		**42-46**
1 - 6		42
7 - 16		43
17 - 22		43, 44
23 - 27		44
28, 29		44
30 - 33		44
34 - 38		45
39 - 43		45
44 - 48		45, 46
XI		**46-48**
1 - 10		46
11 - 18		46, 47
19 - 21		47
22 - 26		47
27 - 30		47, 48
XII		**48-50**
1 - 4		48
5 - 9		48
10		48
11 - 17		49
18, 19		49
20 - 25		49, 50
XIII		**50-53**
1 - 3		50
4 - 12		50, 51
13 - 15		51
16 - 20		51
21 - 25		51, 52

INDEX

	PAGE		PAGE		PAGE
26 - 41	52, 53	**XIX 67-70**		**XXIV 81-83**	
42 - 52	53	1 - 7	67	1 - 4	81
		8 - 13	67	5 - 9	81, 82
XIV 53-55		14 - 17	68	10 - 16	82
1 - 7	53, 54	18 - 20	68	17 - 23	82, 83
8 - 10	54	21, 22	68	24 - 27	83
11 - 13	54	23 - 27	68, 69		
14 - 18	54, 55	28 - 37	69	**XXV 83-85**	
19 - 22	55	38 - 41	70	1 - 6	83
23 - 28	55			7, 8	83
		XX 70-73		9 - 12	84
XV 55-58		1 - 5	70	13 - 21	84, 85
1 - 4	55, 56	6 - 12	70, 71	22 - 27	85
5	56	13 - 16	71		
6 - 12	56	17 - 21	71	**XXVI 85-88**	
13 - 18	56, 57	22 - 24	71	1 - 3	85
19 - 21	57	25 - 31	72	4 - 7	85, 86
22 - 29	57, 58	32 - 38	72, 73	8 - 11	86
30 - 35	58			12 - 18	86, 87
36 - 41	58	**XXI 73-76**		19, 20	87
		1 - 6	73	21 - 23	87
XVI 58-61		7 - 12	73	24 - 29	87
1 - 5	58, 59	13 - 17	74	30 - 32	87, 88
6 - 8	59	18 - 21	74		
9, 10	59	22 - 26	74, 75	**XXVII 88-91**	
11 - 15	59	27 - 36	75	1 - 6	88
16 - 18	60	37 - XXII :2	75, 76	7, 8	88
19 - 24	60			9 - 13	88, 89
25 - 34	60, 61	**XXII 76-78**		14 - 20	89
35, 36	61	2 - 5	76	21 - 26	89, 90
37 - 40	61	6 - 13	76, 77	27 - 32	90
		14 - 16	77	33 - 38	90
XVII 61-64		17 - 21	77	39 - 41	90, 91
1 - 3	61, 62	22 - 24	77, 78	42 - 44	91
4 - 9	62	25 - 30	78		
10 - 14	62			**XXVIII 91-94**	
15	63	**XXIII 78-81**		1 - 6	91, 92
16 - 21	63	1 - 5	78, 79	7 - 10	92
22 - 31	63, 64	6 - 11	79	11 - 16	92
32 - 34	64	12 - 15	79	17 - 19	92, 93
		16 - 22	80	20 - 22	93
XVIII 64-67		23, 24	80	23 - 27	93
1 - 3	64, 65	25 - 30	80, 81	28	93
4 - 11	65	31 - 35	81	30, 31	94
12 - 17	65, 66				
18 - 23	66				
24 - 28	66, 67				

INDEX

ROMANS

PAGE

I 101-103

1 - 7	101
8 - 12	101
13 - 15	101
16 - 23	101, 102
24 - 27	102
28 - 32	102, 103

II 103-105

1 - 10	103
11 - 13	103, 104
14 - 16	104
17 - 24	104
25 - 29	104, 105

III 105, 106

1, 2	105
3, 4	105
5 - 8	105
9 - 18	105, 106
19, 20	106
21 - 26	106
27, 28	106
29 - 31	106

IV 107, 108

1 - 8	107
9 - 12	107
13 - 15	107, 108
16 - 22	108
23 - 25	108

V 108-110

1 - 5	108, 109
6 - 8	109
9 - 11	109
12 - 14	109
15 - 17	109, 110
18 - 21	110

VI 110-112

1 - 4	110
5 - 10	110, 111
11 - 14	111

PAGE

15 - 20	111, 112
21 - 23	112

VII 112-114

1 - 6	112, 113
7 - 15	113
16 - 20	113, 114
21 - 23	114
24, 25	114

VIII 114-117

1 - 4	114
5 - 8	114
9 - 13	114, 115
14 - 18	115
19 - 25	115, 116
26, 27	116
28 - 30	116
31 - 39	116, 117

IX 117-119

1 - 5	117
6, 7	117
8 - 13	117, 118
14 - 18	118
19 - 21	118
22 - 24	118
25 - 29	118, 119
30 - 33	119

X 119, 120

1 - 4	119
5 - 13	119, 120
14 - 17	120
18 - 21	120

XI 120-123

1 - 6	120, 121
7 - 10	121
11 - 14	121
15 - 22	121, 122
23 - 25	122

PAGE

26 - 32	122
33 - 36	122, 123

XII 123, 124

1, 2	123
3 - 5	123
6 - 8	123
9 - 18	123, 124
19 - 21	124

XIII 124, 125

1 - 4	124, 125
5 - 7	125
8 - 12	125
13, 14	125

XIV 125-127

1 - 4	125, 126
5 - 9	126
10 - 13	126
14 - 18	126, 127
19 - 21	127
22, 23	127

XV 127-129

1 - 4	127
5 - 7	127
8 - 12	128
13, 14	128
15, 16	128
17 - 21	128, 129
22 - 24	129
25 - 29	129
30 - 33	129

XVI 129-131

1 - 5	129, 130
5 - 9	130
10 - 12	130
12 - 16	130
17 - 20	130, 131
21 - 27	131

INDEX

FIRST CORINTHIANS

	PAGE		PAGE		PAGE
I 137-139		**VII 147-150**		12 - 17	159, 160
				18 - 27	160
1 - 3	137	1 - 7	147	28 - 31	160
4 - 9	137	8 - 14	147, 148		
10	137	15 - 24	148, 149	**XIII 160, 161**	
11 - 17	138	25 - 28	149		
18 - 25	138, 139	29 - 31	149	1 - 3	160, 161
26 - 29	139	32 - 40	149, 150	4 - 8	161
30, 31	139			8 - 13	161
		VIII 150, 151			
II 139-141		1 - 7	150, 151	**XIV 162-165**	
1 - 5	139, 140	8 - 13	151		
6 - 8	140			1 - 5	162
9 - 11	140	**IX 151-154**		6 - 11	162, 163
12, 13	140			12 - 17	163
14 - 16	140, 141	1 - 3	151	18 - 22	163
		4 - 10	151, 152	23 - 25	163, 164
		11 - 14	152	26 - 33	164
III 141, 142		15 - 17	152, 153	33 - 40	164, 165
1 - 7	141	18 - 23	153		
8 - 11	141	24 - 27	153, 154	**XV 165-168**	
12 - 15	141, 142				
16, 17	142	**X 154-156**		1 - 11	165
18 - 23	142			12 - 19	165, 166
		1 - 5	154	20 - 28	166
		6 - 13	154, 155	29 - 34	166
IV 142-144		14, 15	155	35 - 38	167
		16 - 22	155	39 - 41	167
1 - 5	142, 143	23 - 30	155, 156	42 - 50	167, 168
6 - 13	143, 144	31 - XI:1	156	51 - 58	168
14 - 21	144				
		XI 156-159		**XVI 168, 169**	
V 144, 145		2 - 10	156		
		11 - 16	157	1 - 4	168
1 - 8	144, 145	17 - 22	157, 158	5 - 9	168, 169
9 - 13	145	23 - 34	158, 159	10 - 12	169
				13 - 18	169
VI 145-147		**XII 159, 160**		19 - 24	169
1 - 8	145, 146	1 - 7	159		
9 - 11	146	8 - 11	159		
12 - 20	146, 147				

INDEX

SECOND CORINTHIANS

	PAGE		PAGE		PAGE
I 173-175		11 - 17	179, 180	**X 187, 188**	
		18 - 21	180	1 - 12	187, 188
1, 2	173			13 - 18	188
3 - 7	173				
8 - 11	173, 174	**VI 181, 182**		**XI 188-191**	
12 - 14	174				
15 - 20	174	1 - 10	181	1 - 6	188, 189
21 - 24	174, 175	11 - 13	181	7 - 9	189
		14 - VII:1	182	10 - 15	189, 190
II 175, 176				16 - 20	190
				21 - 28	190, 191
1 - 8	175	**VII 182, 183**		29 - 33	191
9 - 17	175, 176				
		2 - 16	182, 183	**XII 191-193**	
III 176, 177					
				1 - 5	191
1 - 3	176	**VIII 183-185**		6 - 10	191, 192
4 - 9	176			11, 12	192
10 - 18	177	1 - 7	183, 184	13 - 18	192, 193
		8 - 12	184	19 - 21	193
IV 177-179		13 - 15	184, 185		
		16 - 24	185	**XIII 193, 194**	
1 - 6	177, 178				
7 - 15	178	**IX 185-187**		1 - 4	193
16 - 18	178, 179			5, 6	194
		1 - 4	185, 186	7 - 10	194
V 179-180		5 - 9	186	11 - 13	194
		10 - 15	186, 187	14	194
1 - 4	179				
5 - 10	179				

GALATIANS

I 201, 202		**III 204-206**		**V 208, 209**	
1 - 5	201	1 - 9	204	1 - 12	208
6 - 10	201	10 - 14	204, 205	13 - 15	208
11, 12	201	15 - 18	205	16 - 21	208, 209
13, 14	201, 202	19 - 23	205	22 - 26	209
15 - 17	202	24 - 29	206		
18 - 24	202				
		IV 206, 207		**VI 209, 210**	
II 202-204		1 - 7	206		
		8 - 11	206	1 - 5	209
1 - 10	202, 203	12 - 20	206, 207	6 - 10	209, 210
11 - 21	203, 204	21 - 31	207	11 - 18	210

INDEX

EPHESIANS

	PAGE		PAGE		PAGE
I 215, 216		**III 218, 219**		**V 221-223**	
1, 2	215	1 - 7	218	1 - 6	221
3 - 14	215	8 - 12	218	7 - 12	221
15 - 23	215, 216	13 - 19	218, 219	13 - 21	221, 222
		20, 21	219	22 - 33	222, 223
		IV 219-221			
		1 - 6	219		
II 216, 217		7 - 16	219, 220	**VI 223, 224**	
1 - 10	216, 217	17 - 19	220	1 - 9	223
11 - 18	217	20 - 24	220	10 - 20	223, 224
19 - 22	217	25 - 32	220, 221	21 - 24	224